Exploring Rural
IRELAND

D1280104

OTHER BOOKS IN THE *EXPLORING RURAL* SERIES

Series Editor: Andrew Sanger

Exploring Rural
IRELAND

ANDREW SANGER

PASSPORT BOOKS
a division of *NTC Publishing Group*
Lincolnwood, Illinois USA

1995 Printing

This edition first published in 1993 by Passport Books,
a division of NTC Publishing Group,
4255 West Touhy Avenue, Lincolnwood (Chicago),
Illinois 60646-1975 U.S.A. Originally published by
Christopher Helm (Publishers) Ltd., a subsidiary of A&C Black (Publishers) Ltd.
Copyright © 1993, 1989 Andrew Sanger.
Illustrations by Lorna Turpin. Maps by David Henderson.

Library of Congress Catalog Card Number: 92-62571

5 6 7 8 9 ML 9 8 7 6 5 4 3 2

For Gerry

ACKNOWLEDGEMENTS

To Irish friends, colleagues and workmates over the years I owe thanks for making me want to know more about their country. While I travelled in Ireland, many people by their abundant generosity and open-heartedness made it easy and enjoyable to write this book. My friend Rachel Magowan has been a great source of information and ideas, and has helped me enormously. I am especially grateful to John Lahiffe, of the Irish Tourist Board (Bord Fáilte) in London, for his invaluable help, knowledge, and kindness. Thanks too to the Northern Ireland Tourist Office; and to Bob Cashman of Aer Lingus for all the assistance he has given me. Most of all, I express love and thanks to my companion Gerry Dunham, whose running commentary, intelligent suggestions, and helpful criticism were essential at all stages.

CONTENTS

Ireland – the regions and the routes

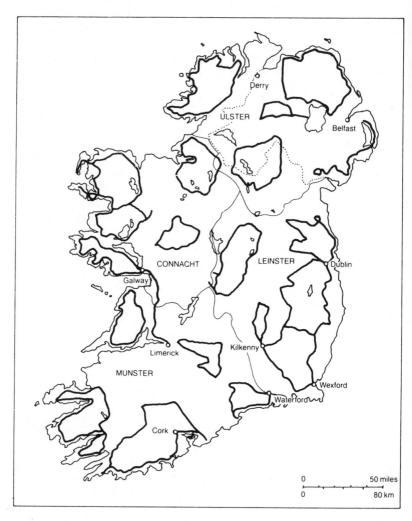

INTRODUCTION

Although Ireland has some of the most astonishingly, extraordinarily beautiful scenery in Europe, as well as an exceptional abundance of reminders of its medieval and prehistoric past, most of the country's attractions are invisible. There's an unpretentious simplicity about Ireland and its people which is delightful and irresistible. There's a marvellous atmosphere here, a sense of being enfolded by myth, in a gentle hold from which one cannot escape back into the brisk modern world of common-sense and rationality.

The Irish themselves (I hope they will forgive me a few generalisations) are certainly an unusual people, with some very engaging and perhaps also some exasperating characteristics. This may be the result, at least in part, of their having entirely escaped colonisation by the Romans, whose disciplined, ordered, and authoritarian society influenced almost every other nation in Europe. It does seem that many of the clichés about the Irish are broadly true. They are amiable, with a streak of melancholy, easy-going, good-hearted, essentially unsophisticated, most of them enjoy a drink, and it's rare indeed for an Irishman or Irishwoman to be at a loss for words. They sometimes seem (to outsiders) to be impossibly credulous—not to say muddled!—with religion, fantasy, legend, and historical fact all merging happily into one. Their view, though, seems to be that a good tale is worth telling—and even worth believing, if it's good enough.

That presumably is why 'the age of miracles' is not yet past, on this dreaming island at Europe's farthest edge, ruled by the vast Atlantic's wind and water. There has been an unbroken tradition over the centuries of Irish country people seeing divine apparitions; almost more than the authorities in Rome know what to do with. And these do tend to be well authenticated: the famous vision at Knock was seen by almost half a village; the modern basilica which stands there now has witnessed dozens of miraculous cures; more recently, moving statues in several villages have been verified by scores of people day after day.

Whatever the explanation for these things, the Church has a powerful appeal to the Irish population as a whole. As the only Catholic country in the English-speaking world, Ireland's churches are full to overflowing every Sunday. Papal pronouncements are taken with earnest seriousness. Divorce and even contraception are still illegal. While no doubt there are many dissenters and atheists, there is a wholehearted devotion to the Church, and a genuine piety, which surprises visitors—even those from

1

other Catholic countries. It has been asserted that the Church governs Ireland, but that is an exaggeration: it rules only the soul of the Irish. Yet Ireland surely is the only republic with a queen; for it is daily repeated ten thousand times or more . . . Hail Mary, Queen of Ireland. Even in the North of Ireland, which remains part of the United Kingdom and where Protestants (divided into a number of more or less austere sects) comprise over half the population, the clergy have immense influence and power.

In the farthest reaches of the country, out west, on the back roads and in the fields and village bars, one occasionally meets a kind of person all but extinct in the rest of the English-speaking world: the true peasant, living on his plot of land from arduous, traditional agricultural work, relatively untainted by fashions or effete modern vanities or the need to 'make an impression' on anyone. Often with a slow, sure, and simple outlook on life and sometimes without a great deal of education to complicate things, yet he may turn out to be startlingly eloquent, or rather, poetic, since often his syntax is idiosyncratic and un-English.

This eloquence belongs to another part of Ireland's tradition, one which has at times been quite at odds with its Christianity: lyricism and literature. A love of ballads and story-telling continues to underlie Irish cultural life. Folk music, whether with new words or old, with modern instruments or traditional, remains for all age groups the real, popular music and song of Ireland, heard everywhere in homes and bars to the accompaniment of much drinking, stamping and clapping. As for writing, since the 19C Revival, Irish authors have made their mark with astounding success on English literature. Even in everyday life, clever words are enjoyed for their own sake, and it's conversation—lively, noisy, witty, relaxed, and good-humoured: what is called 'crack' (Gaelic *craic*)—that is the essential ingredient of an enjoyable evening out.

In Ireland as elsewhere, while some of the large towns contain much of interest, in general the greatest rewards are to be found in touring the countryside, discovering equally interesting sights in uncrowded villages and small towns, and taking in the atmosphere and appearance of the rural areas, with often glorious scenery. In this book Ireland has been divided into its four ancient provinces, Leinster, Munster, Connacht (or Connaught), and Ulster. In each, I have chosen a number of journeys, mostly round-trips of about two or three days, which explore each region and give an opportunity to get to know it more intimately. Every one of Ireland's 32 counties has been included.

There is no need, of course, to follow the routes precisely, nor to complete them in the estimated times. The total distances too, given (in miles and kilometres) at the start of each route, are comfortable, approximate figures. Any of these tours can be cut short, or extended, or simply used as starting points for other rural rides. I have assumed that tours will be done at a relaxed pace, after a leisurely start, with pauses to see anything of interest, with breaks for lunch and for tea, and allowing every day's travelling to end in good time for dinner. As the locals say (for the Irish are full of satisfying aphorisms), 'When God made time, he made plenty of it.' And another, equally to the point: 'If you haven't enough time, then it's something wrong with *you*.'

Getting to Ireland

Car Ferries from Britain to Ireland:

Belfast: from Liverpool—Belfast Car Ferries (9 hrs); from Stranraer—Hoverspeed SeaCat (1½ hrs)

Cork: from Swansea—Swansea–Cork Ferries (10 hrs)

Dublin and Dun Laoghaire (pron. Dun Laira or Dun Leary): from Holyhead—B+I, Sealink (3½ hrs)

Larne: from Cairnryan (Scotland)—P&O (2 hrs); from Stranraer (Scotland)—Sealink (2½ hrs)

Rosslare: from Fishguard—Sealink (3½ hrs); from Pembroke—B+I (4¼ hrs).

Air Services

There are flights to Belfast, Dublin and 7 other Irish airports from 19 British airports. There are direct flights to Dublin and Shannon from a number of cities in North America. The principal British services include:

Belfast: shuttle service hourly from London (Heathrow)—British Airways, British Midland

Cork: from London (Heathrow)—Aer Lingus; from Luton—Ryanair; from Birmingham—Aer Lingus; from Manchester—Aer Lingus

Dublin: from London (Heathrow)—Aer Lingus, British Midland; from London (Gatwick)—Aer Lingus; from Luton—Ryanair; from Birmingham—Aer Lingus; from Edinburgh—Aer Lingus; from Glasgow—Aer Lingus; from Manchester—Aer Lingus, SAS, TAP, Alitalia

Shannon: from London (Heathrow)—Aer Lingus

Knock: from London (Stansted)—Ryanair; from Luton—Ryanair, Manx Airlines; from Manchester—Loganair.

Car hire is available at all airports. The national airline Aer Lingus is also a leading tour operator for holidays in Ireland, and has several interesting Fly-Drive packages on offer. Other options include Aer Lingus' Country Weekends, Farmhouse Holidays, Coach Tours, and Self-Catering programmes.

Roads, Roadsigns, and Maps

Ireland's roads are of reasonably good standard, and they are all numbered and signposted. Yet for some reason, every journey in Ireland is in danger of degenerating into chaos. The simple act of getting from A to B can become impossibly confusing. For travelling on backroads, a decent map is essential. One of the best is the yellow Michelin map no. 405 (Ireland). The Irish Tourist Board (Bord Fáilte) give out a free touring map which is less detailed, but very useful, and which clearly shows the Gaeltacht (Irish-speaking) areas. Small-scale Ordnance Survey maps reveal that Ireland has an unusual density of rural lanes, most not shown on ordinary motoring maps. It is wise to obtain maps before touring, as they are often difficult to find outside the largest towns.

Signposting is clear enough on the major highways between large towns, but on backroads signs give the impression that they exist mainly to let visitors know the Gaelic name for each place, no matter how unpronounceable it looks, rather than how to get there.

Things to beware of with roadsigns are:

1. The *road number* on the sign differs from the map—this is not only because road numbers are occasionally changed but because almost all roads have two alternative numbers (where possible, both have been shown in the text).

2. *Distances* may be shown in either miles or kilometres, and it often is not clear which is being used; as a general rule, where it is not stated, the figure is in miles; often no distances are given.

3. The same place may be indicated in two different *directions*; when this happens, note the distances (although one may be in miles and the other in kilometres)—the longer route is often more scenic; but be wary of signs which say 'Scenic Route' without giving destinations or distances.

4. Many towns and villages are known by *more than one name*; not only do many have both an English and an Irish name, but some have two or three names in both languages, and these may also have alternative spellings; in the text I have given the name most used by residents, with common alternatives in parentheses.

5. In the *Gaeltacht*, only the Irish-language (i.e. Gaelic) name and spelling is given on signs, a perfectly justifiable political move which seems however to defeat the whole object of signposting roads at all, that is, to explain to strangers how to get from A to B (but see the section on reading Gaelic signs, below); a couple of Irish-language signs worth recognising: Dainséar = Danger, and Géill Slí = Give Way.

In the text, Gaelic names have been given where these are still in use, and have been shown as the principal name in Gaeltacht areas, with the English in parentheses. To avoid overcrowding the maps, only the English names have been shown on them.

The proper way to find where you're going is, in any case, to ask someone (though you may get the reply: 'Well, you're settin' out to the wrong place to start with'). People are helpful, and if things get desperate it's never far to a B&B!

Driving

Major highways usually have just two lanes, with a broad hard-shoulder onto which considerate drivers will sometimes move to allow others to overtake. However, these main arterial roads often become congested close to large towns, and standards of driving are not high. By contrast, backroads are delightfully uncrowded, with a slow and congenial pace. It is quite usual, especially in the west, for every driver to raise a forefinger to salute every other, and for pedestrians to lift a hand in greeting. It is wise to keep the speed right down, as every bend (and there are many) could conceal a wavering cyclist, a child playing, or sheep resting on the roadway.

Parking poses no problem at all in most towns or villages. Note however that in Northern Ireland many urban areas are designated as Control Zones (always clearly indicated) in which it is forbidden to leave any unaccompanied vehicle. Control Zones may be closed off altogether at certain times. Northern Ireland towns usually have ample parking facilities on the outskirts of the central district.

Note that garages are usually closed on Sunday, and that credit cards are not widely accepted for petrol.

Crossing the Border

A national frontier separates the British enclave known as Northern Ireland from the rest of the country. This border is guarded by well-protected British soldiers at grim-looking crossing points. However, the crossing itself is easy and for thousands of Irish people is an everyday matter. Usually all traffic is waved through without the least formality, but it is sensible to approach crossing points showly and be prepared to stop if asked. Sometimes drivers may be asked to show identification (passport or driving licence). Whatever your views about the matter, always treat the border security men with courtesy and they will do the same to you.

Where to Stay

The Irish Tourist Board (Bord Fáilte) produces a number of booklets detailing the huge range of accommodation to be found in both town and country. They also publish an annual comprehensive handbook, **Ireland Accommodation**, listing all officially approved accommodation, which is classfied into hotels (graded A*, B, B*, B, C), guesthouses (A, B*, B, C), town homes, country homes, farmhouses, holiday centres, holiday hostels, and youth hostels. There is plenty of rural self-catering accommodation available too, either in specially adapted cottages or in purpose-built houses, including some outwardly modelled on the traditional thatched single-storey dwelling, but with comfortable well-equipped interiors.

There are several different hotel and guesthouse federations, often with broadly overlapping membership. Low-priced bed-and-breakfast accommodation in people's homes is widely available: it is generally clean, simple but comfortable, and friendly, with good plain home-cooking served in generous quantities. Look for the sign 'Bord Fáilte Approved' displayed outside. Approved places are listed in the handbook of the **Town and Country Homes** association.

Although not as widespread as B&Bs, there are also many middle-range country inns or hotels, mainly owned and run by a family. These generally offer homely comfort and a warm welcome; many have an unpretentious dining room and convivial bar. A large number are listed (with photo) in the annual booklet of the **Irish Hotels Federation** (*Be Our Guest*).

In addition to this generally adequate but unassuming standard, Ireland also has a large number of beautiful country houses and imposing castles which have been converted into guesthouses or hotels. These former grand private homes are mostly family-run, and offer a high standard of relaxed comfort and old-fashioned style which compares very favourably to anything available in Britain or Europe. A selection is listed in the little booklet **Irish Country Houses and Restaurants**.

Of the other associations, a couple of the most interesting are the **Irish Organic Farm Guesthouses** (some are simple cottages, others palatial country houses) and the farmhouses of the **Irish Farm Holidays Association**.

Accommodation in **Northern Ireland** is classified into hotels (A*, A, B*, B, C), guesthouses (A or B), farm and country houses, rural guesthouses (sometimes rather grander than the town version), and other approved accommodation (ungraded). All approved places are listed in the Northern Ireland Tourist Board booklet called ***All the Places to Stay***, which includes youth hostels and self-catering holiday homes.

The **Michelin** red guide to Great Britain and Ireland lists a selection of the better hotels and restaurants in the Republic of Ireland and Northern Ireland.

Along all routes, there is plenty of B&B accommodation and usually there are a few small hotels. Any exceptional or above-average establishments which I know personally have been named and described in more detail.

Eating

Eating out is broadly along British lines, though plainer and more filling, with simpler cooking, often fresher meat and fish, and with fewer imported ingredients or Continental influences. Sturdy wholemeal breads, fresh, tender scones for both breakfast and tea, and delicious fresh cream, are specialities, and potatoes are served with almost every meal. Portions are usually astonishingly large. Breakfasts are huge enough to tide you over lunch. At meals, wine is a rarity and sold at wincingly high prices—the more typical Irish custom is to drink tea with meals. The vast majority of eating establishments offer, at best, no more than ordinary home cooking, and quantity not quality is what most of their customers demand. A few such snack bars, cafés, coffee lounges, or restaurants can be found in any town, though often not in villages. One of the most reliable and available places in both town and country to obtain a full meal is the lounge, bar, or dining room of a hotel. About 400 restaurants in Ireland (listed in booklet from Irish Tourist Board) display a sign indicating that they offer a 'Tourist Menu': a relatively low-priced three-course set meal.

Despite the general Irish preference for simple plain food, Ireland also has a handful of restaurants which number among Europe's best, and which could confidently claim to have some of the finest cuisine to be found anywhere.

Names and details are given in the text of any outstanding restaurant along a route.

Pubs

Public houses (pubs, bars, lounges), generally known simply by the name of the proprietor, are the centre of social life in village Ireland. The best are lively, relaxed places where whole families go out to meet friends and neighbours but where strangers are welcome. Often there is live music, with a local group playing traditional Irish music. While in larger towns pubs may be fine old-fashioned places handsome with polished wood and gleaming brass, in small towns and villages they often look like shops. Indeed they may well be shops, with a display of shirts or shoes in the window, but with a small bar inside!

Pubs are licensed for about 12 hours daily, usually 11am to 11pm, or 11.30pm in summer. Dublin and Cork have the 'holy hour', from about 2.30pm to 3.30pm, when pubs close their doors—but let you stay inside to enjoy your drink! Similarly, when it comes to closing time, many places simply lock the front door and open the back, with business as usual until the barman wants to pack up for the night. Nor is it unusual to go into a pub just as the door is being unlocked in the morning, only to find the place already half full with a convivial crowd of drinkers who have come in the back way.

Drinking habits are traditional, and stout beers remain the most popular order—especially Guinness, which, it's true, does taste different in Ireland. Murphy's is another popular stout. When ordering beers, ask for either a pint or 'a glass' (not 'a half' as in Britain). Other favourite drinks include Irish whiskeys (always spelt with an *e*) such as Bushmills or Paddys. Irish coffee is a glass of black coffee with a tot of whiskey in it, and topped with cream to make it look like Guinness.

It's not unusual to see people having a pot of tea in a pub; almost any place which serves food (and most do have sandwiches or similar) will tend to assume that you'll probably want tea with it rather than beer. Tea, incidentally, is usually of the highest quality, and served very strong. The Irish drink a lot of it.

Sightseeing

For the enthusiast of archaeology, Ireland has an exceptional number of prehistoric and early-historic remains. Megalithic dolmens, court tombs of about 4000BC, passage graves of 2500BC, stone circles dating from 2000–1200BC, and pillar stones or *galláns* (or menhirs) are abundant and accessible. Relics of the early Christian and medieval periods too can be seen everywhere, with some—like the tall Round Towers which monks used as lookouts and shelters during the Viking raids—unique to Ireland.

However, when sightseeing, take with a pinch of salt the eloquent hyperbole which attends every ruin, monument, abandoned abbey, birth-place of a national hero, or medieval castle. In general these make excellent points at which to pause on an unhurried journey, an excuse to stretch your legs, little more than that. There are outstanding exceptions though, such as Glendalough, Kilkenny, or Cashel. And the scale of the man-made 'sights' tends to be surprisingly small: few are likely to overawe with their grandeur or majesty. By contrast, some of the work which Nature has made in Ireland, especially along the west and north coasts, is truly breathtaking.

Samuel Johnson dismissed many great spectacles as 'Well worth seeing but not worth *going* to see'. Yet the converse is actually more often true: it is not so much that sights are worth seeing—although some of them most certainly are—but that the journey to see them was well worth making.

Caravan Dwellers

Camping on town boundaries or roadside verges for months at a time, hoarding scrap from which to recycle a living, 'Travellers' are often seen in Ireland, especially in the western counties and on the outskirts of Dublin. In general their caravans are seen in ones or twos rather than several together, and these makeshift camps are characterised by lines of washing, playing children, often a couple of horses. These people are the victims of considerable hostility and discrimination, and the commonest myth circu-lated about them is that, despite their apparent poverty, all caravan dwellers have thousands of pounds hidden away. Unrelated to Romany Gypsies (whatever some may claim), and looking nothing like them, many are likely to be descendants of the uprooted famine survivors. Although Travellers dislike the name Tinkers, it is interesting that the Report of the Travelling People's Review Body (Irish Government publication, 1983), interviewing over 3,000 Travellers, found that of the 769 who claimed to have a trade, 600 were indeed tin-smiths or tinkers, one of those age-old occupations open to itinerants, though there is no call for it now.

The Famine

This relatively recent catastrophe had a profound, permanent effect on Irish life and society, and in some ways the country is still reeling from its impact. There were a number of famine periods in nineteenth-century Ireland, but none as bad as the 'Great Hunger', the Famine of 1845–8. In the decades beforehand, millions of poor tenant families lived on over-crowded and largely unproductive land, exporting almost all their produce to pay rents to absentee landlords in England. Tenants had few rights: for example, any improvement which they made to their premises led to an increase in rent, while non-payment generally led to immediate and unceremonious eviction. To help him survive, the tenant farmer would let the least productive corner of his smallholding to the even poorer 'cottiers'.

In this context, most peasants in 19C Ireland endured unthinkable hardship and had to live almost entirely on potatoes, which were a useful crop because they are filling to eat, and cheap and easy to grow. The Famine resulted from a period of crop failures and blight. It led to about one million deaths from starvation, and even more massive emigration and abandonment of farms as people took to the road or fled to North America (in so-called 'coffin ships'), many so far gone in health and hunger as to die on the way. Meanwhile the English and Anglo-Irish landlords, with some notable exceptions, still insisted on their rents and evicted those who could not pay. The 'emptiness' of the west, which was the worst-affected region, largely results from this. The population of Ireland before the Famine was 8 million; afterwards it stood at 6½ million, of whom 1 million were living in workhouses. Today, owing to a process of emigration which has continued ever since, it is just over 5 million, including 1½ million in Northern Ireland.

The Gaeltacht

The two official languages of the Republic of Ireland are English and Irish. Ireland was still almost entirely Irish-speaking in the 16C, and even in the 17C some of Gaelic's best ballad poetry was being composed and per-formed. The formation after Cromwell of an English upper class in Ireland encouraged the widespread learning of the English language. In the 19C, the Irish language suffered from two important events: first the establish-ment by the English of a compulsory National School system (1831) in which all teaching was in English, and secondly the Famine, which had its most destructive impact on those regions of the country and those parts of the population which were still most deeply rooted in Gaelic culture and language. Later 19C and then 20C pressures on the language have made

English overwhelmingly pre-eminent. It is believed that the proportion of the population who speak Irish as a first language is now no more than 1%. However many more, perhaps a majority, have some understanding of the language. The government of the Republic is determined to keep the national language alive, and it is a compulsory subject in schools. In addition areas with a high proportion of native Irish-speakers have been designated as **Gaeltacht**; these districts are given concessions in tax, government employment, grants to business etc. to encourage their development. The principal Gaeltacht areas are in the west, although there are smaller *Gaeltachtaí* in several other parts of the country. County Donegal contains the largest number of native Irish-speakers, while County Galway has the largest single area of Gaeltacht.

It is noticeable though that, even in the Gaeltacht, all advertising and all signs over garages, pubs and shops are in English, and almost all the people one overhears speaking are talking English. It remains true nevertheless that the Irish language is more widely known and more used in these districts than elsewhere.

Within each Gaeltacht region, roadsigns are usually in the Irish language only, which can be puzzling. In the route descriptions, I have given the Gaelic name as the principal name of any village in the Gaeltacht, and have put its most common English names in parentheses.

Reading Gaelic Signs

Those baffling roadsigns in Gaelic, especially in the Gaeltacht where no English equivalent is given, can be read and understood with a little effort. Irish lettering is based on medieval handwriting of our present roman alphabet (and there are no capital letters except for R and S). Traditionally the letters of the alphabet were named after trees—*aelm*, *beith*, *coll*, etc. (elm, beech, hazel . . .), but modern Gaelic-speakers use the same names as in English. Rules of pronunciation (and the spelling which indicates it) are complex:

Every consonant has both a 'broad' and a 'slender' form, indicated by the adjacent vowels. A, o, u make consonants broad; e, i make them slender. But the differences between a broad and a slender pronunciation are actually very slight, with a few exceptions which are:

slender d—*d* as English 'do'; broad d—rather sibilant *d* as in 'dress'
slender s—*sh* sound, as in English 'sure'; broad s—*s* as in 'soon'
slender t—breathy *t* as in French *très*; broad t—sharper *t* as English 'tool'.

Some consonants (b, c, d, f, g, m, p, s) become aspirates when followed by h (in roman lettering) or with a dot over the letter (in Gaelic lettering).

In certain consonant combinations, only the first letter is sounded: bp, dt, gc, bhf (= v, because v is written bh in Irish), mb, nd.

The Gaeltacht: Irish-speaking areas

Other sounds to watch out for are ch (hard *h*, as in Scottish loch), broad r (always trilled as in Scots speech), slender r (almost like a trilled *z* or th).

With vowels, a long vowel is indicated with the acute accent; others are very short. Diphthong ao sounds like *ai* as in English 'hair', except before a slender consonant, when it becomes like *ee* in 'see'. Usually when two or more vowels appear together, one or more is merely an indicator of whether adjacent consonants are broad or slender.

Actually, there's more to it than this! These are just the most elementary basics. And note that as in English there are numerous exceptions to these rules and marked local differences in pronunciation. In addition, the spelling was revised in 1948 but many signs are still in the old form.

If still undaunted, take a look at the useful book *Teach Yourself Irish*, by Miles Dillon and Donncha ó Cróinin to learn more.

Public Holidays

The Republic

1 Jan. — New Year's Day
17 Mar. — St Patrick's Day (big national celebrations, processions, etc.)
Good Friday (not a statutory holiday)
Easter Monday
1st Mon. in June (June Holiday)
1st Mon. in Aug. (August Holiday)
Last Mon. in Oct. (October Holiday)
25 Dec. — Christmas Day
26 Dec. — St Stephen's Day

The North

(NB: *Days marked*, not statutory holidays, are the 'Marching Season' when businesses may be closed and there is a risk of civil disturbance.*)
1 Jan. — New Year's Day
17 Mar. — St Patrick's Day
Good Friday (not a statutory holiday)
Easter Monday
1st Mon. in May (May Day)
Last Mon. in May (Spring Bank Holiday)
12 Jul.* — Orangeman's Day, 'The Twelfth' (big colourful parades to celebrate the victory of Protestantism and the humiliation of Catholicism at the Battle of the Boyne in 1690)
13–17 Jul.* — Local Protestant parades and festivals to celebrate victory at the Boyne
15 Aug.* — Feast of the Assumption — Catholic parades
Last Mon. in Aug. (Summer Bank Holiday)
25 Dec. — Christmas Day
26 Dec. — Boxing Day

(Republic and North: when 1 Jan., 25 or 26 Dec. fall at a weekend, days off *in lieu* are given in the following week.)

Touring Information

The **Irish Tourist Board** (*or* **Bord Fáilte**, pron. Bord Falltcher) is the national tourist organisation of the Republic of Ireland. Its offices abroad have an abundance of information, maps, vacation ideas. ITB in Britain is at 150 New Bond St, London W1Y 0AQ (071–493 3201). In the United States contact ITB at 230 N Michigan Ave, Chicago, Il 60601 (312–726 9356); 590 Fifth Ave, New York, NY 10036 (212–869 5500); 1880 Century Park E, Suite 314, Los Angeles, Ca 90067 (213–557 0722); 681 Market St, San Francisco, Ca 94105 (415–781 5688). In Canada at 69

Yonge St, Toronto M5E 1K3 (416–364 1301. In Australia at MLC Centre, 37th Level, Martin Place, Sydney 2000 (02–232 7460). In New Zealand, 2nd Floor, Dingwall Building, 87 Queen St, PO Box 279, Auckland 1 (09–793 708).

Among the Irish Tourist Board's most useful publications are: a map of the country; the annual Calendar of Events; annual handbooks *Guest Accommodation* and *Dining in Ireland*; *Ireland Guide*; *Ireland's Heritage*; and the 26 County Guides.

Information about Northern Ireland is available from the **Northern Ireland Tourist Board**, St Anne's Court, 59 North Street, Belfast BT1 1NB (0232 246609). They have an office in the USA at 40 W 57th St, 3rd floor, New York, NY 10019 (212–765 5144). Alternatively contact any of the offices worldwide of the **British Tourist Authority**. Useful publications include the annual guides: *Stop and Visit*; *Let's Eat Out*; *All the Places to Stay*.

Within Ireland, the main information office of the Irish Tourist Board is based at 14 Upper O'Connell St, Dublin (01–747733). There are about 75 other tourist information offices in towns around Ireland, but many of the offices are open only on certain days, or during certain months. They are known and signposted locally by various names—Visitor Centre, Tourist Office, Visitor Information, Tourist Information Office, etc. *In the text I have pointed out locations of these where they exist and have referred to all of them as Tourist Offices.*

Abbreviations

CI	Church of Ireland (Anglican)
Co	County
ft	feet
km	kilometres
RC	Roman Catholic

AN IRISH GLOSSARY

Many Gaelic (i.e. Irish) words to describe architecture, topography, etc. have passed into English as it is spoken in Ireland, and many distinctive English and Irish terms are used to describe the typical habitations and structures of Ireland's history and prehistory. A knowledge of certain Irish suffixes and prefixes also helps to understand the present-day names of towns and villages, which were given garbled and meaningless English appellations by the British military men who surveyed the country. In the political sphere too, a number of Irish and English words in common use may need explanation.

aglish	church
Anglo-Irish	generally a Protestant landowning family of English descent
Anglo-Norman	invaders from Britain after the Norman settlement of England and Wales; they combined French, Viking (i.e Norman) and often Welsh origins
ard	high place
Ascendancy	'rule' or the ruling population, as in Protestant Ascendancy
ath, atha	river crossing
avon	same as: owen
baile	settlement, village
bailey	see: motte
bal	mouth of a river
ballina	ford, crossing, opening
bally	Anglicised rendering of baile (q.v.)
bawn	enclosed yard joined to a fortified house
beg	small
ben	peak, summit
Black and Tans	British soldiers transferred to police duty in Ireland, so-called because they wore a mixture of army and police uniform; notoriously undisciplined and brutal
bog	very moist terrain with a thick spongy layer of mosses etc.

booley	summer pasture; 'booleying' is the moving of cattle between summer and winter grazing areas
Bord Fáilte	(pron. Bord Fall-ch) Irish Tourist Board
boreen	a quiet country lane
bullaun	artificially hollowed stone
bun	end of something, e.g. of a road or river, or the foot of a hill
caher, cahir	a large cashel
cairn	pile of stones marking a (usually prehistoric) grave
carrig, carrick	literally, rock; usually refers to a stone rampart encircling a settlement, village, fort, etc.
cashel	a fortified settlement within high ramparts, i.e. a fort or castle
castle	not always what it suggests—often only a landowner's fortified house
cathair	(pron. caher) same as: caher (q.v.)
ceidhle	(pron. caylee) a bit of a party, generally with traditional Irish music and dancing
Church of Ireland	exactly the same as the Church of England; Anglican
CIE	*Cora Iompair Eireann*, the State transport company (operates buses, trains, boats)
cill	same as kill (q.v.)
clachan	small hamlet
clochán	primitive dry-stone dwelling in beehive shape; also, stepping stones across a stream
clogh	stone
clogher	stone place
clon	meadow
cnoc	same as: knock (q.v.)
court cairn	frequent in Ireland: a cairn with ritual galleries leading off
crack	from Irish *craic*, lively convivial company and conversation
crannóg	a prehistoric settlement, village, house, etc. built on an artificial island in a lake
currach	a small boat made of tarred canvas (formerly skins) over a light frame
curragh	low flat land, often marshy
Dáil	(pron. Doil) lower house of Parliament of the Irish Republic
Dainséar	(roadsign) Danger
demesne	the lands or estate belonging with a building; in England normally a lawyers' word, in Ireland it is in common use
derg	red
derry	oak

Diamond	main square of Ulster Plantation town
dolmen	(archaeological) stone-age grave made of a large horizontal stone placed across smaller uprights
drum	small hill or raised ground
drumlin	small egg-like hills, common in parts of Ireland
du, dub, duf, duv	black
dun	a fort
Eire	Irish name for Ireland, often used to mean the Republic
Éirann	refers to something national, Irish
ennis	island
Erse	(word not heard in Ireland) a name for the Gaelic language
fáilte	(pron. fall-ch) (greeting) welcome
feis	(pron. fesh) a gathering or assembly
feis ceoil	(pron. fesh cayle) festival with music
Fenians	Irish Republican Brotherhood, militant nationalist group founded 1858
Fianna Fail	(pron. Feeanna Foil) centrist political party with roots in that section of the Nationalist movement which did not accept the continued British rule in the North
Fine Gael	(pron. Feena Gale) centrist political party which grew out of a temporary acceptance of the division of Ireland into two in order to achieve an independent republic
fir	men—used on toilet door
fleadh	(pron. flah) music festival; plural *fleadhanna*
Gaelic	the Irish language, always referred to in Ireland as Irish; anything traditionally Irish
Gaelic Football	a traditional Irish sport (rather like rugby football)
Gaeltacht	(or *Ghaeltacht*) (pron. Goiltohht or Gaeltahht) districts officially designated as Irish-speaking—see p. 9
gallan, gallaun	standing stone, menhir
gallowglass	literally, a foreign mercenary soldier (Irish *gall óglach*), originally brought from Scotland by Irish clan chiefs, and now refers to any heavily armed foot soldier in medieval Ireland (or a statue of one)
Garda, Gardai	(pron. gorda, gordee) the police, also known as the Gards (pron. as English 'guards')
Géill Sli	(roadsign) Give Way
glen	valley
Home Rule	self-government
Hibernian	in political or architectural usage, means Irish
High Cross	common in Ireland: a tall stone cross, usually

	richly carved, generally 8–12C
hurling	a traditional Irish sport (rather like speeded-up hockey)
innis, inis, inch	from *inis*, island; sometimes from *inse*, water meadow
IRA	Irish Republican Army, militant nationalist organisation which fought for Irish independence (see Northern Ireland Glossary below)
keel	narrow
kelp	type of edible seaweed, much used as a fertiliser
ken	head
kill	simple church, small monastic site; also means narrow
knock	hill (in principle, the *k* is sounded)
Land League	founded 1849, to fight to protect destitute farmers from eviction
leiter, letter	hillside
lis, liss	an area enclosed within earth ramparts, often a fortified field for animals
lough (or loch)	lake
mac	(in personal names) son, descendant
Mass rock	open-air altar used secretly after Catholicism made illegal under the Penal Laws, 1695–1829 (see Irish History, p. 171)
mona	peat, or peat bog
monastir	from *mainistir*, monastery
mor	large (or important)
motte	a Norman defence: fortified mound with flattened top; often combined with a bailey, a fortified enclosure; a bailey can also be a courtyard within a castle
mná	women—used on toilet door
Northern Ireland	the 'six counties' of Derry, Antrim, Tyrone, Fermanagh, Armagh, and Down, which remained under British rule following the Government of Ireland Act 1920 and the Anglo-Irish War (1919–21) which together brought about the independence of the rest of Ireland; the inhabitants may be correctly referred to as Irish, as the area is part of the United Kingdom (of Great Britain and Northern Ireland) but not part of Britain (i.e. the mainland of England, Scotland, and Wales) or Great Britain (which includes offshore islands except Ireland), while the term British Isles is geographical, not political, and refers to the whole of Great Britain, Northern Ireland,

	and the Republic; see: Ulster
ó, ua, ui	(in personal names) descendant (in English language, written as O')
Ogham	system of writing, used about 5C; an Ogham stone is a stone with an Ogham inscription
Oifig an Phoist	Post Office
oughter	higher, upper
owen	river
The Pale	the area around Dublin under the full control of the Anglo-Normans and later, the English; 'beyond the pale' meant the chaotic and ungovernable regions in the rest of Ireland
Pattern	festival day of a local patron saint
peat	fibrous brown 'earth' made entirely of decayed bog vegetation
Plantation	the organised settlement of Protestant colonists from Scotland and England on land confiscated from conquered Irish lords, esp. in Ulster
Planter	one of the Protestant settlers 'planted' in Ireland
poteen	strong potato spirit, brewed illegally
Progressive Democrats	centrist political party favouring a secular Irish Republic with no territorial claim to the North
rath	rampart around settlement or village
roe, rua	red
ros, ross	a promontory of land, a wood, or a copse
Round Tower	a distinctive feature of many medieval Irish monastic sites: a tall narrow cylindrical tower, usually with a conical roof; the doorway was high off the ground and accessible by a rope ladder; when threatened (usually by Viking raiders) the monks could take refuge inside the tower; between raids, a look-out could be posted at the top
shane, shan	old
sheila-na-gig	female figurine with exaggerated sexual characteristics
sidecar	pony and trap, jaunting car
skerry, skerrig	craggy rock
sláinte!	(pron. slawn-ch) Cheers!
slane	special spade for digging or cutting turf from the bogs
slieve	mountain
souterrain	(archaeological term) underground chamber
strand	usual Irish word for a beach
Taoiseach	(pron. Tee-shuck) Prime Minister
TD	Teachta Dala, i.e. Member of Parliament
teampull	church

Tholsel, Tolsel	the old administrative building of a town, often combining town hall, guildhall, customs house, and court room
tober, tubber	a well, often considered holy or magical
tower house	common in Ireland: a fortified lordly domestic dwelling of several stories, resembling a small but tall castle—and most are locally known as castles; family life was conducted in the relative safety of the upper floors
townland	a district, an area of land with a name, but not necessarily occupied by a town, or even a village
tra	beach (or strand)
tull, tully	small hill
turbary	an area of bog rented by a small farmer to supply himself with peat
turf	the more usual Irish name for peat
tyr	land, country
Ulster	one of the 4 provinces of Ireland, containing 9 counties, but the name is often used (especially by the British administration) to mean the 6 counties of Northern Ireland (q.v.); the 3 Ulster counties in the Republic are Cavan, Monaghan, and Donegal
victualler	a butcher's shop

A Northern Ireland glossary

Anglo-Irish Agreement	1985 treaty between Britain and Ireland allowing the Dublin government a consultative role in N. Ireland—strongly opposed by Protestants
Catholic	descendant of native Irish population pre-dating 17C—see Protestant
IRA	Irish Republican Army, intent on achieving unity and independence for Ireland by force; now active only in Northern Ireland and divided into Provisional and Official factions by ideological differences—illegal
Loyalist	one who wants Northern Ireland to remain part of the United Kingdom (usually a Protestant)
Nationalist	formerly an advocate of Irish independence, now means one who wants Northern Ireland to become part of the Irish Republic (usually a Catholic)
Orange Hall	local meeting hall of the Orange Order
Orange Order	fanatical Protestant secret society, founded

	1790s, now highly influential in Northern Ireland affairs
Protestant	descendant of the English and Scots who took over the land of defeated Irish and colonised Ulster from 17C—see Catholic
Provo	(= Provisional) see IRA
Republican	since the formation of the Irish Republic, means the same as Nationalist
RUC	(= Royal Ulster Constabulary) the police
Sinn Fein	(pron. shin fain) literally 'we ourselves', political party committed to uniting Northern Ireland to the Republic (divided into Official and Provisional factions in line with the IRA division)
UDA	(Ulster Defence Association) Protestant paramilitary terrorist organisation—made illegal in 1992
UDF	(Ulster Defence Force) British Army regiment recruited and stationed in Northern Ireland
Unionist	same as Loyalist
UVF	(Ulster Volunteer Force) Protestant paramilitary and terrorist organisation—illegal

1 CONNACHT

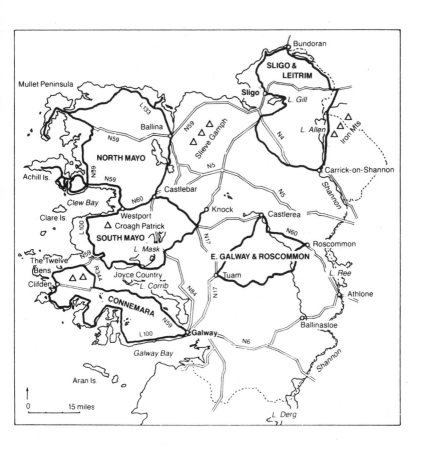

Connacht, or **Connaught**, wildly beautiful but largely uncultivable country in Ireland's far west, was where the dispossessed Irish were forced by Cromwell after their lands had been taken from them in 1652–4. The choice Cromwell gave these Catholic landowners was 'To hell or Connacht'—and for many of them the latter was only marginally preferable. Later, overcrowded and unproductive, the province was hit badly by the Famine. So for two reasons it symbolises Ireland's suffering. Yet this now largely depopulated landscape of peat and rock and wind and water also captures the positive side of Ireland's spirit, a haunting emptiness, a quiet lonely longing, a sense of a time passing without making any mark, and of a humble good-hearted people's endurance and survival. Many who live here or visit the area fall deeply in love with its distinctive atmosphere.

Much of Connacht remains Irish-speaking, with large areas of Gaeltacht in the north west (Co. Mayo) and around Galway City and along Galway Bay. Religious devotion too continues at a high level. This is accentuated by the importance of the shrine of Knock, which attracts tens of thousands of pilgrims annually, and by the 'holy mountain' Croagh Patrick.

North Mayo

3 days/220 miles (367km)/from Westport

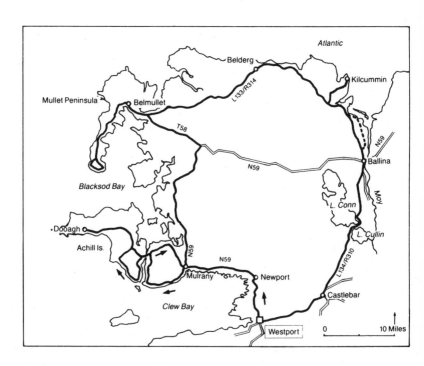

Large areas of County Mayo, with its vast 'desert' of peat bogs and its smooth green, featureless hills, are little visited and indeed barely inhabited. This route gets into the heart of that region. It has a superb, lost, far-away feeling. The small towns and villages are utterly provincial, the people unassuming and rustic. Much of the area is classified as Gaeltacht (Gaelic-speaking), and it was here that I began to notice that speaking the Irish language seems to give people a slightly different character and demeanour. Hard to pinpoint precisely, the difference is of a certain inner quiet, a touch more initial shyness and reserve, opening into a heightened air of frankness. Or perhaps that is just the effect of living in such a remote and tranquil region.

For more about **WESTPORT** (pop: 3,500), our starting point on the shore of Clew Bay, see p. 42.

Take N59/T71 north from the town, through a green countryside of drumlins just inland, to **NEWPORT**. This village, popular with anglers, looks forbidding at first because everything is built of dark stone, but turns out to be a pleasing little place. It rises attractively up the slope from the bank of a broad waterway which flows into the bay. For this is a former seaport whose prosperity was never quite as great as had been planned. To the right of the handsome bridge which enters the village there is a second bridge, which once carried a railway but is now grass-covered. While to the left is **Newport House** (098–41222), for two centuries seat of a branch of the noble ó Donel family, and now an enticing country house hotel (member of the Relais et Châteaux federation).

Although they successfully established themselves here, the ó Donels were originally from Ulster, where they had been defeated and forced out by the Cromwellian confiscation; as the local saying has it, 'When ó Donel first came into it, ó Malley was here to welcome him.' For this is traditional ó Malley country. Even today, 80 per cent of ó Malley (now written O'Malley) births occur in Connacht — their annual clan gathering is usually held in Westport. The most famous or infamous of them was surely Connacht's wild and indomitable 16C queen, Grace ó Malley, also known as Grainne Uaile (or Grainne ui Mhaille or Grania Wael). She has become an almost mythical heroine locally. The whole of this part of the Connacht coast is dotted with the fortified refuges which she used as the need arose, but her home was Clare Island, far out in Clew Bay where it opens into the Atlantic. (More about Grace, and Clare Island on p. 40).

Newport House today is a fine Georgian mansion draped in gorgeous Virginia creeper, standing in grounds beside the tidal river and quay. Inside there are elegant lounges and a magnificent central stairway and hall. The bedrooms are not especially large, but they are unpretentiously comfortable and very quiet. They are free of phone and television. The restaurant offers the best type of Irish cooking, with absolutely fresh local ingredients, well prepared and served in abundant quantities. For breakfast, brought to the bedroom, there was coffee and milk in silver-plated jugs, fresh breads, home-made marmalade, a big bowl of fresh butter (*not* foil-wrapped 'portions'), rashers and free-range eggs (we knew they were free range because we could see the hens from our room — however they were penned up overnight to prevent them waking the guests!).

On the top of Newport's little hill, a grim dark church in neo-Romanesque style (built 1914) has some remarkably good stained glass.

The three windows over the altar are among the best modern stained glass I have seen anywhere. In the street nearby, a wall-painting in naive style shows Father Manus Sweeney being captured and hanged by the British in 1799. More about Father Sweeney in a moment.

If you want to spend some time at Newport, it makes a good base for some superb walks and drives. Our road (N59/T71) continues winding through picturebook countryside, over green hills dotted with white cottages. On the day we drove it, a mist hung over higher hills in the distance, while above us the pearly sky was patched with blue and white. Everything was satisfying to the eye and the soul.

Just 2 miles up the road, a small sign on the left points out a turning for '**Burrishoole Abbey**'. The lane leads down to the waterside, where the small 'abbey' turns out to be the church of a small 15C Dominican priory called St Mary's Priory. A few rowing boats are pulled up alongside its sheltered inlet. Quite apart from the lovely setting, the church itself is rather beautiful, with walls in good condition, but roofless. Part of its cloisters survives, and its cemetery is still very much in use. Inside the church, among several 18C graves, Father Manus Sweeney, aged 36, was buried in his family tomb. A cross was erected by parishioners of Burrishoole with the words

> *To the memory of Father Manus Sweeney*
> *a holy and patriotic priest*
> *who was hanged at Newport*
> *June 8th, 1799,*
> *because he had joined with*
> *his countrymen*
> *in the Rebellion of 1798.*
> *His name shall be in request*
> *from generation to generation.*

This suggests that he was perhaps one of those Mayo men who joined the French Revolutionaries who landed at Kilcummin (farther along this route) in 1798 and led a military campaign against the English.

Return to the road, and soon another sign on the left points the way down to **Carrickhowley Castle**, otherwise known as Carrigahooley, Carrigahooly, Carrickhooly, and Carraighooley Castle . . . and also as Rockfleet Castle! Reached down a long track, standing on a broad flat rock in a wildly rocky sea inlet, this 'castle', one of Grace ó Malley's boltholes, is in fact a waterside fortification suitable only for an emergency retreat. It consists of nothing but a small square tower in excellent condition, and is virtually impregnable. Indeed the English forces who besieged it in 1574 were decisively beaten off by Grace, who—unlikely as it seems—made her home in these cramped quarters for a while. For it was in this tiny fortress that she so notoriously 'pulled a fast one' on the man who had married her, Richard Burke, also called MacWilliam Oughter, whose family had built and owned Carrickhowley tower. The unfortunate fellow, it is believed, actually married her for love, and Grace accepted him on condition that the marriage could be terminated by either party after one year.

During that year she garrisoned this and all MacWilliam Oughter's other fortresses with her own loyal soldiers, refused to let the man near her, and at the end of the year installed herself at Carrickhowley and declared the marriage over by shouting 'I dismiss you' at him from its upper window. Of course she had no intention of giving back his fortifications and it was impossible to take them from her. MacWilliam, whom we may consider as an altogether nicer if less exciting person that Grace ó Malley, went on to found Burrishoole Abbey, and retired to live there for the last four years of his life. The key to the Carrickhowley tower is kept by one or other of the nearby residents, and can usually be borrowed between 10am and 6pm (enquire on the spot for current details). The little shore road continues past Carrickhowley around a beautiful sheltered bay.

Return to the main highway and continue towards **MULRANY** (or Mulranny, Mallaranny or An Mhala Raithni), the road along here being thickly edged with wild fuchsias. Mulrany, standing right on the narrow isthmus which connects the **Corraun Peninsula** to the rest of the mainland, offers little beside some holiday accommodation, petrol station, and supermarket. It quickly becomes apparent that this is something of a holiday area, with more visitors than locals. Here N59/T71 turns away northwards; take L141/R319 onto the Peninsula. The Corraun coast road (follow sign; do not attempt this road if misty or dark), which runs around the south side of the Peninsula, is very attractive, with unkempt masses of fuchsias in places, good views of the sea and Clare Island, and cattle meandering on the road. It eventually opens out to a refreshing airy landscape of heather, moss and peat. On the approach to **ACHILL** village this is marred by the multitude of holiday cottages. Achill stands on the Corraun side of Achill Sound, the narrow waterway which separates the mainland of Ireland from **Achill Island**, its largest offshore island.

The road continues straight across the water onto the island as if unaware of the change, and on the other side is the small village of **ACHILL SOUND**, which has a handful of dwellings and shops including one called *Lavell's Grocery Drapery Lounge Bar and Solicitors*.

Turn left here for the 'Atlantic Drive' (not recommended if misty or dark), a spectacular coast road, much of it on the sheer edge of high winding cliffs. It rejoins L141/R319 near Cashel; carry on to **KEEL**, a large sprawling village in an exposed coastal setting, geared up for tourism. Beyond it is **DOOAGH**, which is similar but more attractive with its white cottages on the green shore. Look back from here for a good view of the impressive Cathedral Cliffs on the coast south of Keel. Corrymore Lodge, near Dooagh, used to belong to Captain Charles Boycott, a Mayo land agent in the 1880s. When he defied the Irish Land League's demands for better conditions of tenancy for local farmers, he was so resolutely spurned and ostracised that his name became part of the English language.

Rising to the right of Dooagh is the summit of Slievemore (2,211ft), on the lower slope of which, reached by a 1½ mile drive along an appallingly rough track (starts opposite Dooagh post office), lies the so-called **'deserted village of Slievemore'**. This is the minimal stone skeleton of a former simple village, abandoned during the Famine. My own view is that unless one is doing a postgraduate study of abandoned villages, and has a car which can be wrecked with impunity, this excursion is perhaps not worth the trouble. Nevertheless, it is true what one local writer has said, that the sight of Slievemore's village, where the daily round must have been cruelly poor and hard, 'at once seems to sum up the history of the West of Ireland, landlordism, famine and emigration'. Some, reasonably enough, see here a symbol of oppression, but it brings to mind with equal force the unimaginable improvement in life and society since those days. Slievemore's scenery, seen from this far off the road, is very fine, and not yet intruded upon by holiday cottages. There is intensive peat-cutting in the area. Underground and underwater caverns beneath Slievemore, called the Seal Caves, can be approached from the sea (boat excursions from Dugoort, on Achill's north coast, 2½ miles from Keel).

Achill's improvement in living standards and its tourist industry should indeed be uttered in a single breath. For the island has little cultivable land, hardly even any much suited to pasture, so until tourism began to 'spoil' the place it was desperately poor. Today, apart from welfare benefits, peat-cutting and fishing, visitors from outside provide the islanders with their only significant source of income. During the summer, local fishermen often catch shark around this coast; the shark are a harmless variety, and may occasionally be seen basking in shallows close to the beaches.

Return through Cashel to Achill Sound. In places rhododendron bushes densely line the road. Stay on L141/R319 as it curves round the northern side of Corraun Peninsula. At Mulrany, turn left onto N59/T71 (signposted Belmullet).

Follow this unfrequented 'main' road across open and desolate peat bogs. Resist the temptation to pick up speed: you may be confronted suddenly by a group of sheep or even (it happened to us) a couple of immobile donkeys rooted to the middle of the roadway. Here and there clusters of rhododendrons suggest a possible threat to the future of these bogs—but no one here seems aware of how destructive yet indestructible the rhododendron is when it establishes itself. Around the gloomy-looking village of **BANGOR** there is industrial peat-cutting which makes the landscape ugly. Turn left at Bangor (onto R313/T58) for Belmullet. Along this road peat bogs give way to farmland. The contrast, after so many miles of the peat's dull monotony, is striking. This soon becomes a Gaeltacht area, so roadsigns are confusing. The road passes along the edge of Black Sod Bay to reach **BEAL AN MHUIRTHEAD (Belmullet)**, the main town of the Mullet Peninsula.

Belmullet is a small, villagey, one-horse town enveloped by watery coastal countryside. At the edges of the town are modern houses and bungalows, some with B&B accommodation, as this is an area which attracts a certain amount of budget family tourism. Holidaymakers here tend to be Irish, quiet, outdoorsy.

Mayo turf

The **Mullet Peninsula** is a narrow flatland, windswept and reedy, yet surprisingly densely populated considering its remote and lonely situation. At its southern tip (15 miles south of Belmullet) there are marvellous sea views, while at the Mullet's northern edge the Atlantic beats the cliffs of Erris Head. Though the water is chilly and the waves strong, Mullet also has some good sandy beaches, and 'not a sinner on them except yourself', as our B&B landlady (Mrs Maguire-Murphy at Belmullet) put it. She and her family were Irish-speakers; it was interesting to stay at her house and hear them, through the kitchen door, chatting in this rare language. Then the door would fly open and out the lady herself would come bearing steaming hot dishes of her really excellent cooking. She and all her family—except the youngest child, who spoke only Irish—could talk to us with ease in an English rich with imagery.

Return along R313/T58 from Belmullet, turning left after about 3 miles onto L133/R314. The junction is poorly signposted and could be passed inadvertently. This road travels long miles across the peat 'desert'. [For an enjoyable departure from our road, turn left at Glenamoy to travel the 8 miles to the attractive fishing harbour at Portacloy and the surrounding cliffs of magnificent Benwee Head. A briefer excursion from the road is just before Belderg where the sign points to Belderg Pier: this is a small simple Atlantic fishing harbour.] **BELDERG** (or Belderrig or Béal Deirg) is just an uncaptivating bogland village. It was Sunday when we visited the place, and the whole population of the district was standing in groups along the road idly chatting after Mass.

Just after Belderg is where, in December 1986, 'the bog moved'. This curious event, which in due course will no doubt lead to signposts and local legends, was a sudden and powerful 'landslip' of peat bog (although the land is quite flat here) that pulled down telegraph poles and fences and entirely covered the road.

The bog movement, properly known as a bog 'burst', revealed yet more traces of iron age habitation in this area, which is arguably the most extensive neolithic site in Europe. The thick and homogeneous cover of peat—known as blanket bog—which covers large areas of Ireland, has concealed but preserved all the evidence of pre-peat habitation and farming. Lifting of the peat cover by archaeologists in many parts of the country, though nowhere more so than in this corner of Mayo, has uncovered 5,000-year-old fields, dividing walls, ploughing traces, mill-stones, remnants of houses and huts, grave sites, tools and jewellery. Also discovered are vestiges of oak and pine woods which pre-date the neolithic farms.

It appears that before the formation of the peat cover these now empty parts of Ireland were quite densely inhabited by a farming people who raised beef cattle on grass pasture which, in the climate of the period, kept growing all year round. It was their own farming practice which was to begin the peat-growth that eventually drove the people out. Excessive forest clearance and replacement by grass destroyed the recycling process which had hitherto protected the soil from the effect of the frequent rain. Without the tree cover, the eroding, leaching power of the rainwater made the soil increasingly acid and unworkable—and unsuitable for grass. The eventual result was the development of a wet, acidic terrain in which only mosses thrived. These bog mosses, growing layer upon layer, feeding upon their own organic decay, are the basis of peat.

Take a short walk anywhere in this bog country, and you find a mossy cover with plenty of 'give'; it lies over a squelchy soil, exposed where peat-cutters have been at work. This damp and dark earth is a humus formed by the quickly decayed mosses of previous weeks. Peat is cut in small blocks, either by one man with his narrow spade, or a team, or, in places with industrial peat-cutting, by machine. The pieces are piled up to dry, which they manage to do despite the climate. The solitary peat-cutters, whose wave seems like a greeting from the distant past, and their stacks of cut peat, are both distinctive features of these boglands. For most of the 10 miles between Belderg and Ballycastle the road runs close to beautiful high sward-topped cliffs with magnificent ocean views. At the same time it is passing, on the landward side, the excavated neolithic site of Behy (not signposted) a megalithic tomb at Ballyglass, and other archaeological finds. The plain and simple village of **BALLYCASTLE** marks the end of the bog country, and the road beyond runs through more developed farmland. There is a second 'village' of attractive holiday cottages at Ballycastle. They are outwardly in the traditional style, low white thatched dwellings, but in fact are much better designed inside and far more comfortable than genuine old cottages. Perhaps the hope is unrealistic but one wishes that country people moving out of their pictur-esque but outdated accommodation into new modern homes were moving into places rather like this instead of ordinary unsightly houses and bungalows.

About 5½ miles after Ballycastle a left turn marked 'Humbert's Landing' leads some 3 miles or so off the 'main' road to a simple little fishing harbour hamlet, delightful and untouched, called **KILCUMMIN**. Here a monu-ment in Irish and French—the English don't have much to say on the subject—records the landing on 22 August 1798 of General Humbert and his Revolutionary troops who came over from France to help the Irish cause (as they perceived it) in the 1798 Rebellion. They found the Irish un-Revolutionary, undisciplined, and too religious.

Humbert brought some 1,100 men with him, and his plan was to aid the Irish insurgents in a military attack on the English. It was assumed that this would spark off an Irish rising along French Revolutionary lines. Unfortunately he arrived after the Rebellion had already been all but crushed elsewhere in the country. Humbert's first forays caught the English by surprise and he did have initial success, but there was little Irish enlistment to the cause, and as soon as the English had organised their forces the Franco–Irish group were swiftly defeated. They surrendered on 8 September. The French were returned to France, and the Irish hanged.

Years later, Napoleon expressed regret that he had not taken more seriously the idea of invading Ireland, and led an expedition himself. But by the time he had these thoughts Napoleon had discovered that he could not fulfil his ambition to invade Britain, which would have been much easier if he had first taken Ireland.

Although such a short-lived adventure, the unexpected arrival of the French troops, complete with Revolutionary fervour, into the midst of this remote corner of a poor country, has sparked many imaginations. W.B. Yeats' play *Cathleen ní Houlihan* has the French invasion in the background, and the events are retold in *The Year of the French*, a novel by Thomas Flanagan, which has been translated into French and made into a film for Irish and French television.

Return from Kilcummin to the main road (R314/L133) and carry on into **KILLALA**, a village on the coast of Killala Bay. Humbert came straight here from Kilcummin, taking the village and making it his base. The village is dominated by a striking Round Tower (86ft high), of no great significance except as a lookout and refuge in time of battle. Close to it is a small Anglican church grandly called a cathedral. It was indeed the seat of an ancient bishopric (now moved; Catholic to Ballina and Protestant to Tuam), supposedly founded by St Patrick himself. The present structure dates mainly from 17C, the Gothic south doorway and the crypt surviving from a previous building. [A possible detour after leaving Killala is the minor road on the left which goes to Ballina, passing close to the ruins of 15C Moyne Abbey (fine cloisters) and well-preserved but roofless little Rosserk Abbey, dating from 1400.]

Continue into **BALLINA** (pronounced Bally Na), which was taken by Humbert. Today it is a provincial town (pop: 6,850), with an old-fashioned feeling, on the wide and pleasing river Moy. There is a 19C cathedral, ruins of a 14C friary, and a dolmen. The dolmen stands near the railway station, south of the town centre. Despite its obviously greater antiquity, it is called the Dolmen of the Four Maols and is commonly believed to mark the grave of four brothers all called Maol who in 6C killed their teacher, Bishop Ceallach of Kilemoremoy, and were hanged by his brother. [At Cairns (or Carns), east of Ballina is the site of a series of apparations of the Virgin Mary, St Bernadette, sacred hearts, luminous crosses in the sky, etc., seen by many people over a period of several days in 1985. These visions have not been 'approved' by the Church.]

Pass the Ballina railway station and dolmen on N56/T40 and soon take minor R310/L134 on right (direction Castlebar). After **KNOCKMORE**, beside large Lough Conn on right, the countryside and hills beyond are very beautiful. There are excellent views from here to **PONTOON**, where two lakes (Conn and Cullin) meet and have been joined at a narrow isthmus. The water flowing between them changes its direction according to which lake is currently fuller. The road then winds exquisitely round the edge of Lough Cullin, passing well-placed **Healy's Hotel** (094–56443) at the waterside. Eventually the road turns away from the lough and crosses a peaty moorland before reaching Castlebar.

For another possible place to stay in the area, instead of turning off to Pontoon, stay on N57, Soon after Carrowntrela, there's an unusual country house hotel on the right, **Mount Falcon** (096–21172), an imposing castle-like 19C mansion. It is run and in every way dominated by Mrs Aldridge, whose home this has been since 1932. It is in effect a guest house or B&B, though an exceptionally grand one. The house is tremendously comfortable in an old-fashioned way. When we arrived, tea was brought to us at once and a blazing log fire lit in the sitting room, which is full of deep armchairs, huge gilt mirrors, antique mahogany tables, bookshelves, and altogether a pleasant chaotic disorder more reminiscent of staying with aristocratic relatives than visiting a hotel. The other rooms too have sturdy doors, massive wardrobes, everything well and solidly made. And in the evening everyone sits down together at a long polished candlelit table. There's good food and plenty of it. To retrieve the route from here, either return to the Pontoon turning or go on to the Knockmore turning on the right after Mount Falcon. This brings you to Lough Conn and the Pontoon road.

Compared to the small places seen along the way, **CASTLEBAR**, County Mayo's capital, is quite a large town (pop. 6,500), with an agreeable atmosphere. There is a tourist information phone number in summer: 094–21207. The town was taken by Humbert's Franco–Irish force with such ease that the retreat of the large number of English troops stationed here has ever since been gleefully known by local people as 'The Races of Castlebar'.

The captors held the town for just one week, during which they declared the founding of the Republic of Connaught, part of the United Republic of Ireland. There's a pleasant green in the town centre called The Mall, at one end of which stands a monument to the 'Battle of Castlebar' and the tomb of John Moore, who according to the inscription was 'Ireland's First President and Descendant of St Thomas Moore'. He was 'captured in the 1798 French–Irish rebellion and died in Waterford Gaol'. It seems that following the taking of the town and the setting up of their premature Irish Republic, the Revolutionaries, there and then, appointed Moore as their head. He was one of a wealthy but politically radical family of wine-merchants (their business was based in Spain). They were certainly the richest and most influential Catholic family in the district. The Moore family continued to prosper and to be active in Republican politics during the 19C.

Just 7 miles south of Castlebar on the Ballinrobe road, Ballintubber Abbey is worth a visit (see p. 37). From Castlebar take N60/T39 back into Westport.

South Mayo

2–3 days/145 miles (240km)/from Knock

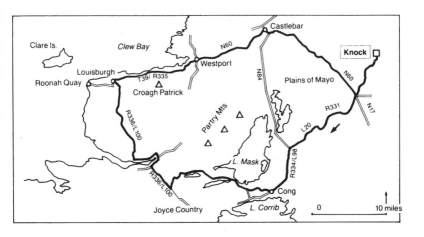

Life in southern Mayo follows a conservative and traditional pattern, and the population seem even more deeply religious than elsewhere. The area has two of Ireland's most important Catholic sacred sites, the holy mountain of Croagh Patrick, and the modern basilica and shrine at Knock. In the east and south of the area, where Mayo merges into the rocky land of Connemara, the scenery is spectacular, with lakes, green-sloped mountains, scores of clear clean streams, and hills which seem inhabited only by sheep.

This route starts from the small airport (car hire available) on N17 north of Knock village, but could equally be started at Knock itself (or for that matter, from any other point along the route).

The tiny Connaught International Airport or Horan International Airport, better known simply as **Knock Airport**, is not just an airport. It is also a great *cause célèbre* of national and local renown, and has been for years, both before and after its completion in 1986. This is not at all the usual airport story of local opposition, but rather a religious matter. Devout Catholics regard the airport as a symbol of something vague but important—God's will, perhaps—or a further authentication of a divine vision allegedly seen in Knock church in 1879. They envisage planes full of pilgrims arriving from all over the globe to see the holy place where this apparition occurred. Sceptics see the airport as a massively expensive 20C folly, a white elephant. A third view—which seems to have been vindicated, although the effect has been small as yet—is that an airport will stimulate local business and encourage non-pilgrim tourism in remote county Mayo.

Feelings about the airport are still intense. At a B&B where I was staying on a visit to Connacht, a fellow guest asked me which route I took to Ireland. When I answered that I had flown to Knock, he leapt from his seat to shake my hand and cried 'Did you now! Good man yourself!' Later, my chambermaid in a country house hotel described Knock Airport, with great sincerity, as 'a miracle, a gift from God'.

Take N17 south from the airport via Kilkelly to **KNOCK** (Gaelic *Cnoc*, hill). This village has turned itself over entirely to tourism, but of a different kind from most resorts. For nearly all the people who come here are fervently religious, and believe that a divine presence manifested itself on the south wall of Knock's old parish church, on the evening of Thursday, 21 August 1879. The vision, seen by 15 people all at once, was of Mary (wearing a crown), Joseph, and St John the Evangelist (holding a book) standing by an altar on which were a lamb and a crucifix, with angels floating above. The vision was not static; the figures appeared to have some movement. And this was no fleeting spectacle: it lasted a full two hours, during which the villagers came and went. At first some of the witnesses did not think it was a divine or miraculous event. Some went away and came back later. Some tried to get the parish priest to see it but he refused to come.

Whatever one may think about the likelihood of such sights really physically being there, the fact is that the 15 witnesses—closely questioned by two Ecclesiastical Commissions—all agreed that they had seen this vision. It may be a factor that they were all simple, poor villagers living in a small community in one of the most remote and unsophisticated parts of Ireland. However, after careful consideration by the Commissions, who are understandably anxious not to be deceived, their evidence was accepted.

It should however be realised that apparitions were common in Ireland at the time, just as, say, moving statues are now. The *Illustrated Monitor*, a Dublin religious magazine, refers to several during 1875. A comparison of the witnesses' statements (printed in *Weekly News*, 21 and 28 Feb. 1880, and in the book *The Apparition and Miracles at Knock*, by J. MacPhilpin, published 1880) also shows some minor but telling inconsistencies. And the autobiography of a nun, Sister M.F. Cusack, who lived and worked at Knock immediately after the apparition (*The Story of My Life*, 1891) relates how—admittedly this was post-Vision—one evening in the church a bright light appeared above the altar. Everyone in the church began to exclaim that they were seeing the Vision, and to describe it, although according to Sister Cusack it was nothing but a bright light. On walking up to the altar she was able to discover how a 'very large glass stone', as she describes it, was catching the light of the setting sun and refracting it onto the wall. And there is some hearsay evidence that the images on the south wall of Knock church were cast by a magic lantern—a trick which might easily deceive people of that time and place. These explanations sound improbable, but so does the 'divine' alternative.

Whatever its cause, 100 years after the apparition Pope John Paul II visited the shrine—the airport was built for him to use—and said an open-air Mass here for half a million people.

The old parish church still stands as before, though looking a trifle out of place in today's touristic Knock. The south wall where the figures were seen had to be rebuilt after souvenir-hungry pilgrims had almost dismantled it stone by stone. The site of the vision is now contained within a glass chamber—the Shrine—which serves as a transparent chapel; white marble statuary inside it recreates what is supposed to have been seen.

Standing close by, the modern Basilica (completed 1976) is an octagonal concrete structure, large and functional, capable of holding a congregation of 20,000. Its proper name is The Basilica of Our Lady Queen of Ireland. The interior has a pleasing light sobriety; there is a central raised altar in a circular auditorium. Mass is often attended by thousands of visitors, and loudspeakers relay services to crowds outside.

To cope with the great numbers of pilgrims, huge car parks have been built around the village centre, and there is a whole area designated for souvenir stalls. Nearly every souvenir has a religious component. And so great is the demand for 'holy water' that it is available from nine ordinary taps in a row alongside the large 'processional square' in front of the shrine.*

If anyone doesn't know what Catholicism is, this is the place to come and see it. The visitors' devotion and piety is astonishing. An endless procession of worshippers makes its way round the exterior of the old church, each person repeating the rosary. Many individuals kneel down on the outside steps of the Shrine, or even in the adjacent tarmac wastes of the 'processional square' or the street, to face the place where the apparition occurred and pray to the Virgin Mary.

One of the most marvellous, thought-provoking things about Knock is that, whereas a visit to the great Christian centres in other countries is almost always in a sense a look at the past, here that 'past' is still alive. At Knock one comes face to face with the medieval mentality which inspired pilgrims to walk across Europe to pray at famous shrines, a view of the world which is not straightjacketed by rationality, a simplicity of attitude which accepts without argument or question anything which emanates from the Church, and willingly gives more credence to the impossible than to the obvious.

* 'Holy water' is ordinary water which has been blessed for religious use and declared 'holy' by a priest. In this case it is the taps and water supply which have received the necessary blessing.

Knock Shrine

Also interesting at Knock is the Folk Museum to the south of the Basilica.

Continue south on N17. This is flat green country called the Plains of Mayo. **CLAREMORRIS** (Clár Chlainne Mhurris) is a small crossroads town. Here pick up minor R331/L20 (direction Ballinrobe).

[Off to the right of the route from here is the small village of **MAYO**. In 1570, when County Mayo was given its name, Mayo was an important town with a monastery and a cathedral. All its ecclesiastical buildings were demolished following Henry VIII's Reformation and the town sank into obscurity.]

BALLINROBE (Baile an Róba) is a popular angling centre, with good access to the attractive lakes Lough Mask, Lough Carra and Lough Corrib.

[**Ballintubber Abbey** (or Ballintober, Ballintobber, etc.), about 10 miles along the Ballinrobe to Castlebar road, deserves a visit. Although it is closer to Castlebar, easiest access is from Ballinrobe as there is less traffic to deal with. Take N84/T40 (direction Castlebar). The road passes between Mask and Carra loughs, crossing a small Gaeltacht district. At Partry (or Partree) stay on N84 for another 3 miles to Ballintubber (Ballintober), from which take a right turn to reach the abbey about 1 mile away. In a land where fact and fantasy, history and myth, become very muddled, many places claim to have been blessed by a visit from St Patrick. However, there is clearer evidence that Patrick did indeed found a monastic community here at Ballintubber in 5C. In 1216, Cathal 'Crobhderg' ó Conor, King of Connacht, founded a new Augustinian community here. The original structure was damaged by fire and rebuilt in 1270; several additions and alterations were made in succeeding centuries. Cathal's soubriquet Crobhderg (pronounced Crovdearg and sometimes written that way, although also sometimes spelt Croderg or Crobderg) means Red Hand, and he was far better known in his day for destroying abbeys than building them. It is thought that Ballintubber was the result of his efforts to turn over a new leaf. Despite the damage done during the 16C Reformation and 17C Cromwellian period, and its present state of neglect, the abbey has stayed in continuous use right up to the present day. It was restored—some say excessively—in 1966, during which work a papal seal of 1463 was discovered. This simple church and 15C cloisters in their countryside setting make a pleasing contrast with so many of the other Irish monastic structures which have fallen into ruin.]

From Ballinrobe, take R334/L98 (direction Cong). The road passes through little **NEALE** (pronounced Nail), to the west of which Loughmask House was one of the residences of Captain Charles Boycott, who was ostracised by the local people for his opposition to the Irish Land League, and so gave his name to the language. From Neale take R345/L101 to **CONG** (Gaelic *cunga*, isthmus, i.e. between loughs Mask and Corrib), a pretty village in a lovely waterside location. A restored 14C stone cross stands in the main street. This is not the Cross of Cong (also known as Bachall Buidhe, the yellow crozier), a finely decorated ornamental processional cross of oak, copper, and gold, made in 1123, guarded by monks of Cong Abbey until 1840, and since housed in the National Museum in Dublin. Although the monks had custody of the cross—which supposedly contained a particle of the 'True Cross'—they did not have an abbey. Their original premises were founded as an Augustinian community in 1128 by Turlough ó Conor, King of Connacht and all Ireland, on the site of a previous 7C monastery. It became one of the most important spiritual centres in the country and a number of Kings of Ireland were buried here. Cong Abbey was closed down in 1542 during the Reformation. It was soon reduced to ruins, and these remain, close to the village. They are attractive, with partly reconstructed cloisters.

Close by, **Ashford Castle** (092–46003), at the edge of Cong village, is a massive and impressive grey pile rising with story-book grandeur beside a river and on the bank of Lough Corrib. Though all in remarkably consistent style, the building includes three very different periods—a small 13C Anglo-Norman castle, 18C Guinness family country house, and 1970s hotel extension. It is hard to pick out which part is which, although it is plain enough that the overall appearance owes more to late 18C extravagance than medieval fortification. It is now one of Ireland's most superbly luxurious hotels. A number of well-known people have stayed at the hotel, including President Ronald Reagan and his team during Reagan's visit to Ireland in search of forebears. The hotel is promoted with much sentiment in the USA by its American owners. For all that, the building, grounds, and setting are magnificent. The interior is palatial, with masses of wood pannelling, 2-inch-thick solid wooden doors, brass fittings, chandeliers, thick carpets, etc. There are two elegant restaurants, both with good food served in huge quantities.

The castle looks out on glorious, tranquil Lough Corrib, in which, a local man informed me, there's 'an island for every day of the year—365,

Ashford Castle

and 366 on leap years'. (This joke must be an old one, since I was later told the same thing about Clew Bay!)

This is limestone country, very porous, and the narrow strip of land between the two loughs is riddled with eroded underground water channels, caverns and hollows. Best known is Pigeon Hole, an opening in the ground which is descended by a flight of steps to reach a swift underground stream which runs between loughs Mask and Corrib. Daftest result of the limestone's porosity is the Dry Canal, commissioned during the Famine by no doubt well-meaning persons who, rather than simply give money to the starving, preferred to make them work for their bread. The work, each man being paid about fourpence per day for five years, was to construct this fine canal, complete with necessary locks, which connects the two lakes and touches Cong Village. At a proud opening ceremony the canal was filled with water, which promptly disappeared into the ground. It has remained perfectly empty ever since.

An undulating leafy road (R345/L101) goes on to **AN FHAIRCHE (Clonbur)**, a fishing village which lies in a supposedly Gaeltacht district. However, every indication (i.e. from nosily eavesdropping) is that the people here are English-speakers. The village is actually in Galway, not Mayo, and in the next 25 miles our road goes to and fro across the Galway border. The high green hill country far ahead and away to the left (west) is Connemara. Rising up closer to the village is the lovely region of pasture and glens called **Joyce's Country**—nothing to do with James Joyce, it was colonised by the proud and fierce Joyce clan who came here from Wales during the 13C Anglo-Norman invasion of western Ireland.

At the junction in the middle of Clonbur, turn right following a sign to 'An Chloch Breach'. (On the Michelin map this is the road which appears to pass through 'Finny'.) This is hardly more than a back lane, little used; it is lined by enormous wild fuchsias in places. At a fork, do *not* take the road signposted Gleanntreig, which might appear to be the obvious direction (it is a dead end). Our route threads between two lakes, and follows a long, narrow lake on the left, then a silvery stream below heather-covered hills, and eventually skirts a larger lake on the left (Lough Nafooey). Along this road there are really beautiful views of hills, flowers, and lakes. There are small bright green fields within walls of heaped stones. This is the very heart of Joyce's Country.

Follow signs to Leenane; where the road meets a T-junction (with R336/L100), turn right (signposted An Líonán). **AN LÍONÁN (Leenane)** is a small village, a little touristy, beside the waters of a long, fjord-like sea inlet. Here join N59/T71, turning right (direction Westport); within the mile, turn left onto R335/L100 (direction Louisburgh) which crosses the inlet. Rising on one side of the water is the curiously named mountain Devil's Mother (2,140ft), and on the other side, Ben Gorm (2,310ft). According to maps there should be a village called Aasleigh, complete with a supposedly picturesque little waterfall just across the inlet, but I did not find anything there at all; surely though, in such a country, it requires but little faith to believe in an unseen waterfall!

The road now rises gently, alternating lake and stream, along the pretty

Delphi valley. Rhododendrons grow riotously along parts of the route. **DELPHI** itself, a scattering of buildings, exists really only as a place for angling holidays. The name is no mere coincidence: it actually was named after the famous Greek oracle, by a Marquess of Sligo who built a fishing lodge here after completing his Grand Tour of Europe. The country becomes less attractive around **LOUISBURGH**, another place named after somewhere else, in this case Louisburgh, Nova Scotia, by an uncle of another Marquess of Sligo. Louisburgh is a resorty village near the Clew Bay coast. Five miles west of the village is Roonah Quay, from which there are boat connections to Clare Island.

Mountainous **CLARE ISLAND** in Clew Bay was the home of Connacht's formidable first lady of local legend, Grace ó Malley or Granuaile (or Grainne Uaile or Grainne Ui Mhaille or Grania Wael; born 1530, died about 1600). She raided and ruled this stretch of coastal Connacht, and her stormy life and adventures have become almost mythical in this part of Ireland. The true story is that her father was a Connacht chieftain, a distinguished ó Malley; at the age of 15 she was married off to a neighbouring chief, Donal ó Flaherty. She totally dominated him, his domaine and his soldiery, to such a degree that when Donal was untimely killed in an accident, all his men vowed continuing loyalty to her rather than his successor (Grace herself could not take over his title, which under Celtic law could not be inherited by a woman). She set up residence on Clare Island, and by trade and piracy along these Connacht shores managed to maintain a certain prosperity. It was during this period that she temporarily acquired another husband, MacWilliam Oughter (also known as Sir Richard Burke) whom she divorced after one year, keeping all his useful coastal fortification in the process.

A constant thorn in her side was the encroaching might of the English, with whom she battled frequently and furiously. In September 1593, by now aged over 60 and having just had a very trying sea-battle with Sir Richard Bingham, Governor of Connaught, Grace sailed from the west of Ireland to England, making her way grandly up the Thames and mooring her Celtic warship at Greenwich, where Queen Elizabeth I was in residence. How on earth it happened still puzzles scholars to this day, but the uncrowned pirate queen talked her way into a private audience with the reigning monarch of Britain and Ireland. Elizabeth recorded simply that 'an aged woman Grany O Malley came to see me'. What was said by each party is not known, although witnesses recalled that the Irishwoman showed no deference to the Englishwoman, and they seemed to regard each other as equals. Grace returned home with a royal promise that she would not be bothered again by the English fleet in western Ireland. Nevertheless her seafaring and unscrupulous livelihood was not an easy one to maintain in her old age, and at 70 she died in her Clare Island fastness. Her castle can be seen on the eastern end of the island.

Also on Clare Island are ruins of a Carmelite friary of 1224, behind which an ó Malley grave is believed to be that of Granuaile. Her ancient clan—now written O'Malley—is still more numerous in this area than anywhere else in the world. Each year they have an annual gathering, usually in Westport.

From Louisburgh, take R335/T39 towards Westport. The sea comes into view at **LECANVEY** (or Leckanvey, Lekanvy, etc.), soon after which the black conical hill **Croagh Patrick** (2,518ft) rises on the right. It is often mist-shrouded. At **MURRISK**, a path starting beside Campbell's Bar (or, alternatively, from 15C Murrisk Abbey), ascends Croagh Patrick. Known as 'the Reek' hereabouts, the hill is one of Ireland's most sacred sites. It is widely believed that St Patrick climbed to the summit and spent the whole 40 days of Lent in the year AD441; while here he reputedly, by casting a bell down the mountainside (it was returned to him by various unchristian-sounding spirits), managed to banish all reptiles from Irish soil. (What part this has in God's plan of things is not explained!) He had countless other trying experiences while on the mountain, including being beset by whole clouds of demons in the shape of vicious black birds, and an encounter with another non-Biblical personage, Corra, the Mother of Satan. These tales sometimes tend to be related here as if they were literally true rather than symbolic of spiritual struggle.

It is viewed as an act of piety to climb to the top of Croagh Patrick.

Croagh Patrick

There is an annual pilgrimage starting at dawn on the last Sunday in July, attended by many tens of thousands of the devout, some of whom walk up the path in bare feet. The way is marked by various 'stations'—shrines and monuments—which the most pious encircle (sometimes on their knees) seven times while repeating the Lord's Prayer and Ave Maria. The last 1,000 ft is rough cutting shale, awkward even in shoes. The summit (superb views of Clew Bay and Connemara) is a flat area with a small chapel at which Mass is said every half hour during the pilgrimage. In pre-Patrick days the mountain was called Croagh Aigli and was even then the scene of an annual pilgrimage at that time of year—a jolly Celtic festival called Lughnasa.

The road continues towards Westport. About 1½ miles before the town, sadly abandoned Westport Quay, still with some of the original 18C warehouses, recalls Westport's past hopes of importance. There was some transatlantic trade, although even at the height of its fortunes the harbour was not put to any much greater use than it is now—by fishermen heading out to sea. Close by, **Westport House** (open May–Sept. afternoons) is an imposing mansion built in 1734 by Colonel John Browne, ancestor of the present proprietor, the Marquess of Sligo. Browne was a Jacobite, and had fought at the Siege of Limerick in 1690. His wife was one of many Irish noblewomen who claimed to be descended from Grace ó Malley.

Thomas de Quincey (*Confessions of an Opium Eater*, etc.) and William Thackeray (*Vanity Fair*, etc.) both enjoyed long stays at Westport House as guests. Thackeray in particular was impressed by Clew Bay, 'which was of a gold colour'; he was moved to declare that 'It forms an event in one's life to have seen the place, so beautiful is it.' The Bay's flock of little islands he fancifully likened to 'so many Dolphins and Whales basking there'. The house is grandly furnished, has a good collection of silver, and is beautifully located, but the effect is not enhanced by the incongruous tourist attractions, including souvenir shop, animal enclosure, and tea shop.

WESTPORT itself is a bustling town, seeming largish by local standards, despite a surprisingly small population total (3,500). It is something of a holiday centre and has a **Tourist Information Office** (in The Mall). Countryside can be seen at the end of all its streets. Westport was built in 1780 for Peter Browne, 2nd Earl of Altamont, as a sort of adjunct to Westport House. It still benefits to some degree from a certain 18C dignity and style. The wealth of the Earl's wife, which had been derived from slave-worked West Indian sugar plantations, paid for the whole ambitious project.

Westport's little main square, called The Octagon—and it actually is octagonal—is dominated by a granite plinth from which the statue (it was of a philanthropic banker called George Glendenning) has long since been removed. In this town square, in 1879, a public meeting gave birth to the Land League, which encouraged Irish tenant farmers to rebel against their extremely repressive terms of tenure, and became an important part of the Home Rule Movement. From The Octagon, short (delightfully named!) Shop Street leads down to another small 'square' with in its centre a marvellous confusion of signposts and a funny little clock tower. Bridge Street and James Street lead to The Mall, prettily lined with lime trees, which follows both banks of the canalised river Carrowbeg through town.

Take N60/T39 from Westport to **CASTLEBAR** (see. p. 32). The simple way to return from here to Knock is N60 to Claremorris where pick up N17; or for Knock Airport, from Castlebar take N5 via **TURLOUGH** (unusual round tower beside ruins of church) to Charlestown, where find N17 heading south to airport.

Connemara

2–3 days/140 miles (235km)/from Galway

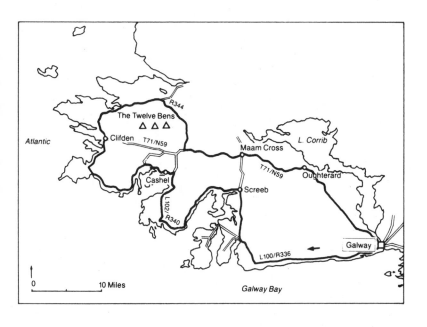

> There's something in the core of me
> That needs the West to set it free.
> ('Connemara', Oliver St John Gogarty)

Connemara is the western part of County Galway. Its rocky, mountainous countryside, much of it matted with peat (or turf, as the Irish call it), is one of Ireland's most affecting and beautiful landscapes. It is almost entirely uncultivated, a strange wilderness both watery and stony, inhospitable yet gentle. Certain parts can be used for pasture, and one meets unfenced cattle wandering freely. Along Connemara's southern and western shore, the Atlantic bites deep into the land, making a glorious coastline of bays and inlets, among the most magnificent scenery in Europe. The northern boundary is made by the waters of vast and sprawling Lough Corrib and the valley of the river Joyce. Throughout much of the region the summits of the Twelve Bens, the dozen peaks grouped together in Connemara's north west, remain in view. Thousands of rough stone walls make an intricate tracery over the terrain, demarking pitifully tiny fields, always hopelessly unproductive and now abandoned, dating from pre-Famine days.

In some ways Connemara feels as if it contains the heart and soul of Connacht. It has been at times the very symbol of Irish misery, a place of banishment, of struggle, of overcrowding and exploitation by absent landlords. In the 18C and early 19C, though so unsuitable for agriculture, Connemara was densely populated with wretchedly poor tenant farmers. The Famine and its desperate aftermath changed all that: most died, many fled, and the land has finally been left with little but its bare beauty.

Today, although the worst of the poverty has been eradicated—indeed the view is marred at times by prim new cottages—much of the population still have as old-fashioned an existence as can be found in Ireland, living in conditions of the most unostentatious simplicity. Typical older dwellings are thatched single-storey cottages, often with grass growing on the roofs. Beside the house will be a pile of drying turf for use as fuel in the hearth. Connemara, also known as Iar-Chonnacht (west Connacht), embraces one of the country's largest Gaeltacht districts, and the road-

Connemara

signs, though fascinating, abandon all attempt to be of any use to travellers!

GALWAY (Gaillimn) pop: 37,900 Largest city in western Ireland, pleasant and bustling, centred on large grassy Eyre Square (**Tourist Office**). First established as a fortress of the ó Conors of Connacht around 1100; conquered and colonised 1232 by Anglo-Norman Richard de Burgo (or de Burgh); grew into a prosperous seaport. Leading family for centuries was the Lynches, whose fine 16C mansion ('Lynch's Castle'; now a bank) stands on corner of Abbeygate St. Conquered by the English in 1652, it went into rapid decline. This is a town with frankly only modest attractions, but see: Galway's Silver Sword (1610) and Great Mace (1710) in bank at 19 Eyre Sq.; 14C St Nicholas Church. The town is noted for oysters and salmon, and its university is a centre of Gaelic studies. Nora Barnacle (1884–1951), constant companion of James Joyce, was born here.

There are ferry and air connections from Galway to the **Aran Islands** (**Oileáin Árainn**). The three islands—Inisheer (Inis Oirthir), Inishmaan (Inis Meáin), Inishmore (Inis Mór)—are starkly beautiful, rocky and treeless, covered by a web of loosely heaped stone walls separating tiny fields. Stones are so abundant here, and everything else so scarce, that these fields do not even have gates: to take animals out or put them in, a few feet of wall are peremptorily knocked down and can be as quickly rebuilt. Although often visited, the islands preserve much quiet dignity and unspoiled character; nearly all inhabitants are Irish-speakers and just a few still wear the traditional cowhide shoes (no heels; called 'pampooties') and clothes (men: distinctive dark blue shirt, thick tweed trousers, unbleached woollen waistcoat, and coloured woollen belts; women: thick fringed shawls and long full skirts dyed red with madder). And of course this is the place for best quality Aran sweaters. There is some farming, the 'soil' being a fertile mixture of sand and seaweed (supposed to produce excellent potatoes), but the men earn their livelihoods largely from fishing, for which they often still use *currachs* (curious black tar-covered rowing boats made of canvas stretched over a light frame).

The islands have numerous remnants of old fortifications, early-Christian churches, historic monuments, of which the most impressive is the superbly situated **Dún Aengus**, a magnificently constructed pre-historic stone fortress with concentric defences, overhanging a high cliff on the south side of Inishmore (5 miles west of Kilronan, or Cill Ronáin). The author Liam O'Flaherty was an Aran native, and J.M. Synge was a devotee of the islands and gathered much of his inspiration and dramatic style from them. Not only some of his best plays are set here (*Riders to the Sea*, etc.) but some of Synge's lesser-known prose writing describes in close detail life on the Aran Islands at the turn of the century.

From Galway town take 'Coast Road' R336/L100 (direction Barna). This runs close to Galway Bay, with some pretty stretches of road and many good ocean views. It enters the Gaeltacht almost immediately on leaving the city. At **CASLA (Costelloe)** there is the option of travelling out on R343 across rocky Carraroe Peninsula to Gorumna Island, reached by bridges. This bleak, rocky corner is noted for its poteen (illegal home-distilled whiskey). Costelloe is the base of national Irish-language broadcasting service Radio na Gaeltachta which makes such fascinating listening (even when one cannot understand a single word!).

Continuing from Costelloe, stay on R336/L100 which here begins to penetrate somewhat bleaker, boggier country. At Scríb (or Scríob or Screeb) take R340/L102, the coast road on left, which circles Kilkieran Bay, staying close to the water, and gradually returns to more attractive country. Along the Kilkieran shore there is commercial gathering of seaweed, which is used for health foods, medicines, certain local snacks, and also for fertiliser. At **AN CAISEAL (Cashel)**, beside Bertraghboy Bay, top quality country house hotel, **Cashel House** (Relais et Châteaux; 095–31001) received praise from Géneral de Gaulle who stayed here with his wife for two weeks in 1969. It is noted for fine food and comfortable accommodation.

Take R342, pretty waterside road. Pass through **TOOMBEALA** (R341), near which (not on our route) is **Ballynahinch Castle** (095–31006), now a top-grade country house hotel but formerly the home of the Martin family who owned almost the whole of Connemara from 1700 up to the 19C Famine. One of the last to occupy the house was the notoriously irascible Richard Martin, who disliked people but loved animals. He used to imprison his poor tenant farmers in his own private jail for being cruel to their wretched livestock, and was also noted for his murderous duels with members of his own class. Nevertheless he ended up with the nickname Humanity Dick because he did so much to relieve the suffering of animals, and was instrumental in the setting up of the Royal Society for the Protection of Animals in 1824.

Carry on to **CLOCH NA RÓN (Roundstone)**, an attractive planned village built in the 1820s and now a lobster-fishing community with a certain amount of new development. From here westward the land catches strong, refreshing Atlantic breezes, so invigorating and exhilarating that this has been called the 'brandy and soda road'. Just after **BAILE CONAOLA (Ballyconeely)**, beside Mannin Bay, a monument off the road shows where Alcock and Brown landed in the midst of bog in 1919 after making the first trans-Atlantic flight (it took 16½ hrs). Mannin's signposted 'coral strand' here is a lovely white beach made not of ordinary sand but created by a coral-like species of seaweed. Most of Connemara's sandy white beaches are made of this 'coral'.

AN CLOCHAN (Clifden), the next place along the coast road, is considered as the 'capital' of Connemara, although it is hardly more than a village (pop: 1,400), just a pleasant little resorty country town resting gently below lovely green hills and above the water of Clifden Bay. Built in the early 19C it retains something of its Georgian character. Clifden has some inexpensive accommodation, and makes a good base for walks in the hills or by the sea or for touring western Connemara. It is at the very foot of the **Twelve Bens** (or Twelve Pins; Gaelic *ben* means a peak) and close to the boundary of **Connemara National Park**, a 5,000-acre conservation area extending from nearby Letterfrack village to the heart of the Twelve Bens; another good excursion with superb cliff and ocean views is the so-called Sky road from Clifden to Kingstown. Towards the end of summer Clifden suddenly bursts into activity for its festive Connemara Pony Show, a traditional event which still attracts locals from all over Connacht. Clifden's Catholic church stands on the site of the *clochán* which gave the town its Gaelic name.

Continue along the coast road (now N59/T71), lined with wild fuchsias in places, through the little villages of **MOYARD** and, soon after, **LETTERFRACK**, where the road crosses into the National Park (Visitor Information Centre in the village; open 10am–6.30pm daily May–Sept., 095–41054). Founded as a Quaker settlement in the 19C, Letterfrack today has its craft shop and tourist information board, yet remains ingenuously pretty and rustic in a beautiful waterside setting. An access road from Letterfrack leads through private grounds to **Rosleague Manor** (095–41101), a country house hotel embraced by its surroundings of wonderful quiet hills, the wind and the trees, and the calm view across a big Atlantic inlet to misty lines of hills ranged behind. The Foyles, Rosleague's brother and sister proprietors, are unaffected, likeable, and competent. They bought the house in 1969, at which time it was still the home of its original 19C owners, an Anglo–Irish family named Brown whose fortune came from Indian tea-plantations. Rosleague offers informal, relaxed, unpretentious elegance and comfort; attentive but friendly service; and in the dining room, imaginative and delicious food and good wines.

[A picturesque lane leads from Letterfrack along the **Rinvyle (or Renvyle) Peninsula** to a dolmen and a ruined fortress (held in turn by the competing Joyce, ó Flahertie, and Blake clans) at Rinvyle Point. **Renvyle House**, now a hotel (095–43511), at Renvyle was formerly the home of Oliver St John Gogarty, writer and wit who appears in Joyce's *Ulysses* as Mulligan. His other guests here included fellow writers W.B. Yeats and G.B. Shaw and the painter Augustus John. Another notable holiday visitor to remote Renvyle was the philosopher Wittgenstein.]

Leave Letterfrack on the main road (N59/T71), soon reaching the white towers of fantastic 19C Kylemore Castle on the left, now called **Kylemore Abbey** as it has been a Benedictine convent since 1920. It is startling to note that this extraordinarily over-elaborate mock 'castle', built for millionaire MP Mitchell Henry, is described by the Irish Tourist Board as 'a building of unsurpassed beauty'. Yet there is undoubtedly something splendid about the place, its well-built self-importance and magnificent location. Visitors are welcome. Adjacent Kylemore Lough gives superb views towards the Twelve Bens. After the lough, leave the main road, following R344 round to the right (direction Recess).

This lonely road was built in the 1840s as a famine relief scheme. It skirts between the wild slopes of the lofty Twelve Bens and the Maumturk (or Maamturk) range, running across deserted open country with unfenced sheep grazing. Shortly before Straith Salach (or Recess) join N59/T71 (direction Galway). This makes its way into a bleak empty landscape dominated by Lackavrea (or Corcogemore) Mountain, standing north of the road. Maam Cross, much signposted, turns out to be nothing but a bare crossroads. Beyond it, N59 runs beside a string of lakes along the Owenriff river to little **OUGHTERARD (Uachtar Ard)** (pronounced Ookterard) on the shore of Lough Corrib. Two miles after the village, sturdy four-storey **Aughnanure Castle**, beside the Lough at the mouth of river Drimneen, is the handsome remnant of a 16C fortified tower of the dreaded ó Flaherties, the Connacht clan who so frightened the ruling Anglo–Norman families of Galway that they inscribed above one of the city gates 'From the fury of the O'Flaherties good Lord deliver us'!

Passing Ross and Ballycuirke lakes, and the village of Moycullen, where **Drimcong House** (091–85115) is an outstanding restaurant, the road returns the short distance into the city of Galway.

Aughnanure Castle

Eastern Galway and Roscommon

1–2 days/71 miles (115km)/from Roscommon

This eastern, inland part of Connacht is surprisingly unlike the rest of the province, lacking any of the hills and grandeur of the west coast. Almost the whole of this part of the country is gentle, barely undulating, undramatic, a landscape with few features. Partly bog, partly rough heath and

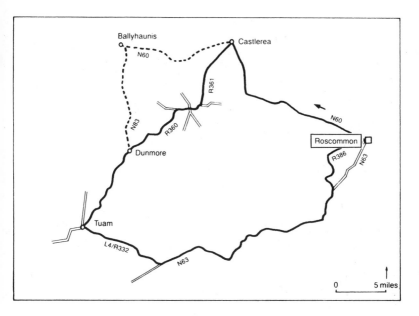

moor, partly grassy farmland, it none the less has some appealing little towns and villages and some interesting historic sites.

For anyone who has enjoyed reading Trollope's *The Kellys and the O'Kellys*, a novel set in 1844, there is the added interest that most of the action takes place in this area: the main characters live at the village of Dunmore, and their nearest 'big town' is Tuam.

ROSCOMMON (pop: only 1,700, though it seems larger) is a quiet country town. An unusual spire on its impressive Church of the Sacred Heart (1903–25) is visible from afar. In front of the church a small grotto has a crucifixion scene constructed inside. Note the gilded tympanum over the church entrance. The town takes its name from Ros Comain, Comain's wood, after Abbot Comain, founder of a monastery on the site in 745. Considerable remnants of a later Dominican Priory (founded 1257, rebuilt 1453) can also be seen. In the town's small main square with its cross, the Bank of Ireland is housed in the former Courthouse, a fine 18C grey stone building in classical style, while opposite is the forbidding 18C exterior of the once-notorious County Jail, later a lunatic asylum, and now unused. This jailhouse was where all the county's hangings took place, and for a time the executioner was one legendary 'Lady Betty', who had her own death sentence commuted in exchange for taking the unwanted hangman's job.

Take N60/T39 (direction Castlerea). Just on the edge of Roscommon, set back behind an impressive old gateway on the left of this road, are ruins of a large imposing castle. Originally built in 1268 (rebuilt 1280), numerous damaging attacks over the centuries took their toll, especially the capture by Cromwell's forces in 1652, yet a good deal has survived.

Roscommon Castle

Carry on towards Castlerea through not-unattractive wooded and heathy country. Just off the road to the right (on R367/L98), some 6 miles before the town, is ruined **Ballintober Castle** (or Ballintubber). From the time of the Anglo-Norman invasion until the early 18C this was the seat of the ancient ruling family of the province, the ó Conors of Connacht. The ó Conor (or O'Conor) family then moved to Clonalis House, at nearby Castlerea.

CASTLEREA (pronounced Castleray), a largish provincial town on the river Suck (again population totals are deceptive—only about 1,850), has little of interest except for **Clonalis House** (signposted: off Castlebar road just north west of the town). This elegant 19C house, with excellent furnishings and decor, is the present-day seat of the O'Conor family who were the Kings of Connacht for centuries until the English takeover. Inside the house (guided tours throughout day) visitors can see the sumptuously furnished rooms and the library with its astonishing family records, consisting of over 100,000 original archive documents. Bettam's study of the O'Conor genealogy (on display) traces the line back to 1100BC—making it the oldest recorded family in Europe (although some other ancient Irish families dispute this and claim the honour for themselves).

The head of the O'Conor family—he who would in former times have become the King of Connacht—is always known as the O'Conor Don.

The ancient direct line was brought to an end by a 19C Don who became a Jesuit priest and therefore remained childless. The present occupant of the house inherited the property through the mother's side, and therefore could not hold the title, which passed to a cousin. The present O'Conor Don apparently lives in Dublin and is said to take little interest in the family or its history.

Also in the library: hundreds of documents recording events in Irish and local history, and (on display) original handwritten letters to the O'Conors from distinguished friends and guests including Trollope, Douglas Hyde, Gladstone, and Parnell. The house has its own chapel with a 'Penal Altar' (a secret altar used during the years of the 18C Penal Laws which were designed, among other things, to prevent Catholics from being landowners). In another room can be seen the harp of Turlough O'Carolan (1670–1738), so-called 'Last of the Irish Bards', a blind traditional musician whose compositions included the tune of 'The Star-Spangled Banner'. Outside the front door of the house is the ancient, though unimpressive, Coronation Stone of the O'Conor Kings.

From Castlerea travel towards Dunmore. There are two possibilities: either take the country lanes (R361 to Trien and Williamstown, then R360/T11[A] through Kilnalag to Dunmore); or use the main roads (N60/T39 almost into uninteresting Ballyhaunis, then south on N83/T11 to Dunmore).

The village of **DUNMORE** has a pleasant little central esplanade or square, around which are at least half a dozen places to get a drink. Indeed, almost every business combines its main function with selling a few pints of Guinness. Some seem uncertain whether they are primarily bars or something else. It's a convenient arrangement though, for shoppers who feel like a drink while buying a pound of tomatoes. They can get both at Thomas Byrne's 'Grocery and Lounge', for example, or at 'The Corner Shop' (Grocery and Newsagents), which is also a bar. Even the drapery is a bar.

Anthony Trollope, describing Dunmore (as it was in 1844) in *The Kellys and the O'Kellys*, was less charmed by it than I: 'It is a dirty, ragged little town, standing in a very poor part of the country, with nothing about it to induce the traveller to go out of his beaten track. It is parcelled out among different owners, some of whom would think it folly to throw away a penny on the place, and others of whom have not a penny to throw away.' His main characters, the Kellys, have just such a combined shop–bar–hotel as one can see today. 'The shop occupied the most important part of the ground floor. Next to the shop, and opening out of it, was a large drinking-room, furnished with narrow benches and rickety tables; and here the more humble of Mrs Kelly's guests regaled themselves.'

A description of Mrs K's kitchen is fascinating: 'The difference of the English and Irish character is nowhere more plainly discerned than in their respective kitchens. With the former, this apartment is probably the cleanest, and certainly the most orderly, in the house. It is rarely intruded into by those unconnected in some way with its business. An Irish kitchen is devoted to hospitality in every sense of the word. Its doors are open to almost all idlers and loungers. It is usually a temple dedicated to the goddess of disorder. All you see is a grimy black ceiling, an uneven clay floor, a small darkened window, one or two unearthly-looking recesses, a heap of potatoes in the corner, a pile of turf against the wall, two pigs and a dog under the single dresser, three or four chickens on the window-sill, an old cock moaning on the top of a rickety press, and a crowd of ragged garments, squatting, standing, kneeling, and crouching, round the fire, from which issues a babel of strange tongues, not one word of which is at first intelligible to ears unaccustomed to such eloquence.'

Curiously, Trollope does not mention Dunmore Friary, the small ruin of a monastery dating from 1425. It was founded by Walter de Bermingham, of the Anglo-Norman family who controlled this area from 13C until Cromwellian times. A short way out of Dunmore on L27 (Ballindine road), a small ruined castle on a mound to the right of the road was the de Bermingham's fortified mansion (or 'castle', as it is called). This building, originally constructed in 1225, partly rebuilt in 16/17C, was inhabited until 19C and has only become a ruin since then.

Take N83/T11 across gently undulating green country to **TUAM** (pronounced Tyoom or Choom), a pleasant bustling provincial town (pop: 4,350) founded as a religious community in 6C by St Jarlath. Its two main shopping streets, High St and Shop St, converge on the triangular main square in the middle of which stands a 12C Celtic High Cross. Inscribed on the cross are words in praise of Turlough ó Conor, the King of Connacht at that time, who based himself here and became High King of Ireland. A lane turning off the High St leads to the Mill Museum, housed in a former 17C corn mill and showing how it operated; inside the museum is a **Tourist Office**. Tuam is the present ecclesiastical capital of Connacht for both Catholics and Protestants. At the far end of the High St, little-used 19C St Mary's Cathedral (Church of Ireland) incorporates a lovely chancel arch of the 12C. Part of an earlier cathedral on the same site, the red sandstone arch is interestingly decorated, but has been very damaged by damp—it was exposed to the weather for 500 years; structurally it is odd in that it has no keystone.

Take R382/L4 from Tuam, via Barnaderg, to N63/T15, where turn left (direction Roscommon). Follow this road as it makes its way erratically back to Roscommon. For a more rustic alternative along a short part of the way, at **ATHLEAGUE** (5½ miles before Roscommon), noted for horse fairs, turn left onto the Fuerty road (R366). Pass through **FUERTY**, a quiet hamlet. In the graveyard of its curious ruined church, two interesting early Christian fragments of stone carving are displayed, while in the church itself, it is said, 100 local Catholic priests were imprisoned and massacred during Cromwell's time by a Colonel Ormsby, still spoken of and hated (and becoming mythical) in this district. The graveyard contains many intriguing old tombstones, some 17C. The Fuerty road continues into Roscommon.

Sligo and Leitrim

2 days/120 miles (200km)/from Sligo

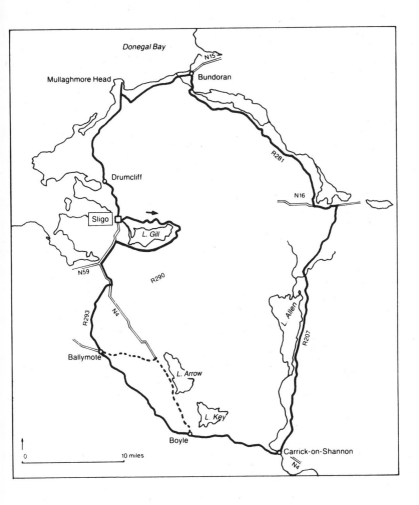

Beautiful lakes and forests descending to superb Atlantic coast, separated by expanses of bog-covered plain reaching up onto mountainous slopes, and yet with rich undulating farmland in other areas, the Sligo and Leitrim region is perhaps the most varied and certainly the most contented and productive-looking corner of Connacht. It has supported a considerable population since times long past, and County Sligo especially has a startling abundance of prehistoric remains. Pronounce their names as Sly-go and Leetrim.

The maternal grandparents (the Pollexfens, prosperous shipowners) of the extraordinary Yeats family lived in Sligo, and the visiting junior members of the family were strongly inspired by the surrounding country-side. The poems of the Irish nationalist and Nobel Prize winner (for literature) W.B. Yeats (1865–1939) and the oil paintings of his brother Jack B. Yeats (1871–1957) dwelt often upon its life and landscapes.

SLIGO pop: 17,300 A large, pleasant market town on the (mainly southern) bank of the Garavogue river, in an attractive strip of wooded country squeezed between the Atlantic (Sligo Bay) and Lough Gill. Historically it was an important fortified river ford much fought-over by rival tribes and plundered by Vikings. Its unusual 19C Courthouse (Lower Market St), in style similar to the Law Courts in London, looks like a cross between a medieval fortress and a Renaissance mansion. The County Library (Stephen St) contains paintings and drawings by Jack B. Yeats and John B. Yeats (W.B.'s father, famous as a portrait artist) and other members of the Yeats family and other Irish artists, as well as a Museum concerned mainly with memorabilia of W.B. Yeats. In the Anglican cathedral there is a memorial to Susan Yeats, mother of W.B. and Jack. See also: ruins of 13–15C Sligo Abbey (originally founded 1252), with good cloisters. A couple of possible places to stay: the **Silver Swan** (071–43231), right beside the Hyde Bridge in the middle of town, or the **Sligo Park** (071–60291), a couple of miles out of town on N4. Both are fairly characterless, but reach a decent middle-range standard, with com-fortable rooms and with bars and restaurants popular with local people. **Tourist Office**: Temple St (071–61201).

[Visible from Sligo town is the huge flat 'cairn-heaped grassy hill' of Knocknarea (1083ft), which captivated W.B. Yeats. At its summit a huge cairn stands in memory of Maeva, 1C Queen of Connacht (known to the English as 'Queen Mab'). In Red Hanrahan's Song, Yeats describes how

The wind had bundled up the clouds high over Knocknarea
And thrown the thunder on the stones for all that Maeve can say.

'Passionate Maeve' fired Yeats' imagination, and features in both his early and late work, although perhaps ancient Maeve symbolised for him the Irish revolutionary Maude Gonne with whom he fell in love. She did not return the sentiment. Close to Knocknarea, Carrowmore is a site with several megalithic dolmens, cairns, etc.].

Leave Sligo town centre on N16 (Enniskillen road), then follow signs to Dromahair on L16/R286. This pretty drive runs through the country north of **Lough Gill**, passing little Colgagh Lake on left. Behind it is the so-called Deerpark Monument (signposted), a court cairn (prehistoric burial chamber with ceremonial enclosure) among several other stone-age re-mains, now enclosed by a forest plantation.

A little farther along the road you'll see across a corner of the lake to **Parke's Castle** standing impressively on the water's edge. This was the heavily fortified private house of a rich 17C English merchant who obviously set his heart on living in this lovely spot despite the difficulties of the period. It is built on the site of a fortress of the ó Rourke chieftains, Gaelic rulers of the Sligo region; in their time the area was known as Breffni or Breffni ó Rourke. From this shore, and as you continue towards Dromahair, are some lovely views of the lake and its many islands, which include tiny Innisfree, Yeats' dream of a tranquil refuge when he was in Dublin: *'I will arise and go now, and go to Innisfree . . . And live alone in the bee-loud glade.'*

The road turns away from the lake into the agreeable village of **DROMAHAIR**, where the ruined 16C mansion Old Hall (no visits) occupies the site of another ó Rourke stronghold. This particular Breffni fortress had witnessed a great turning point in Irish history, for it was from here in 1152 that Tiernan ó Rourke's wife Devorguilla vanished—eloped or abducted—with Dermot MacMurrough, King of Leinster, when he attacked the castle. The attack was all in the normal course of Irish regional conflicts, but taking his wife particularly infuriated ó Rourke who set out with renewed vigour to capture and punish MacMurrough. MacMurrough called upon the French King of England, Henry II, for help. Henry agreed to let the powerful fighter Richard Fitz-Gilbert de Clare, the Earl of Pembroke (usually known as Strongbow) go to MacMurrough's aid. However, Strongbow's arrival was effectively only the beginning of a full-scale Anglo-Norman invasion of Ireland. Meanwhile, satisfied with the turn of events, MacMurrough returned Devorguilla to her husband (though she went straight to live in the nunnery at Mellifont) and even paid him a handsome compensation. Strongbow married MacMurrough's daughter (that was all part of the deal between the two men), so that on MacMurrough's death he became King of Leinster.

On the opposite bank of the river are impressive ruins of Cleevelea Friary, founded for Franciscans by the ó Rourkes in 1508—making it the last monastic community established in Ireland before the Reformation.

Just after Dromahair, take L117/R287 (direction Sligo; soon changes to R290). After 3 miles, at a rather complicated junction, a turning on the right signposted **Innisfree** leads down to the lakeshore for a view of this endearing little island.

Return to the junction and carry on (towards Sligo) through an interest-ing, pleasing terrain of woods and rock and little fields of pasture among miniature hills. The road returns to the lake again. From a car park signposted **Dooney Rock** you can scramble up to the place where Yeats supposedly sat and daydreamed by the water.

On reaching N4, turn left (direction Dublin). Just beyond Collooney, opposite where N17 goes off to the right (signposted Knock), a lane leads to the immensely grand—yet unpretentious and welcoming—**Markree Castle** and **Knockmuldowney Restaurant** (071–67800) in a vast private estate. A little further down N4, turn left at the sign 'R293 Ballymote'. Continue into the quiet village of **BALLYMOTE**, noted for Richard de Burgo's sturdy fortress dating from 1300, now just a ruined shell but still

Temple House and Temple ruin

impressive. Access to the castle is from St John of God Nursing Home on the Bunnanaddan road. Adjacent are ruins of a Franciscan Friary (locally called 'the Abbey'), founded about 1450 by the MacDonaghs when they were in possession of the castle (which they held for two centuries). It was either in the castle or in the friary that the important 15C Book of Ballymote was compiled. This was the manuscript which showed how to read the strange Ogham alphabet, a system of 20 letters made up of lines and dots, used on many ancient Irish and British stone monuments.

A little drive away from Ballymote (follow signs to Temple House Lake along back roads from the village), **Temple House** (071–83329) is one of the most remarkable places I have ever stayed in anywhere. This vast Georgian mansion standing in its 1,000 acres of (organic) farm and woods was built in 1780 and refurbished in 1864—and has had almost nothing done to it since. Its owner Sandy Perceval and his wife Debonnaire are a fine example of the genial, cultured and unpretentious, and now frankly not terribly prosperous, land-owning Anglo-Irish gentry. The house is almost like a museum, with all its Victorian accoutrements and furnishings, even curtains and cutlery, unchanged for more than a century, and as Sandy commented, 'many people consider us as a museum piece too'. The Percevals, resident at Temple House since 1665, are cousins to the O'Haras, whose ancestral home this used to be. (The O'Haras are another of the ancient Irish families who claim to be the oldest family in Europe.) In the grounds are lakeside ruins of a Knights Templar castle dating from

1200, which subsequently formed part of an O'Hara mansion. Although Temple House has a total of over 90 rooms, including 18 bedrooms, only four are let. Bedrooms are huge, facilities adequate, food excellent, surroundings magnificent, and prices astonishingly low. Sandy plays the spoons at local Irish music evenings.

There are two possible routes from Ballymote to Boyle:

Leave Ballymote on the signposted Castlebaldwin road; at Castlebaldwin turn right onto N4. Carry on over the ridge of the Curlew Hills, with some good views of the lakes, into Boyle.

Or, a simpler route to Boyle is to leave Ballymote on the signposted Boyle road. This country road winds through rich farmland dotted with sheep and cows all the way into Boyle town.

BOYLE (in Co. Roscommon) is a bustling little local centre (pop: 1,750), on the river Boyle, with handsome waterside ruins of a Cistercian Abbey (built 1235; badly damaged by Cromwell's forces 1659). Curiously, the north side of its impressive church building is Gothic and the south Romanesque. Note also some fine stone carving.

Take busy N4 east (direction Longford, Dublin). On the left, Lough Key Forest Park is a delightful area of woods on the shore of a very picturesque lake. The road arrives at **CARRICK-ON-SHANNON** (pop: 2,050), Leitrim's quietly busy county town, attractively placed on the banks of Ireland's longest river. Carrick marks the upper limit of navigation along the Shannon, and the town is a popular centre for fishing and boat excursions. Here find T54/R280, the minor road to **LEITRIM** (pronounced Leetrim), now a small ordinary village although once important. It gave the county its name because once the Bishops of Liathdroma (i.e. Leitrim) had their residence here, and there was also a strategic castle of the ó Rourkes here (some ruins can be seen).

Cross the bridge and continue along this minor road, which follows the Shannon upstream, with a big, bare hill—Slieve Anierin—on the right. At **DRUMSHANBO**, with its tractors parked in the street, follow signs to Dowra (left at first T-junction; right at second T-junction; immediately left again). The road winds upwards, and looks down onto the wooded banks of Lough Allen. To the right are bare hills—the Iron Mountains. For this part of the route, the road has crossed briefly into the province of Ulster. At **DOWRA**, a tiny farming village, take L43 over the bridge following signs 'Blacklion 10½' or 'Glenfarne 11¾'. Up on the right is the source of the Shannon, known as the Shannon Pot, or simply The Pot. Carry on to N16, where turn left (the Northern Ireland border is a couple of miles away on the right). The road crosses back into Co. Leitrim and the province of Connacht. Take the right turn signposted Kiltyclogher (R281).

After a short distance a sign on the left points to 'Sean McDermott's House'—presumably the birthplace or residence of this 1916 Easter Rising activist. We followed this sign along a narrow lane into hills beautiful and silent but for the sound of distant sheep, with lovely views into Fermanagh. But we failed to find this monument, which is perhaps lost in the mists of Irish legend. **KILTYCLOGHER** is a neat, sleepy village just on the south side of the Leitrim/Fermanagh border, and thus narrowly escaped being included in Northern Ireland; at its central crossroads stands a statue of Sean McDermott, 'patriot executed in 1916 by the British', the same man whose house eluded us. A sign by the village church leads (past the rubbish dump!) to the 'Natural Bridge over which St Patrick crossed'. Its naturalness is debatable; more interesting anyway is the concrete barrier just here marking the border with the UK.

Continue along deserted R281, passing Black Pigs Dyke, an earlier frontier fortification: these earthworks were made by Ulstermen in 3C to defend their boundary with Connacht. At **ROSSINVER** (ruins of early-Christian church) turn right towards Kinlough. (The sign marked 'Unapproved Road' leads the short distance to another yellow and black barrier with the UK. It has a small opening to allow cyclists and pedestrians to nip across to ask neighbours on the other side if they can borrow a cup of sugar. Several little houses stand right next to the border.) Our road runs close to the shore of picturesque Lough Melvin. At unattractive **KINLOUGH**, turn right onto busier T54/R280 to reach the Atlantic at Bundoran.

BUNDORAN (again the road has crossed briefly into the province of Ulster) is a small charmless resort town (pop: 1,600) complete with 'Irish Gift Shop', amusement arcades, funfair, campsites, etc. It does have a few pretty features though, including some thatched cottages with dandelions growing on the roof, and good views along this marvellous stretch of coast.

Ben Bulben

Drumcliff churchyard

Travel south out of Bundoran on coast road N15. Pass through Tullaghan, with its old cross. Along this coastal strip are scattered many ruins of prehistoric, early-Christian, and medieval periods. One of the finest is at **CREEVYKEEL** (signposted, to left of road), an important Late Stone Age (2500BC) settlement with good court cairn and other relics. To the right of the road at this point is **MULLAGHMORE**, a peaceful, if slightly bleak, resort village with cows grazing next to the walled harbour (constructed by Lord Palmerstone, 1842). A road runs round Mullaghmore Head, which would also make a good walk, with splendid ocean views. Mid-19C Classiebawn Castle, the mansion of the Mountbattens, can be seen from a distance, and eventually the road passes in front of its gatehouse; on either side of the gate are monograms of Earl Mountbatten of Burma. It was off this stretch of seashore that Admiral Louis Mountbatten was blown up in his sailing boat by the IRA in 1979.

Return from Mullaghmore to N15, where turn right (direction Sligo). Soon after Grange, a turning on right leads to early-19C Lissadell House, home of the Gore-Booth family, among whom were Eva Gore-Booth, the poet and friend of W.B. Yeats, and her sister Constance Markievicz, first woman elected to sit in the British House of Commons. However, she did not go to Westminster, preferring (as an Irish nationalist) to take her seat in the Dáil at Dublin. Return to N15, which continues to **DRUMCLIFF** (various spellings; also Droim Chliab), at the foot of the imposing table mountain Ben Bulben (1730ft).

An 11C Celtic Cross beside the road here (on right) supposedly marks the site of a monastery founded by St Columbcille (or Colmcille or Columba) in about 575. Almost opposite, and presumed to be standing on the remnants of this monastery, is Drumcliff's parish church of St Columba (Church of Ireland) where W.B. Yeats is buried. Yeats spent his final years on the French Riviera, died in 1939, and was originally buried there. In 1948 his body was brought back to Ireland and buried in the graveyard of this little church where his grandfather had been rector. This was in keeping with the curious 'wish' or fantasy expressed in his poem 'Under Ben Bulben':

Under bare Ben Bulben's head
In Drumcliff churchyard Yeats is laid.
An ancestor was rector there
Long years ago, a church stands near,
By the road an ancient cross.
No marble, no conventional phrase;
On limestone quarried near the spot
By his command these words are cut:
  Cast a cold eye
  On life, on death.
  Horseman, pass by!

Yeats' unostentatious grave lies among the others to the left (north) of the church entrance. The words have indeed been cut. In the same tomb is George Yeats, his wife (Georgie Hyde-Lees). The interior of the small church is plain and new.

2 MUNSTER

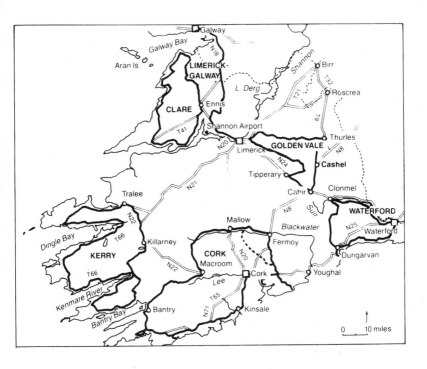

Taking up the whole of Ireland's south and south-west coasts, **Munster** is the largest province and without doubt includes—especially along the erratically indented rocky shore of County Kerry—some of the best scenery in the whole country. It also contains by far the greatest concentration of historic monuments, archaeological sites, medieval castles and landmarks of Ireland's heritage. And although not a wealthy region, it possesses several of the very best restaurants and hotels. Not surprising then, that in a few places—Blarney, for example, or Bunratty or Killarney—it attracts too many tourists for comfort. One can either brave these places just to see the sights, or choose instead to concentrate on the many other places along these routes where visitors are still a rarity.

Clare

2–3 days/130 miles (210km)/from Ennis

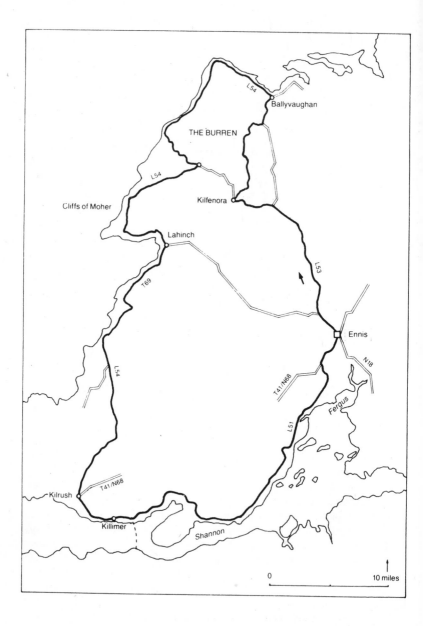

Centuries ago County Clare was part of the Kingdom of Connacht. It later became the separate Kingdom of Thomond, and as time passed found itself absorbed into Munster. Yet even now it still has more in common with that sparse, rocky, majestic province to its north than with the rest of Munster. Cromwell could obviously see the similarity, when he decided to banish the unwanted Irish gentry to a nebulous zone 'West of the Shannon'—which includes Clare. Along the immense estuary of the Shannon, the country is green and productive, but elsewhere the land is rock-hard and unyielding. Its coast rises in spectacular, daunting cliff-faces which take the brunt of the Atlantic's force, while in the north of the county is the eerie Burren region, a harsh limestone desert. In the gentler areas, pastures are broken up by forests of gorse and bracken; sheep graze in little fields enclosed by stone walls or overgrown hedges. In County Clare, sheep are seen everywhere—even on a town-centre football pitch. A few of the Travellers in these parts are still living in painted wooden caravans. Long cut off from its neighbours by the waters of Galway Bay and the broad Shannon, Clare has retained a profound provincial simplicity, unaffectedness and independence. The most remote part, all that which lies west of Ennis, is explored on this route.

ENNIS (or Innis, Inis etc.), on the bank of the river Fergus, is a big town by local standards (pop: 6,300), and is Clare's capital. Though not especially attractive, it has near its centre an interesting ruined 13C friary ('Ennis Abbey'), once a large and important community numbering up to 1,000 residents. Some good stonecarving has survived, and the friary was restored in the 1950s. The only other buildings with anything to recommend them are the Classical courthouse of 1850 and the converted Presbyterian church which now houses the Éamon de Valera Museum and Library. **Tourist Office**: Bank Place.

Leave town on N85/T70 (direction Lahinch) but after 2 miles, at Fountain Cross, head off to the right on R476/L53 (direction Corofin, Ballyvaughan). Another couple of miles reaches a minor left turn along which is **Dysert O'Dea** (signposted). A monastic site founded by St Tola, originally 7C or 8C, this was all long-ago abandoned; what survives now of the monastery are 12C remnants of a Romanesque church, a broken Round Tower, and The White Cross of Tola, an impressive High Cross. The place later became a local defensive stronghold, and it was here in 1318 that a battle between the Gaelic ó Brien and the Anglo-Norman de Clare resulted in a resounding defeat for the Anglo-Normans, who had finally to abandon all attempts to take control of the Kingdom of Thomond. The strong tower house which stands here now was originally 15C, and was where the indomitable and half-legendary Máire Rua (see Lemanagh Castle below) lived with her first husband Daniel Neylon, whose home this was in the early 1600s. It was rebuilt in 1840 by Diarmuid O'Dea, and has lately become a good museum and 'Archaeology Centre'.

Press on to **COROFIN**, a village amid picturesque lakes and woods. The Clare Heritage Centre here gives an overview, using such headings as education, culture, famine, etc., of one of the worst periods of Irish history, 1800–60. Nearby, ruined castles of the ó Briens stand on the bank of Lake Inchiquin (Gaelic *inis ui Chuinn*, ó Quin's island). **KILLINABOY**, beyond the lake, has some unusual religious ruins and must have been a small monastic settlement. There's a relic of a Round Tower, a tower house, and an early church with a (rather weatherworn) *sheila-na-gig*, which is a pre-Christian figurine with exaggerated female features, carved above the door. Another pre-Christian emblem, the Tau Cross, a curious small carving, used to stand close by in a field, but it seems to have been removed. A replica can be seen at Kilfenora.

The road turns towards Kilfenora, passing the imposing remains of **Lemanagh** 'castle' (various spellings). This building started life as a 15C tower house and became a 17C mansion. It was the home (with her husband Conor ó Brien) of Máire Rua, 'Red Mary', a terrible figure of local legend who supposedly had a dozen husbands (or any number up to 25), obliged her servants to dress as women and summarily executed several of them by hanging, and made local people pay tolls to use the public highway. It is even said that her suitors had to prove themselves by riding a wild stallion, and that almost invariably the horse would run straight to the Cliffs of Moher and jump into the sea. She is the proof that myths and fabulous legends do not all date from the distant past, for poor Máire was a real person, living as recently as during the Cromwellian period. She may have been rather tempestuous, forceful and unpopular, but almost everything which is believed about her turns out to be untrue. She was born in 1615, had three tragic marriages (one was arranged by her parents), bore numerous children, most of whom died, was tried for murdering a servant and was pardoned, and with her second husband Conor ó Brien fought hard against the Cromwellian takeover of Ireland. The matter of making people pay tolls is another wild exaggeration from the fact that she and Conor ó Brien enclosed some land as a deer park.

At this point the road is on the edge of **The Burren** (pronounced 'burn'), 100 sq. miles of strange treeless wild landscape with sharp-edged limestone 'pavements', hills, heath, and 'disappearing lakes' —disappearing because rainwater at first gathers, then drains into extensive underground labyrinths. Between the flat rocks, multitudes of tiny plants with beautiful little flowers have gained a foothold; but these are invisible from a distance. Yet inhospitable as it looks, the whole district was formerly densely populated, and is brimming with dolmens and ring-forts and early-Christian remains. Follow the road (L53) into **KILFENORA**, where the **Burren Information Centre** has a useful and informative audio-visual presentation and displays about The Burren. A replica of the Killinaboy Tau Cross can be seen here. Beside the Centre, a small 12C former cathedral has been partly restored and the nave now belongs to the Protestants. The choir remains roofless. Note the odd carvings of 'Cleric's Heads'. The 13ft-tall, unusually carved Doorty Cross in the graveyard is one of seven High Crosses which once stood around the cathedral. It is impressive and interesting. Beside it are 18C and 20C gravestones of the Doorty family, who still have hereditary rights to the

The Doorty Cross

bishopic! Other surviving High Crosses are a simpler one in the north-west corner of the graveyard, while the tallest of them stands in a field near the present Catholic church.

From Kilfenora, turn onto a minor road signposted Aillwee Caves. This goes through the very heart of The Burren. At a T-junction turn right onto T69 (direction Ballyvaughan). You reach Corkscrew Hill, which winds its way up to good views of The Burren landscape and of Galway Bay the north, with the comfortable country-house style **Gregans Castle Hotel** (065–77005) down below. A sign on the right points the way to **Aillwee Cave**. Beneath the surface this limestone terrain is hollowed out like a Swiss cheese, with complex networks of tunnels and caves. Aillwee is not by any means the most impressive of them, but is the one best equipped to deal with visitors. It is by no means undiscovered, and receives occasional coach parties. To be frank, it is not *that* spectacular: a ⅓-mile walk into a narrow limestone cave with modest rock formations. Above the cave is a pleasant snackbar and restaurant, everything home made.

From the Cave, continue to **BALLYVAUGHAN** on the coast. This is a lovely, ordinary little village next to a beautiful bay. There are a couple of good craft workshops, and inevitably it attracts some tourists in summer. Beside the village is a group of pretty, thatched holiday cottages. Follow the coast road (L54/R477; direction Cregg) beside Galway Bay as it skirts the edges of The Burren.

Go through coastal villages Fanore and Dereen, heading towards **LISDOONVARNA**. Although barely more than a village (pop: 700), it has the look and feeling of a rather abandoned resort town, and has lots of hotels. Lisdoonvarna has a great reputation for its traditional centuries-old Matchmaking Festival. Hopeful rustics, male and female, have long gathered here, clean, coiffed, and dressed in their best, to look for a life partner. The festival comes durng the month of September at about the

The main street, Ballyvaughan

time of the Harvest Festival. Professional matchmakers traditionally, for a fee, assist the young (and not so young) aspirants by arranging meetings. Surprisingly, even in this day of 'Lonely Hearts' ads, the festival still has a certain popularity. Some matchmakers in the past became legendary, and one of the most highly praised of them all, Jimmy White, has only just retired; however, it seems that they are a dying breed.

Besides all that, Lisdoonvarna used also to be a popular spa resort, one of very few in Ireland. It still has the baths which were opened in 1845, but today spas are not such big business, and the town shows signs of its decline. Efforts to revive its fortunes may yet prove successful, and among new attractions (still on a spa theme) are saunas, recreation centres, and keep-fit clubs. We paused at The Roadside Tavern on the entrance into town for a drink and a snack, and discovered that the proprietor runs the small tiled pump room opposite (Easter–Sept.). Here he will serve you a glass (for 10p) of the horrible iron-rich water, and relate details of the medical authorities who have sung its praises. He will report the evidence that Lisdoonvarna waters are good for the blood and cure rheumatism, adding his own view however that 'it's a great thing for the health but I don't know about curing.'

From Lisdoonvarna L54/R478 goes on to the **Cliffs of Moher** (access road to cliffs; Visitor Centre, parking, teashop), a truly awesome meeting of land with ocean, one of the most stupendous stretches of coast in Europe. Here 5 miles of absolutely sheer cliffs, in places over 650ft high, curve round to take the full force of the Atlantic's power. As the locals say, 'The next parish to here is New York.' From the car park, walk to the cliff edge and take the footpath which goes to the right. The path, made in 1835 by the land's owner Cornelius O'Brien, leads to O'Brien's Tower, which gives the best view of the cliffs, the ocean below and the Aran Islands out to sea. There is a tremendous screeching and wheeling of sea birds, which nest in their thousands in these wind-battered cliffs.

Continue south on the road to **LISCANNOR** and **LAHINCH**, neighbouring villages on a seashore altogether tamer than at Moher. Liscannor has the best golf course in Ireland, beside a mile-long estuary beach. At the golf course the weather barometer has a sign attached, 'See Goats'. This was explained to me as meaning that if the goats are around the clubhouse, rain's on the way, but if they are not in view fine weather is coming. At the ocean village of Lahinch, massive leisurely Atlantic waves break onto a broad beach. It was in the sea just offshore from these two villages, in Liscannor Bay, that Mulholland invented the submarine. Here, and all along this coastline, gaunt remnants can be seen of a string of defensive towers erected by the ó Briens, whose territories these were.

[If you want to cut the route short at this point, take T67 to Ennistimon, where turn right onto T70, which runs beside the Cullenagh river all the way back to Enis.]

South of Lahinch the countryside appears to be lusher and less stony. At **QUILTY** waves beat at the feet of the village. At a fork after Quilty, take the left turn (L54/R483) signposted to **KILRUSH**, which has little to recommend it. Take the minor road across the countryside to Killimer Ferry (signposted).

[This ferry is invaluable if you do not want to make the return into Ennis but would prefer to move on to County Kerry, south of the Shannon. The crossing takes 20 minutes across the impressively broad estuary. The ferry is a primitive open-deck vessel with a small cabin. Departures are every hour on the hour starting at 7am (9am or 10am Sun.) and finishing at 9pm (7pm Oct.–Mar.).]

From Killimer, minor R486 goes across country to meet, at Kilmurry, the Shannon coast road R473/L51. This follows the attractive estuaries of the Shannon and then the Fergus rivers, passing various ruined abbeys and castles erected (12/13C) by the ruling ó Briens. On meeting the main Ennis–Limerick road, N18, turn left to return into Ennis.

Limerick to Galway

1–2 days/80 miles (130km)/from Limerick (or Shannon airport) to Galway

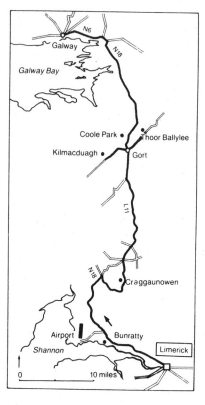

This journey starts in Munster and ends in Connacht. Though largely on main roads it is an interesting route with plenty to see, and one which many travellers in the west of Ireland may find themselves making. Almost two-thirds of the distance is within the borders of Co. Clare, in Munster, but some might argue that it ought to appear in the Connacht chapter. For Clare used once to be part of Connacht, and while a good deal of the interest of the journey lies simply with the calm green countryside, and the remnants which it presents of a turbulent past, much is also in the connection with W.B. Yeats, the Irish poet closely associated with that wild and beautiful province on the other side of Galway Bay.

Lovers of rural Ireland may protest that the city of Limerick is very large and very busy, and that an eventful history does not of itself justify getting caught in traffic and spending much time in crowded streets. If you do find yourself in the town, it has some relics of its past to see and to ponder; and certainly it is useful for shopping or finding refreshment. But it would not, I think, be a sin to by-pass the city of Limerick altogether.

LIMERICK pop: 70,000 County capital. Large industrial town well-sited on the broad Shannon river. Commercial activities range from curing bacon to making fine lace. The old heart of the city is the fortified port at the confluence of the Abbey river with the Shannon. Historically, this was a strategic location on Ireland's west coast: initially a Viking raiding settlement (9C); seized by Brian Ború (AD1000) who made it the capital of the Kings of Munster; taken by King John's forces (1210) who built fortifications. Richard II enlarged the town and fortifications, 1394. Returned to Irish rule under Henry VIII, the city later strongly resisted the 17C English takeover, notably in the violent Siege of 1690 when (after

Battle of the Boyne) King James' Catholic army defended the town against the Protestant forces of William of Orange. The city capitulated under a treaty which guaranteed religious freedom, but the treaty was not honoured. The city's defensive walls were dismantled in 1760.

North of the Abbey river is English Town, the district originally enclosed by King John, where his substantial castle still stands on the bank of the Shannon. See also: 18C courthouse; interesting CI Cathedral, 11C but much changed especially in 19C (note unusual 15C misericords). South of Abbey river is Irish Town, enclosed within Richard II's enlarged fortifications, where see: 18C Customs House, and restored 18C The Granary (with **Tourist Office**). The later Georgian district, Newtown Pery, with some attractive streets surviving, lies south of Irish Town.

Cross the Shannon on Limerick's Sarsfield Bridge, and take busy N18 (direction Ennis). Along this fast and hectic highway, known as Ennis Road, are a number of characterless hotels. About 5 miles from Limerick, 17C **Cratloe House** is a rare survival of the Irish 'long house' style of mansion, standing in its own woods and gardens. After this point the dual carriageway suddenly degenerates into a normal two-lane road.

Bunratty Castle, right beside the road, is the gaunt, sturdy 15C stronghold of the ó Briens, Earls of Thomond (the old province which encompassed Clare). Being close to Shannon airport, and being in fact managed by the Shannon Development authority, Bunratty has been turned into something of a tourist magnet. Mock 'medieval banquets' are given here throughout the season, with entertainers and 'serving wenches' in period costume. These are perhaps slightly absurd but can be appreciated as a bit of fun (061–61788 for details and bookings). The castle itself is really a tower-house (a tall heavily fortified domestic building), five stories high and in a magnificent state of preservation; it was still lived in until the last century, and in 1954 was purchased by Viscount Gort, who restored and refurnished the castle to its original style. Behind the castle, **Bunratty Folk Park**, an ambitious (and successful) museum project, consists of a collection of buildings, some arranged as a village (far too clean and neat to be a real one!), illustrating the architecture and way of life of rural Ireland in late 19C. There are examples of cottages from other regions of Ireland, showing how they differ. Wandering round this artificial village may seem a poor substitute for seeing the real thing, but in truth this is probably as near as any visitor to Ireland can get to witnessing the interiors of these simple long low thatched cottages which are still seen in many parts of the most remote and rustic west.

Walk right through the Folk Park to get to **MacCloskey's Restaurant** (061–364082), serving excellent French cuisine using best, fresh Irish ingredients. The restaurant is hidden away in the well-restored 17C vaulted wine cellars of a Georgian mansion, Bunratty House. The Folk Park also has a tea room with tasty home-made bread and cakes. A replica pub serves food and wine during the day; for more authentic Irish public-house refreshment, pop into **Durtie Nellie's**, a lively, popular and inexpensive pub restaurant right next door to Bunratty Castle.

Bunratty Castle

Continue along N18 (Ennis road). [Just after Bunratty, a left turn goes into **Shannon Airport**. Less used nowadays because planes can travel longer distances without refuelling, Shannon—Europe's most westerly major airport—was for many years a vital stop on flights between Europe and North America. It is still an ideal entry point into Ireland for visitors coming from across the Atlantic. Owing to its previous importance, the airport is large and has good facilities including local hotels. Shannon, opened 1945, was the world's first airport to provide duty-free shopping.]

Pass through **NEWMARKET ON FERGUS**, little town with lots of new houses. Just beyond it, a right turn goes towards Quin, passing **Dromoland Castle** (061–71144), an elaborate Gothic medieval-look 19C country house constructed on the ruins of earlier mansions. It was built for a latter-day O'Brien, Lord Inchiquin. It is now a luxury hotel, member of the Relais et Châteaux federation. A great grey stone fortress replete with turrets and towers, and standing in a vast green estate, Dromoland makes an impressive sight from the road above. Within its grounds, Mooghaun is the largest prehistoric ring fort in Ireland. Obviously a prosperous community lived here in that remote era, for nearby is the site where the Clare Gold Hoard was unearthed by workmen in 1854. This was a vast collection of prehistoric solid gold artwork and ornaments. Unfortunately most of the pieces were disposed of rapidly and privately and soon disappeared, maybe melted down. The few pieces which were recovered can be seen in the National Museum in Dublin.

Carry on along this back road to **QUIN**, which has an exceptionally well-preserved Franciscan Abbey of 1402, beside ruins of a 12C Anglo-Norman castle. Note especially the central tower and cloisters. Despite harassment over the centuries, the Franciscan community stayed in residence right up until the early 19C.

Take R469 towards Kilmurray and Sixmilebridge. This passes in front of **Knappogue Castle**, 15C fortress which, partly to please its Texan owners and perhaps partly for the benefit of tourists, has been made a little too mock-medieval; like Bunratty it has 'medieval banquets' which owe more to the idea of fun nights out than knights in armour. At a junction turn left to **Craggaunowen Megalithic Centre** (or Craiganowen, etc.) (signposted), a remarkable outdoor museum of architecture and lifestyle, built in the grounds of a restored 15C castle. Inside the castle—actually a fortified tower-house—are displays of Irish and English folk art and fur-

Craggaunowen Megalithic Centre

nishings dating back to 14C. Just as at Bunratty Folk Park, outdoor structures vividly and excitingly show the sort of dwellings in which people lived in the past; the difference is that here they are prehistoric reconstructions. Best exhibit is a recreated Bronze Age *crannóg*, a fortified lake dwelling on an artificial island. Teas and home-baked scones are served in the castle's entrance lodge.

Continue beyond Craggaunowen (direction Killeen, Gort, Galway) through Moymore, at first on L194, then turning (after Moymore) onto R462/L11, heading north. Go through Killeen and turn right onto the main Galway road N18. This goes into a landscape of limestone, with all the strange formations and phenomena associated with this extremely porous rock. Beside the road (on right) is a fine Regency mansion, Lough Cutra Castle. From here an underground river flows to Gort, but making sporadic appearances on the way, notably at The Punchbowl, where the river emerges only to disappear underground again almost at once.

GORT is a largish (pop: 1,100) workaday but quite pleasant market town and former garrison. Take the Loughrea road (N66/L11) as far as a left turn, about 2 miles from Gort with a sign pointing to 'Yeats' Tower', **Thoor Ballylee**. This is the old de Burgos tower-house in which W.B. Yeats (1865–1939), and his wife George, spent a lot of time during the 1920s. It is a sturdy little stone fortress beside a stream (one of those which disappears into the ground not much farther along its course). Yeats had bought the place from the Congested Districts Board in 1916, having first seen it some 20 years before while visiting Edward Martyn at Tullira Castle and Lady Gregory at Coole Park (both of which places we see later on the route).

Yeats was obviously very fond of his 'thoor', and worked hard to convert the building and make it habitable. It is described with touching detail in many poems, and he even published a collection called The Tower with a picture of the tall fortified house on the cover. But it was damp and difficult to maintain, and the Yeatses eventually abandoned attempts to make the tower their home. Yeats believed with sadness that after his death it would fall into ruin, but his fame prevented that. It has been preserved and opened to visitors (good teashop and bookshop on the site) who can see now with their own eyes 'This winding, gyring, spiring treadmill of a stair' and the 'chamber arched with stone . . .' as well as the furniture and books which belonged to Yeats. One of his poems is called 'To Be Carved On a Stone at Thoor Balylee', and the words have indeed been carved:

> *I, the poet William Yeats*
> *With old mill boards and sea-green slates*
> *And smithy work from the Gort forge*
> *Restored this tower for my wife George;*
> *And may these characteristics remain*
> *When all is ruin once again.*

Return to Gort. Before continuing northwards, it is interesting to make a little excursion to **KILMACDUAGH**, 3 miles along R460/L55 via Newtown; it has an astonishing set of monastic ruins. The original church was established here in 610 by St Colman; it was replaced by a cathedral in 14C, though keeping some features of the older building (and note: 10C west door; Flamboyant windows; good stonework). All around it are other intriguing buildings: 13C St Mary's Church (or Teampull Muire); O'Heyne's Abbey is a remnant of a 10–13C abbey church; an Oratory which may date right back to St Colman's time; a 14C 'Bishop's Castle': and certainly not least, a leaning Round Tower—112ft tall and 2ft out of true. The angle looks alarming, but has been like that for centuries.

Travel north out of Gort (direction Galway, N18), coming in less than 2 miles to **Coole Park** (or Coole Forest Park). With woods, lakes, and footpaths, this estate is now a National Forest and a wildlife preserve. Attractive as it may be today, it is a mere reminder of greater times. For these were the grounds of a Georgian country house which used to be the home of Lady Augusta Gregory (1859–1932). Lady Gregory, besides being a writer herself, is best known as the person around whom much of Ireland's late-19C literary life revolved. She was quick to spot talent, even in young unknown writers, and invited numerous great novelists and playwrights to Coole Park, whether for a dinner or to spend several weeks. She was greatly admired and liked by many of Ireland's most important writers of that time. Her *Journals* of the period are interesting.

It's strange that it was in this rural corner of Ireland, on the opposite side of the country from the lively and cultured capital, that the Irish Revival—the great 19C renaissance of Irish art and literature—really took place. Lady Gregory helped inspire and organise the founding of Dublin's Abbey Theatre, which was to be (as it still is) the vehicle for publicising some of the best new work by Irish writers. Many came here to meet and discuss and be inspired by each other's creative energy. Indeed, a good deal of the writing itself was done here, as Lady Gregory urged her friends that they would benefit from the peaceful setting and offered them space in which to work. Yeats described in poetry his visits to the house, and of 'a dance-like glory that those walls begot'. When Lady Gregory died he wrote in a sincere lament, 'She has been to me mother, friend, sister and brother.'

After her death, the house came into the possession of the Irish government. With astounding philistinism they allowed the place to fall into decay, and instead of restoring it as either a literary museum or a monument to one of the great turning points in the resurgence of Irish nationalism, decided to sell it to a contractor who dismantled it for building stone (even though Douglas Hyde, another of Lady Gregory's guests, was President of Ireland at the time). What does remain at Coole Park is Lady Gregory's **Autograph Tree**, a sort of living visitors' book, a copper beech on which house guests carved their initials. One can still see where it was 'signed' by George Bernard Shaw, J.M. Synge, 'AE' (George Russell), John Masefield, Sean O'Casey, Oliver Gogarty, Augustus John, Jack Yeats, W.B. Yeats and many others.

Continue along N18, passing (on right) **Tullira Castle**. Behind a confused 19C outer structure, this is in fact a 17C tower-house. It was the home of Edward Martyn (1859–1923), playwright, producer, patron of the arts, and a good friend of W.B. Yeats. It was he, Yeats and Lady Gregory who resolved, at Coole in 1898, to found the Abbey Theatre in Dublin as 'an Irish Literary Theatre', and as things turned out Martyn bore most of the expense of the project. He also took a particular interest in stained-glass design, and revitalised this old craft in Ireland by bringing foreign masters to teach the art. The imaginativeness and creativity evident in modern Irish stained glass are largely due to his efforts and encouragement.

N18 heads north through a landscape marked with the stony ruins of Round Towers, tower-houses, fortresses, and signs of battles long ago lost and won. After Oranmore the road runs beside the short of Galway Bay into the city of **GALWAY** (see p. 45).

The Golden Vale

2 days/110 miles (180km)/from Cashel

This is part of the mild heart of Ireland. Fertile and productive Counties Limerick and Tipperary (known as 'Tipp' to its friends) offer a green, gentle and undramatic countryside. The Golden Vale, or Golden Vein, running right through the region, is a plain of rich and handsome farmland planted after Cromwell's conquest with his loyal Protestant soldiers. Highlight of the route is imposing Cashel, for seven centuries seat of the Kings of Munster and later a great medieval ecclesiastical capital.

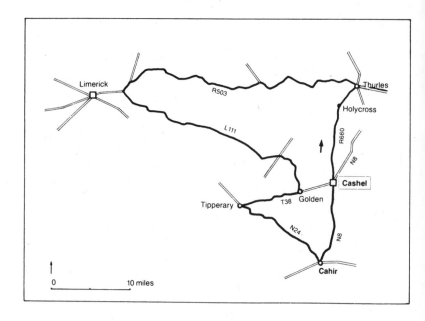

The pleasant, quiet little country town of **CASHEL** attracts large numbers of visitors, both Irish and foreign. Along its main street there's a **Tourist Office**, a number of souvenir shops, a hotel in a 15C tower house (Quirke's Castle), and another much more notable hotel, the Cashel Palace, about which a few words below. The town's great attraction is the remarkable group of buildings which stand on **The Rock of Cashel** (or St Patrick's Rock), a massive block which lies incongruously on the rich green plain. A fortress since long previously, after AD370 the Rock became known as Cashel of Kings (Gaelic *caiseal*, pron. 'cashel', means a stone fortress), and was the seat of the powerful Kings of Munster. These Celtic chieftains embraced Christianity at an early date: it is said that Patrick himself came here to baptise the king in AD450. Among Irish rulers who made their base here was 10C Brian Ború. In 1101, as the Church became more central to national political power, and as the English Crown took ascendancy over the Irish, the Munster kings made the Rock over to the Church and made themselves into a dynasty of archbishops. Cashel remained a place of regal as well as ecclesiastical importance; Henry II came here in 1171 to receive homage from the Thomond king Donal ó Brien. In 1647 the Rock was attacked and plundered by Lord Inchiquin, causing serious damage. Under the 18C archbishops, apparently a pampered and bloated crew, the Rock fell into disuse, and one of them removed and sold the lead roof of the Rock's cathedral building.

The Rock can be reached by road or footpaths from the town. The whole summit is still enclosed by a rampart. To see so many medieval buildings together and in such good condition is exceptional in Ireland. However, almost nothing survives from the pre-ecclesiastical period.

There are marvellous views of the surrounding rich farmland of the Golden Vale and of the roofless but impressive Hore Abbey at the foot of the Rock. Going through the enclosure's main gate (open daily; pay to enter), the following things can be seen:

1. On the right stands the two-storey Hall of the **Vicars Choral**, charming residential quarters of the cathedral cantors, dating from 1420 and carefully restored; the restoration involved removing a whole modern house from the interior of the main hall. Note the superb roof timbers, fine stone fireplace, and a good tapestry. In the undercroft, or vaulted basement beneath the building, a Cashel museum is being installed. One of the exhibits is a curious 12C High Cross ('the Cross of St Patrick'), now broken, standing on a base which some believe to be the original coronation stone of the kings of Munster.

2. Between the Vicars Choral and the roofless cathedral is a replica of the High Cross.

3. The centrepiece of the Rock is the 13C Gothic cathedral, without its roof since 18C; it has large proportions by Irish standards, has no aisle, and there is some good stonecarving.

4. Walking clockwise around the exterior of the cathedral, one passes first the narrow, high fortress which was tacked onto the west end of the building in 15C.

5. Continuing around the cathedral, a number of 16C engraved tombstones and memorials, as well as more recent and some 20C graves (one can still be buried here).

6. Attached to the north-east corner of the cathedral is the Rock's principal landmark, a Round Tower, 92ft high, built in 1101, and still in near-perfect condition.

7. Finally, fixed in the south-east corner between the cathedral's choir and transept, is the most interesting and most beautiful structure of all, **Cormac's Chapel**; built between 1127 and 1134, it is the earliest Romanesque church in Ireland. It is made of attractively laid dressed stone, and has a pair of fine towers and a lovely Romanesque doorway and windows; it is tragic that a later window was cut into the arch of the doorway. Inside, the chapel is sturdy, strong, satisfying, with bold carving in perfect Romanesque style. Although the place is, unfortunately, absolutely riddled with damp and suffering the consequences (assurances have been made that this will be dealt with soon), traces of frescoes have survived above the choir. Note too all the little heads and faces arranged over the chancel arch, and the elaborate sarcophagus, dating from the foundation of the chapel. Despite its age, Cormac's Chapel has kept the whole of its roof, which is entirely made of stone, not wood, and is unusually steeply pitched, enhancing its attractiveness.

From the Rock, a path goes down through handsome gardens to the Archbishops' Palace, a fine Palladian mansion of about 1730, now a superb luxury hotel, **The Cashel Palace** (062–61411). The interior, partly Regency, is sumptuous and extremely elegant. As a hotel, it offers a really exceptional standard of service, comfort and cuisine. There is, however, a certain excessive preponderance of loud American guests. If you cannot

Cormac's Chapel, Cashel

afford an overnight stay, or are just passing through during the day, have a traditional Irish tea in the hotel's Buttery. As well as the first-class cooking, some good Irish farmhouse cheeses may be sampled at the hotel; although Ireland has no long tradition of cheese-making, it now produces a number of delicious cheeses, using unpasteurised cows' or ewes' milk. Some of the best of Ireland's farmhouse cheeses are made in the Cashel area, notably the exquisite Cashel Blue, from the village of Fethard (or Feathart, pron. Fethart), 10 miles from Cashel.

Cashel has also made another important contribution to Irish gastronomy: that rich stout brew called Guinness. In the 1740s, Richard Guinis, the archbishop's agent, planted hops in the grounds of Cashel Palace and from them made a strong black beer. His son, using the same recipe, started brewing the beer commercially, and later founded the Guinness brewery at Dublin.

Leave the centre of Cashel initially on the Dublin road, but on the edge of town, fork left (signposted Thurles and Holy Cross Abbey), then fork right (signposted Thurles). The road crosses fairly flat country of rich pasture. **HOLY CROSS** is the name of the village which surrounds the abbey, as well as the abbey itself. The village is attractively sited on the river Suir; on its outskirts is a picturesque group of thatched holiday cottages (0504-43259 for details). **Holy Cross Abbey** is an impressive restored Cistercian monastery, founded 1180. It purported to possess a fragment of the True Cross. A lot of the original building has disappeared, but what remains, including the very pleasing ruins of the cloisters, rewards a visit. The monastic buildings are open to the public without charge, and for a small fee one can see a short video about their history. Today the Abbey is still a place of worship: it serves as a diocesan sanctuary and centre of pastoral care, and its church is now the parish church of Holy Cross village.

After the Abbey, fork right (signposted Roscrea); at the next fork, take the right turn (signposted Roscrea, with a second, obscured, sign to Thurles).

THURLES (pron. 'Durlas') is a pleasant market town (pop: 7,400) on the river Suir. At one end of its broad main esplanade a ruined 15C tower house, called Bridge Castle, guards the Suir crossing. Swans swim by the bridge. This fortress, belonging to Macrichard Butler, was once much larger, with outbuildings; it was occupied in 1690 by the Williamite force following their Boyne victory and prior to the Seige of Limerick. Another small Butlerite fortress can be seen tucked away at the other end of the main square. Cross the river to see the 19C cathedral, a startling building covered with a lot of ineffective Italianate decoration.

Cross back to the west side of the river, and leave town on the Limerick road (R503/T19). This part of the route runs through the higher, less fertile hills to the north of the Golden Vale. Pass a racecourse just outside Thurles. At Rosmult, follow the Limerick road as it turns to the right. Here the country becomes higher and bleaker for several miles until Milestone, where again veer to the right. Stay on R503/T19, direction Limerick: at the crossroads beyond Inch, the road takes a left turn. At **REAR CROSS**, there's a two-chambered dolmen on the hill rising to the right of the village. Pass through Newport and at Lisnagry, join main road N7; turn left (direction Limerick).

[It is only another 5 miles from here into **LIMERICK** (see p. 68). If you do want to go into this large town, simply remain on N7. To continue the route afterwards, return towards Lisnagy on the same road.]

Turn left just outside Lisnagy (or right, if coming from Limerick), onto L111/R506. Continue to Cappamore, after which the road number is L111 or R505. This road runs through the heart of the green and satisfying fertile Golden Vale. There is little to see except countryside, although some of the villages signpost a modest local sight or two. This area, 'planted' not with great landowners or prosperous speculators as in some other places but with more modest Protestant citizens, saw a lot of fighting during the Civil War and other disturbances earlier this century. Continue through Annacarty and Dundrum (direction Cashel). After Dundrum, take the right turn (direction Ballygriffin, Golden) to **GOLDEN**, a village well placed on the river Suir, crossed by an old bridge. On an island in the river stands a gaunt pillar of stone, last remnant of a Norman fortification, on which is now a memorial to Thomas MacDonagh, local commander of the 1916 Easter Rising. According to the inscription, 'he died like a prince'.

In Golden, on the west side of the river, a lane is signposted to **Athassel Abbey**. This leads to the extensive, very ruinous remains of what was once a prosperous and important priory, the largest in Ireland, surrounded by a thriving little town. The priory was founded for Augustinians in 1192 by the Anglo-Norman William de Burgo (or de Burgh). The town was destroyed during long periods of fighting in the early 14C, and the priory eventually suffered the fate of the Dissolution. There is still plenty to see (note some fine stonecarving, cloister, and the main doorway), and the ruins give a clear impression of how great the place once was. They are now abandoned, deserted, uncared-for, and access is over a stile and across a muddy field.

From Golden, on N74/T36, it's not a long way to **TIPPERARY**. The town, with a certain amount of industry and not especially attractive, like many Irish provincial towns, looks larger than its population total (5,000) suggests. It has a strongly nationalist history, and there is a public park named after Sean Treacy, the Tipperaryman who, it is said, fired the very first shots in the Anglo-Irish war (1919–21). It was apparently chance alone that chose the town's name for use in the famous army marching song—Harry Williams and Jack Judge, the authors of the lyrics, had never been to the town and probably didn't even know where it was.

Take N24 (direction Clonmel) across rolling country of rich green fields of pasture and woods and overgrown hedges. [At Bansho, and again beyond it, small signs point to **Glen of Aherlow** on the right, a lovely scenic drive with views along the valley of the gleaming Aherlow river.] N24 continues to **CAHIR** (or Caher, Cathair, etc.; pron. 'Care'), by-passing remains of a 13C Augustinian Priory just before entering this small town on the shores of the river Suir. Cahir, with its pleasant main square and riverside mall, would be an agreeable place but for the endless procession of lorries passing through. But dominating everything else about the town is its great stone castle (Gaelic *cathair*, pron. 'care'), which has managed to escape the worst ravages of history and remains in astonishingly good condition.

Cahir Castle stands on a rocky islet in the midst of the Suir; at its foot a broad weir divides the brown swirling waters. A sturdy high stone rampart with towers protects the tall battlemented keep within. It's a pity about the factory which has made itself look like a castle, standing on the riverbank behind the real castle! Cahir Castle was built, probably by Conor ó Brien, in about 1142 and was enlarged in 15C. The ground plan follows the shape of the island on which it stands, and the defences are cleverly designed, being divided into separately fortified sections (or wards). It withstood frequent attacks until the advent of cannon, for

Cahir Castle

which it was not quite so well equipped. In 16–17C, as English rivals competed for control over the region, Cahir Castle found itself more vulnerable. Robert Devereux, 2nd Earl of Essex, confronted and conquered it within three days in 1599. In 1641, the notorious Lord Inchiquin ('Murrough of the Burnings', who destroyed many towns and fortifications in Ireland), achieved the same task within just a matter of hours. In 1650, Cromwell arrived here in person. He being unwilling to engage in what he thought might prove a long struggle to subdue the stronghold, and its occupants believing that he would ultimately be successful in such a battle, terms were offered and accepted which allowed the castle garrison to leave unmolested with all their flags and weapons. This is perhaps one of the main reasons for the castle's relatively undamaged state, since it was Cromwell's men who reduced most of the country's other old fortresses to their present ruinous condition. Cahir Castle was restored in 1840 and 1964, is now open to the public, and houses a modest local museum.

Travel the 11 miles back to Cashel on main road N8.

Waterford

1–2 days/110 miles (180km)/from Waterford

Tucked away in Munster's untypically balmy and gentle south-east corner, green and hilly County Waterford was an early victim of Danish and Viking attacks (the name itself, originally Vadrafjord, is Norse), and later was the first part of Ireland to be settled by Anglo-Normans. In few parts of the country can Celtic, Norse, and Norman remains be seen in such close

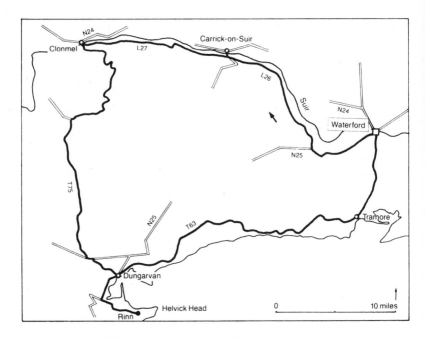

juxtaposition. The county proved difficult for the English to subdue initially, and during the Cromwellian era the Great Rebellion made Waterford into a virtually independent stronghold loyal to the displaced Catholic monarchy in England. During the early decades of this century, the county was fiercely nationalist, and saw considerable fighting. Today, it is a relatively prosperous region, with Waterford city a leading commercial and industrial centre. Despite that, the county preserves an important and influential little Gaeltacht district based on the village of Rinn. County Waterford is bordered by the Atlantic in the south, and inland by the beautiful rivers Blackwater and Suir (which Spenser knew as 'the gentle Shure'). This route also ventures across the Suir a couple of times to take a look at interesting provincial towns which belong to neighbouring County Tipperary.

WATERFORD (or Port Lairge) pop: 38,500 Large industrial town on the Suir river, with quayside main street (The Quay; **Tourist Office** at no. 41) on the south bank facing the busy commercial port on the north. At the end of the main street, Reginald's Tower is a circular stone fortification, built by Ragnvald son of Sygtrygg ('Reginald the Dane') about 1003 as part of the original fortifications of the Norse settlement. The tower was attacked and taken by the Anglo-Normans, including in 1170 Strongbow (Earl of Pembroke), who was married here to the daughter of the King of Leinster. Over the centuries it afforded a local base for numerous English lords and monarchs, including Henry II, King John, and Richard II. It is said that King James climbed to its roof for a farewell look at Ireland when fleeing after his defeats at the hands of William of Orange. The tower today houses an art gallery and an interesting museum of Waterford's eventful history. Among the exhibits are the ceremonial sword and mace of King John; city charters dating back to Richard II; and 'The Nail', a brass plaque of the city's arms, on which cash transactions and trade were legalised and made binding, and from which comes the expression 'cash on the nail'. Other fragments of the city ramparts survive at the top of Castle St. See also: ruins of 13C Blackfriars Priory (O'Connell St); ruins of 13C Franciscan Friary, 'The French Church' (the Quay); 18C Renaissance CI cathedral, Christchurch, with several interesting items from 11C cathedral formerly on the site (note 15C Rice Monument, of a decaying corpse complete with crawling vermin). There are several handsome buildings around town, including 18/19C RC Holy Trinity cathedral (the Quay), and 19C Courthouse (the Mall).

Highlight of the town is the **Waterford Crystal factory**, away from the centre on the main Cork road N25. Coming from Waterford, the factory entrance is on the right. There are free 40-minute tours, and a free video explaining the manufacture of Waterford glassware, among the finest and most beautiful in the world. The tour is worthwhile. The factory opened in 1783, and the same techniques of production have been used ever since. Every piece of Waterford ware is made individually by hand. To watch the skill of the glass blowers and cutters is astonishing; for example, it takes four skilled craftsmen and their seven assistants to make a single decanter. The pieces are then fired in furnaces at 2,500°F. There are no 'seconds'—anything below standard is destroyed at the factory.

Continue on main road N25 beyond the Waterford Crystal factory (direction Cork), going into rich and rolling green farmland. A clear sign indicates the right turn to Carrick-on-Suir (no road number is given; it is L26 or R680). Follow this pleasant leafy road beside the river. At a fork, take the right (direction Carrick).

Cross the river (which takes you over the border into County Tipperary) to enter **CARRICK-ON-SUIR** on its 'new' bridge, with a good view of the town and of the medieval bridge a little farther upstream. The main landmark is the unimpressive 18C Tholsel with its curious clock tower rising above the low houses and shops. Carrick is an ordinary workaday town (pop: 5,600) in a lovely setting: the Suir is very handsome at this point. There's a **tourist office** (signposted) just off the main street (one way, east to west). Go to the end of the main street, pass the Tholsel (or 'Town Clock', as it is called), which at ground level looks more like a closed-down cinema; turn right and right again into a street, parallel with the main street but with traffic going west to east. Turn left at the end; then right into the main road (N24, main Waterford road); take the next right, a little backstreet, to the 'castle' (signposted).

Carrick is Gaelic for a circular stone rampart, and presumably something along those lines once stood where Carrick's **Ormond Castle** can be seen today, but the present building is far from what one normally considers to be a castle. It is a substantial but delapidated Elizabethan mansion (16C), tacked on to a ruined 13C tower house. The older part was built by the

Glassworker at Waterford Crystal factory

Butler family, and the once-fine Elizabethan house, now looking grey and sad and shuttered, was constructed for the 10th Earl of Ormonde. The interior, though somewhat decaying, has some impressive original features.

Return to Carrick's main street, and take the road (almost opposite the Tholsel) which goes down to the medieval bridge. Note that on the downstream side the bridge has seven arches, while on the upstream, thanks to the shape of the riverbank, it has eight! Cross the river and immediately turn right—the turning is literally just on the far side of the bridge. It has no signpost. This backstreet passes an old Franciscan friary, still occupied by Franciscans. On faith alone, since there is still no signpost, follow this road as it leaves town. This is a lovely stretch of country, a broad rich green valley of woods and meadows, the road giving views of ruined tower houses on both sides of the river. We are now back in County Waterford.

Eventually a signpost declares that this is the L27 to Clonmel. At a fork, take the left, marked 'Comeragh Drive' (the right turn says 'Kilsheelán ½' and leads over a hump-backed bridge onto major N24). This makes a gorgeous drive. It comes to an unusual junction of two hump-backed bridges: take the left (signposted 'Clonmel'). Turn right over the next bridge into Clonmel, which again is in County Tipperary.

CLONMEL (or Cluain Meala) pop: 12,500 Big, lively, industrial, largest town in Tipperary. It has a pleasant air and a tree-lined main street. The run-down-looking Tholsel (17C), known here as the Main Guard, stands prominent at one end of the main street. At the other end, the narrow West Gate, a handsome structure with a little turret rising from one corner (and in fact dating only from 1831, despite appearances) straddles the street. On the West Gate there is a plaque to Laurence Sterne (1713–68), the author, who was born here—but I am sure even his mother would not have been pleased by the portrait represented of him. Other literary connections in the town: the wanderer and writer George Borrow had a short spell at a grammar school near the West Gate about 1814, while Anthony Trollope also lived briefly in Clonmel 1844–5.

Leave Clonmel by the same road that was used to come in. On crossing the bridge back over the Suir, turn right to follow the sign to 'The Nire'— this refers to the river Nire or Nier. This is a marvellous drive over hilly country at the edge of the Comeragh and Monavullagh ranges. The road meets larger T27/R671, where turn left (direction Dungarvan). Follow the road round to the left as the road number changes to T75/R462, continuing towards Dungarvan. On meeting N72, turn left, and right to rejoin the Dungarvan road.

DUNGARVAN, well placed on the shore of the large natural bay Dungarvan Harbour, is a thriving town (pop: 6,700) with some character. It preserves remains of a castle built by King John (and known as Prince John's Castle), which was a stronghold of the anti-Cromwell Great Rebellion in the 1640s. However it eventually surrendered to him without a fight, and so escaped much damage. Across the river Colligan is the district called Abbeyside, where parts survive of a 13C Austin friary and 13C fortress of the MacGraths (known as Dungarvan Castle).

A worthwhile excursion from Dungarvan is out to Rinn, on the other side of Dungarvan Harbour. Leave Dungarvan on N25, the main Cork road; after 2½ miles turn left onto a small road to RINN (Ring, or An Rinn, or Ringville). The whole neighbourhood of the village is sometimes known as the Rinn (Ring) Peninsula. This is an Irish-speaking enclave, known as the Deisi Gaeltacht, after the original Gaelic tribe who lived here, the Deisi. There is a Gaelic College here for those pursuing further education in the language. Beyond the village are the Atlantic cliffs of **Helvick Head**.

Return to Dungarvan and leave town on the east side of the river, taking coast road R675/T63 (direction Tramore). This passes through a few resort towns or villages all of which look as if they have, to a greater or lesser degree, been declining in recent years. The largest of them, TRAMORE (or Trá Mór) (pop: 6,700), lies in a sandy bay overlooked at each end by ruined fortifications. Stay on the same road as it makes its way back into Waterford.

*

If travelling on from Waterford to Rosslare or Wexford (or beyond), far more enjoyable than the main road is to take L157 (south of the Suir) to **PASSAGE EAST***, from which a small car ferry goes to and fro across the Suir–Barrow estuary, landing at pretty* **BALLYHACK** *on the other side. From there take L159, a direct road with little traffic to Wexford, with a turn-off for Rosslare.*

Cork

3 days/245 miles (390km)/from Cork

The largest Irish county, Cork possesses a range of landscapes from the wildest and rockiest Atlantic shore to sublime, gentle coasts, or inland from the mildest and most tender green farmland, to bleak and haunting areas of bog, heath, or hills. The climate, though moist, is generally balmy and temperate all year round. This journey around Ireland's south-west

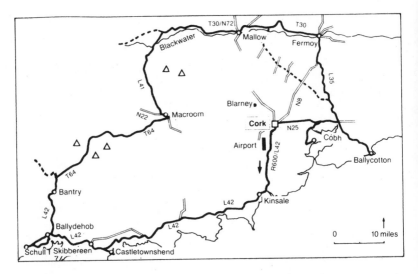

corner is one of the most satisfying routes of all. It also, surprisingly perhaps, offers some of the country's best hotel-restaurants.

CORK pop: 136,500 Ireland's third city (after Dublin and Belfast), grew across the banks and islands of two arms of the river Lee after the founding of a monastery on its south bank in about AD600 by St Finbarr. The name comes from Gaelic *corcaigh*, a marsh. Now highly industrialised and densely populated, yet with some attractive Georgian streets and old quays at its centre. The waterways give it a particular charm. Historically, it was the scene of frequent conflict between local tribes, Norsemen and Anglo-Normans, and later became a bastion of nationalism. During the 1920s, it suffered at the hands of the Black and Tans, the notoriously savage and uncontrollable British police who openly murdered the city's mayor and on 12 December 1920 went on the rampage, setting fire to a large part of the city centre, destroying, among other things, its famous Carnegie Library. Hardly anything in Cork has survived its violent history, but see: Red Abbey Tower, last remnant of an Augustinian abbey; ruins of 17C Elizabeth Fort; the columned Courthouse of 1835; and the imposing CI St Finbarr's Cathedral of 1878. Note that the main thoroughfares, Grand Parade and curving Patrick St, are actually built upon filled-in sections of the river Lee.

At the city's Opera House there are two annual seasons of high-quality ballet, theatre and opera. There are also three interesting art galleries. There's a big covered market each Saturday, with an astonishing number of butchers' stalls: meat, sausages, and 'drisheen' (a kind of blood sausage) are especially popular at Cork. Murphy's Stout, the excellent milder and mellower rival to Guinness, is brewed here. **Tourist Office** in Grand Parade.

Ascend steep Summer Hill into the suburb of Montenotte, where in Middle Glanmire Rd, one discovers the Ryan brothers' **Arbutus Lodge**

(021–501237), an outstandingly good family-run hotel, friendly, civilised and comfortable. Its dining room (open to non-guests) is among the best restaurants in Ireland. Trained in three-rosette French kitchens, the Ryans provide a truly exquisite and imaginative meal with unfussy elegance and professionalism, using only the best fresh local ingredients. The wine list is a formidable document, over 20 pages long, including many rarities which they 'secretly hope no one will order'. With deceptive modesty the Ryans describe their first-class little hotel as a *restaurant avec chambres*, which hardly does it justice. It is worth staying overnight just for the generous and delicious breakfast.

An all-too-popular excursion from Cork is to **BLARNEY**, about 5 miles north west on L69. At this unappealing village, 15C Blarney Castle (hefty entrance fee) is the goal of anyone who seeks to acquire the Irish 'gift of the gab', supposedly given to all who lean over backwards and succeed in kissing the difficult-to-reach **Blarney Stone**, part of the structure of the castle. If the legendary qualities of the Stone seem rather unbelievable, that could be because the whole idea was dreamed up only about 150 years ago. Nevertheless, the use of the word 'blarney' to mean persuasive and eloquent nonsense, is much older than that. It probably dates back to Elizabeth I who found difficulty negotiating with the smooth-talking clan leader MacCarthy, lord of Blarney Castle.

Leave Cork on L42/R600 (signposted to the airport). Pass Cork Airport and continue on this road to **KINSALE**, a pretty and interesting old fishing village on a big tidal river estuary. It's the home of a Jazz Festival and a Food Festival. As well as having a reasonable hotel, **Acton's** (021–772135), Kinsale has a surprising number of decent restaurants—at the time of my visit there were 14 (and I probably missed some!), mostly specialising in fish dishes. It also preserves a few ruins of its old fortifications, and an unusual church, St Mulrose's (12C, with later additions). The Tholsel, now housing a museum of local history, dates from 1706, and there's an 18C fishmarket. Desmond's Castle ('the French Prison') was originally a 16C mansion. In 1601, a Spanish fleet pulled up outside the harbour intent upon doing battle with the English, and formed an alliance with disgruntled Irish earls for the purpose. The Spanish tactic, however, proved both treacherous and misconceived: they tricked the Irish into launching an attack on their own against the English, thinking that they could go in afterwards to mop up. However, the Irish were soundly beaten; and the Spanish had to take flight having achieved nothing. After that incident, the English made Kinsale into a naval base, and barred any Irishman from living within its walls until the end of 18C. An access road leads to **Charles Fort**, a large star-shaped fortress which the English built in 1680 to protect the harbour. It remained in continuous occupation by the British navy until Irish independence in 1922.

Cross the Bandon river on the main road L42. A left turn goes to the dramatic cliffs of the **Old Head of Kinsale**, off which the Lusitania was sunk by a German torpedo in 1915, with the loss of over 1,000 lives.

When returning from the Head to the main road, it is more direct to take a left turn to **BALLINSPITTLE**. There is a Moving Statue here, seen on 22 July 1985 by some 20 people. Since then, there have been almost daily reports of its moving. To try your luck at witnessing this 'miracle', follow signs (½ mile before the village) marked 'Grotto', to a little cavern on a hillside just off the road. Here is a miniature representation of the apparition at Lourdes, with a statue of Bernadette gazing at another of the Virgin Mary. It is said, though, that Mary only moves for believers, which seems rather counter-productive. Wouldn't it make more sense for Mary to move for sceptics? I sat and stared to no avail.

The travel writer Eric Newby and his wife also went to see what they could see. Newby looked hard at the concrete stone, and 'just as during the war I had gazed out fixedly into the darkness of the night so many times while acting as a sentry, eventually imagining I saw movement, so I gazed at the statue of the Mother of God in Ballinspittle, waiting for a sign. And suddenly, when my eyes had begun to ache with the effort of concentration, it began to move, not just backwards and forwards, but from side to side. It was extraordinary, but no more extraordinary in its way than seeing movement taking place in the dark as a sentry, and sometimes actually shouting, "Who goes there?" '

Once back on L42, continue west through **TIMOLEAGUE**, with interesting ruins of a 14C Franciscan friary once well known for its abundant stocks of imported wines, and 13C Barrymore Castle, which has attractive gardens. Go straight through **CLONAKILTY**, a small market down, to **ROSCARBERY** (or Ross Carbery, etc.), shortly after which turn left onto R597/L191 (direction Union Hall and Castletownsend).

Pass ruined and ivy-smothered 17C mansion Coppinger Court, and go through villages **GLANDORE** and, facing it across Glandore Harbour, **UNION HALL**. Follow signs carefully (via Rineen, after which fork left, then turn left) to descend into **CASTLETOWNSHEND** (or Castle Townsend). This picturesque and rustic little village has a beautiful CI church in which it is plain that God himself was considered less important than the local ruling English families, the Coghills and Somervilles and above all the Townshends (or Townsends). The writer Edith Somerville is buried in the churchyard. Jonathan Swift stayed here in 1723—or it may have been at nearby Union Hall: he spent the time composing a poem in Latin, 'Carberiae Rupes' (Carbery Cliffs). The whole district suffered terribly in the Famine, and there have been several accounts published of the unimaginable conditions of the broken hovels in which the peasantry struggled to live and prematurely died in the mid-1840s, at which time the Reverend Townshend, Protestant vicar of Castle Townshend, was earning £8,000 a year (a lot of money) from crippling rents on such properties from here to Mizen Head.

Double back out of the village, but at a junction instead of turning towards Union Hall, carry on to **SKIBBEREEN**, busy little local centre on the river Ilen (**Tourist Office** in Town Hall). Take L42/N71 along the wild and rocky coast, with good views over Roaringwater Bay. At

Ballydehob bar

BALLYDEHOB, the quiet main street rises up prettily from a tributary of the Bay, passing between plain-fronted houses, each painted a different colour. Something of a hippy mecca for a while, this village has reverted gradually to its original character. In the **Ballydehob Inn** (028–37139), or Nora Morris's as everyone calls it, one can get a good drink and a good dinner, and there are basic, comfortable rooms upstairs.

A minor road turning left off the beginning of the Schull road (L57/R592) is a little-used back way from Ballydehob to Schull. It's the perfect country lane, threading for miles between banks of bramble, nettles, primroses, bluebells and buttercups, overlooking the islands and broad waters of Roaringwater. Beyond the fishing village of **SCHULL** (or Skull) scenic, sometimes dramatic, lanes continue out to the Atlantic cliffs of Mizen Head. This whole area suffered very badly during the great Famine; densely populated at the start of the 19C, after the Famine it was deserted.

Return to Ballydehob. Take L42/N71 (just east of the village, off the Skibbereen road) to Bantry. Just before the town, Bantry House, a fine 18C mansion, has pleasing gardens and views across Bantry Bay, while inside the house, good paintings, tapestries, and furnishings can be seen. After the small town of **BANTRY**, centred on its spacious marketplace, take T65/N71 around the head of Bantry Bay to **BALLYLICKEY** (alternative spellings). Top quality place to stay here: **Ballylickey Manor** (027–50071), a country house hotel and restaurant, member of the Relais et Châteaux federation, with 10 acres of parkland on the edge of Bantry Bay. At this point one has a choice.

One possibility is to go from County Cork into County Kerry, via Glengarriff and Kenmare (p. 93), and the glorious road from there to Killarney (p. 92). Beyond Killarney, take N72 along the Blackwater Valley towards Mallow. This, I must confess, would be my own preference. It makes for a longer but more beautiful journey.

Alternatively, one could remain within County Cork, turning right at Ballylickey onto R584/T64 and heading inland (direction Macroom) along the Owvane valley. After Kealkill, the road rises left through the wild **Keimaneigh Pass** through the Shehy Mountains. [A side road on the left leads down (2 miles) to the strange phenomenon of **Guagán Barra** (or Gougane Barra), a dark lake in a deep hollow almost enclosed by sheer mountain slopes.] Descend into a Gaeltacht district, going through **BÉAL ATHA AN GHAORTHAIDH (Ballingeary)** and **INCHIGEELAGH**, with its tower. Skirt The Gearagh, a scrubby, bushy, marshy area, and Inishcarra Reservoir, and on meeting major N22 (the main Cork–Killarney road) turn left into **MACROOM** (or Maigh Chromtha). This modest little market town on the Sullane river has kept a few Georgian facades, some pleasing shops, and a remnant of castle standing on its estate.

Leave Macroom on the main road (N22, Killarney direction), soon turning right onto L41/R582 which climbs through stony hilly country, with the low Boggeragh Mountains (marked footpaths) rising to the east. It descends into **MILLSTREET**, a good centre for local walks or drives. Take the Mallow road (L71/R583), passing Drishane Castle, a 15C tower house with later additions. Cross the Blackwater, and on meeting N72 turn right (direction Mallow). The route is now in the **Valley of the Blackwater**, delightful countryside threaded-through by the lovely little Blackwater river, although the best of the valley drive is farther east, beyond Mallow. Here N72 goes through green and wooded country.

Shortly before Mallow, a sign points left to **Longueville House** (022–47156), an imposing country house hotel standing in its own 500-acre farm beside the river Blackwater. It is a member of the Relais et Châteaux federation. The setting is utterly quiet and peaceful. Bedrooms, bathrooms, lounges are all comfortable. Service is attentive, friendly and competent. The house stands on a small rise, with marvellous rustic views of woods and farms and green rolling pasture, and sheep grazing just outside the door. The dining room offers good and generous meals.

Built in 1720 and clearly Georgian in style, with a lovely Victorian conservatory at one end, Longueville was a private home until 1968. The present proprietors Michael and Jane O'Callaghan bought the house, so fulfilling an ambition, because the estate had belonged to the O'Callaghans before being confiscated by the English during the Cromwellian era and given to the 'planted' Longfield family. The grey ruins of the original O'Callaghan fortress (Dromineen Castle) stand within sight, beyond trees on the far side of the Blackwater. Perhaps the most remarkable thing about Longueville today is that it is Ireland's only

Longueville House with the O'Callaghan mansion in the foreground

vineyard, growing and making its own wine, available in the Longueville restaurant. When it comes to cultivating grapes in Ireland, Michael O'Callaghan says, 'Winter's no problem. The main thing is to get the temperature high enough during the July flowering. Then it must be over 19°C for a week. If you get that you've a very good chance for the harvest. Sometimes we do have bad years, with summers hardly good enough for hay, let alone wine.' He devotes 3 acres to grapes, mainly a little-used German variety called Reichensteiner. The result is distinctive, dry and crisp; it's rather thin and by no means a great wine, yet perfectly drinkable, and that in itself seems like an achievement.

From Longueville House turn back onto N72 and go into **MALLOW**, an agreeable and moderately large industrial country town (pop: 6,700) on the Blackwater. In 18–19C it was an elegant spa resort, and retains several fine town houses. Its riverside 'castle', still privately owned by the original family, is a 16C fortified house incorporating part of an earlier fortress on the site. For the Irish perhaps Mallow is best known for its notorious 'rakes', whose antisocial antics are spelled out in the popular song 'The Rakes of Mallow', written during the spa's heyday. Fortunately the behaviour of young men in Mallow seems to have been moderated since then!

Take N72/T30 east from the town, towards Fermoy. (But see below for an alternative route across the Nagles hills.) The road veers away from the Blackwater to **CASTLETOWNROCHE** in the Glen of Awbeg. The 'Roche' in its name refers to the Roche family, descended from the Anglo-Normans, who controlled large parts of this region right up until the Cromwell invasion. Castle Widenham, the Roche's ancestral family home in the village, combines their medieval tower house with a later mansion. Outside the village (to north) the superb, fascinating gardens of 18C **Annes Grove House** (signposted) are open to the public—they deserve an unhurried visit.

Keep to the Fermoy road, which returns to the Blackwater valley. Pass an old Roche tower at **BALLYHOOLY**, and, just before Fermoy, Georgian mansion **Castle Hyde**, home of the family of Douglas Hyde, first president of the Irish republic.

Bright, bustling **FERMOY** (pop: 3,000) on the Blackwater was founded in 1791 by a Scots businessman (as we would say today) called John Anderson. He purchased the land and constructed a small town with army barracks, hotel, houses, and shops. He then started a mail coach service from Cork to Dublin which halted at his hotel in Fermoy, so ensuring its success. Turn south here onto the main Cork road (N8). After Rathcormack village take the left turn to **MIDLETON** (pron. Middleton).

[Michael O'Callaghan of Longueville House suggested a more rural route than this: 'There's a very wonderful way to go that's over a mountain . . . that's the beautiful way to go . . . but how do you ever find it? I know the place you're going to very well—and I know it's very hard to find. And if I tell you the way, you'll get lost. But you've all day to do it in, and I'm sure you'll retrieve the situation.' We did follow his directions, through pretty upland farm country among the Nagles hills, and we did get lost, wandering along leafy quiet country roads of cowparsley and buttercup, eventually finding ourselves in a narrow muddy lane behind a broken-down tractor. Its driver was a young man wearing an old-fashioned smock or tunic tightened with a broad leather belt. He had an amicable, open manner, and chatted to us about how he couldn't move the tractor at all and didn't see how we would ever get past, then promptly told us the way, and effortlessly pushed his tractor to one side so that we could pass. Thus we did 'retrieve the situation'.

If you want to try this alternative route, take N72/T30 as far as a small right turn which crosses the Blackwater to Killavullen, with its two old castles. Carry straight on to Beennaskehy, where turn left towards Glenville and Watergrasshill. On the way, this minor lane twice meets slightly larger backroads (which signpost Cork to the right): at both of these keep straight on by turning right and then left. At Watergrasshill, cross N8 (direction Leamlara, Lisgoold, Midleton). Follow signposts which mention Midleton. At Lisgoold, rejoin the main route, turning right along the Owenacurra to Midleton.]

From Midleton aim for **Ballymaloe House** (021–652417) between Cloyne and Shanagarry. It can be difficult to find. From Midleton, at the roundabout out of town on N25, take the Whitegates road, soon turning left onto the Cloyne and Ballycotton road; at Cloyne take leafy tranquil R632/L35^A (direction Ballycotton). Just 2 miles out of Cloyne, at a fork and bend in the road, a gateway opens into the Ballymaloe estate. Ballymaloe is a relaxed, cheerful, thoroughly civilised and enjoyable country house hotel, one of Ireland's best. The large mansion, incorporating a 14C tower house, stands in 400 acres mainly employed as a farm. Crows call out from the tall trees, sheep gently wander and nibble at the grass, children play in the garden and pool. The house is beautifully decorated and furnished. Rooms are supremely comfortable, elegant, and none has a TV or radio or a lock on the door. In the dining room first-class imaginative Irish (and French) cooking is served. There's an extensive wine list with an unusually good selection of half-bottles. Ivan and Myrtle Allen and family are the likeable, competent hosts, who run, in addition to the hotel and restaurant, a craft shop, a farm shop, and a renowned cookery school. Accustomed to the restraints of normal hotel life, we asked 'What is the latest time at which we can order breakfast?' To which Myrtle Allen replied—'Well, lunch is at one, but I should hope we've never been known to refuse anyone their breakfast.'

There are numerous pleasant walks and drives and cycle rides (bike hire at Ballymaloe) to be made in the lush, peaceful countryside of this immediate area, one of the best being to the exquisite village of **BALLYCOTTON** on the coast.

If you don't want to visit Ballymaloe House—and it is expensive—it's still enjoyable to go to Ballycotton on the direct road from Cloyne.

Return from Ballycotton to Midleton, where turn left onto N25, busy main Cork road. On the way back to the city, an interesting excursion may be made to **CÓBH** (pron. Cove), signposted to the left. This major commercial port on an island in Cork Harbour has a certain appeal, and makes a fairly popular outing for Cork residents. Off the Cóbh road, **Fota House** (open to public) is a grand Regency mansion, lavishly furnished and decorated in the style of the time, with some good landscape paintings. In the grounds are gardens, arboretum, and a most unexpected Wildlife Park. There is no direct route from Cóbh to Cork, so go back to N25 and turn left to return into the city.

Kerry
2–4 days/260 miles (410km)/from Killarney

County Kerry consists of a little land and a lot of water. The powerful Atlantic waves cut deeply inland, creating three rocky peninsulas pointing into the sea—Dingle, Iveragh, and Beara. Each is astonishingly beautiful, with pearly air veiling idyllic landscapes of dark forests, wild rocky slopes and motionless lakes. The coastal road encircling the Iveragh peninsula is known as the Ring of Kerry, and is a popular route for coach tours. Although the other two peninsulas are much less well known, sometimes all three peninsulas are called Rings of Kerry. Behind the coast, narrow lanes run through dense leafy woods and around tumbled moss-covered rocks, cross tiny stone bridges over brisk little streams, pass miniature churches, and cast glimpses between the hills at lakes, waterfalls, or sea

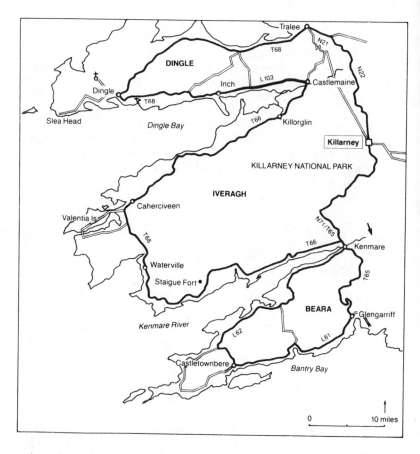

inlets. Parts of the countryside are thickly covered with huge rhododendron bushes, spectacular when in bloom (though posing a threat to the rest of the local plant and animal life). The whole region combines the majestic with the pretty.

KILLARNEY is not to everyone's taste (one could start the route at Kenmare, see below, if preferred). A bustling country town (pop: about 8,000) in a lovely setting, it is over-run with tourists. Absurd entertainments have been provided for them, such as the horse-drawn 'jaunting carriages', although it should be admitted that this form of transport offers good views and an agreeable pace, and the driver (called a jarvey) generally knows the best places to go. **Tourist Office** in the Town Hall along the main street.

There are many magnificent excursions to be made near the town by car, pony trap or on foot. One of the best is through a dramatic gorge called the **Gap of Dunloe** (organised trips from Killarney combining pony trap and boat). Even close to Killarney, the scenery is marvellous, right beside the town is picturesque Lough Leane, a large expanse forming the centre of Killarney National Park. Beneath its waters, it is said, local clan leader ó Donoghue still lives on, emerging briefly at sunrise on May Day. The lake is almost cut in half by a densely wooded peninsula called Ross Island, at the head of which there are attractively restored ruins of a 14C ó Donoghue castle. Cromwell's men managed to arrive here by ship, knowing that the local tradition had it that the stronghold could not be taken until strange ships were seen sailing on the lake: as soon as the vessels were sighted the castle's defenders laid down their arms. At an abbey (now in ruins) on Inisfallen Island, in the lake, the 13C Annals of Inisfallen were written, giving much information about local Celtic history and myth.

Leave Killarney on T65/N22 (direction Kenmare) which passes Ross Island and runs through lush forest. Part of the distance is within the Bourne-Vincent Memorial Park, in which are the considerable remains of a fine 14C Franciscan monastery, **Muckross Abbey**, with handsome cloisters half Gothic and half Romanesque; close by, in splendid gardens, is the 19C mansion Muckross House, now a museum of local arts and crafts.

Continue over pretty Galways Bridge, and soon after, pause at **Ladies View**, one of the best viewpoints along this road. The immense and complex scenery of lakes, of hills beyond hills, of the lofty Macgillycuddy's Reeks in the middle distance, really is quite wonderful. The Reeks, pronounced Maclycuddys, are Ireland's highest mountains, up to 3,414ft high. Carry on towards Kenmare, passing through Molly's Gap. This is an amazing beautiful part of the journey, the narrow winding road working its way through high rocky country above lakes of steely waters. Deciduous trees cling tenaciously to precipitous hillsides.

The modest, peaceful village of **KENMARE**, traditionally a lace-making centre, is blessed with one of Ireland's best hotel-restaurants, **The Park Hotel** (064–41200). With old-fashioned charm and style, furnished with antiques, standing serenely in its own private parkland, this grand country hotel has no crass modern ideas about luxury: everything here is calm, discreet, sumptuous. Obviously it is not cheap, yet neither could it be considered at all overpriced; the restaurant offers excellent, imaginative Irish cuisine with a French inspiration, and continues to win its well-deserved annual Michelin rosette.

Cross the Kenmare river on the suspension bridge (T65/N71; direction Glengarriff), and stay on this road as it climbs the Sheen valley, passes in tunnels beneath the barren summits of the Caha Mountains, and, after some magnificent scenery, descends through dense woods into **GLENGARRIFF**. This agreeable small resort town, on a protected corner of Bantry Bay, is noted for its mild climate and lush vegetation. Take L61/R572 (direction Castletownbere) along the sparsely inhabited south side of the **Beara Peninsula**, travelling between barren mountains and the sea. At **ADRIGOLE**, there is the option of turning inland and crossing, via the spectacular Healy Pass, over the Caha Mountains to the peninsula's north side. Our route continues (signposted Coast Road) to

Between Killarney and Kenmare

CASTLETOWNBERE, former British naval base and still a busy harbour. Double back from the town to turn inland on L62/R571, which crosses the Slieve Miskish Mountains to arrive in just 4 miles at the peninsula's north side. At **EYERIES** the road veers round to the right (signposted Kenmare). The Beara's north is greener and arguably more beautiful than the south; the drive from Eyeries to **ARDGROOM** is superb. Beyond, after views of Kilmackilloge Harbour (part of the broad Kenmare River sea inlet), the road arrives at **LAURAGH**. On the outskirts of the village, the wooded parkland of Derreen Gardens rewards a visit: as well as fine old oaks, etc., the tree ferns and azaleas are striking (tea room). The house whose estate this was has been rebuilt since being destroyed during the 1922 uprising, and it remains in the family of the man who laid out these gardens, the 5th Lord Lansdowne. The Kenmare road climbs inland and descends again to **ARDEA**. After the Ardea Bridge, the road follows the coast back to Kenmare.

Leave Kenmare on the Killarney road, turning left in ½ mile onto T66/N70. Our route now begins to circle the Iveragh peninsula—this is the ever-popular **Ring of Kerry** drive, and in summer one should be prepared to meet a certain amount of traffic. For much of the way the landscape is of thrillingly beautiful watery mountain scenery.

Pass Dunkerron Castle, then the ruins of Dromore Castle in its wooded estate (separate entrance to Dromore Wood picnic site). Cross Blackwater Bridge and continue to **PARKNASILLA**, a small village resort with woods, picnic spots, bathing beach and accommodation. Trees line the road as it goes on to **SNEEM**, a delightful village with mountains ranged behind. After a short inland stretch, first wooded, then rocky, the road returns to the bank of Kenmare River at **CASTLE COVE**. A lane leads from the village up to **Staigue Stone Fort**, a fascinating, and magnificently well preserved, 2,000-year-old circular stone fortress—probably the best example in Ireland. Its stupendously thick outer wall still stands 18ft high in parts. From Castle Cove, pass through West Cove (with abandoned copper mines) to **CAHERDANIEL** (or Catherdaniel), on the seaward side of which is **Derrynane National Historic Park**. The Park is essentially the house and extensive grounds of 17–19C Derrynane House, home of Daniel O'Connell ('The Liberator'). The house contains its original furnishings, and is preserved as a Daniel O'Connell museum. A re-erected Ogham stone can also be seen at Derrynane.

From here to **WATERVILLE** the scenery is breathtaking. Before entering the pleasant litle resort, two menhirs (prehistoric standing stones) and a stone circle can be seen. The town stands between Ballinskelligs Bay and Lough Currane, with hills rising behind. **The Huntsman** makes a good lunch stop here. Continue through a Gaeltacht district towards **CAHIRCIVEEN**, birthplace of Daniel O'Connell (1775–1847) and now a thriving local agricultural centre. There are several medieval and prehistoric ruins in the immediate area. An excellent excursion from here is to **Valentia Island** (or Valencia, Béal Inse, etc.), with quite astonishing subtropical gardens! A narrow winding channel of water separates Valentia from the mainland. The island can be reached by ferry from Reenard (3 miles west of Cahirciveen), or by road from Portmagee (10 miles south west of the town).

T66/N70 now turns back towards the east (direction Tralee, Killarney), passing the picturesque remains of Carnan House, in which Daniel O'Connell was born, and soon reaching the banks of Dingle Bay. Follow the road, with superb views, through Glenbeigh and past Caragh Lake. About 5 miles beyond Caragh, **KILLORGLIN** (or Kilorglin, Cill Orglan, etc.), has a ruined Knights Templar castle and is the setting every August for a colourful cattle fair. There are some good possibilities for food and drink in the little town. Continue on T66 (NB: direction Tralee, not Killarney).

Pass through Milltown and cross the river Maine at **CASTLEMAINE** where formerly, as the name makes clear, a fortress defended this once-prosperous little port (now disused) on an inlet off the impressive natural enclosure of Castlemaine Harbour. Turn left onto R561/L103 (direction Dingle) for a tour round the **Dingle Peninsula** (or Corkaguiny, Corca Dhuibhne, etc.). This narrow projection of land, exceptionally beautiful, has a remarkable collection of prehistoric, early-Christian, and medieval remains. The ancient past seems strangly close at hand, in the very air, throughout the area. Half the peninsula is Irish-speaking. It was from Dingle Peninsula that Brendan, the semi-mythical priest-explorer, supposedly set sail on the voyage which landed him, perhaps, in North America in 6C (he was searching for a legendary western paradise).

Head along the bank of Castlemaine Harbour to **INCH**, a village at the end of a long strip of sand—called 'the inch'—which is one of the natural protective walls of the Harbour. At Anascual, follow the road round to the left (R559/T68; direction Dingle/An Daigean). **AN DAINGEAN (Dingle)** is another small town, partly Irish-speaking, on a natural harbour. It has a really superb setting. There are several Irish-speaking villages in stunningly beautiful country beyond Dingle, for anyone who wants to explore further. R559, passing standing stones on the way, skirts naturally protected Ventry Harbour, and reaches down to dramatic **Slea Head**, with views of the Atlantic and the rugged Blasket Islands. Between Ventry Harbour and Slea Head ruins of hundreds of **clocháns** (primitive beehive-shaped stone dwellings, dating from about 6–8C) have been discovered. Life on the Blaskets is the subject of the fascinating autobiography *Peig*, by islander Peig Sayers. Within easier reach of Dingle, standing in open country, **Gallarus Oratory** is a curious and perfectly preserved little windowless stone structure dating from about 8C or 9C. It has similarities with the *clocháns*, but its base is rectangular instead of circular.

From Dingle, climb steeply up towards **Connor Pass** (with panoramic views) and descend again towards the north shore of the Dingle Peninsula. The road continues through Camp village to Tralee. If the weather is very bad or visibility poor, it might be wiser to get to Tralee by going back to

Ancient cross-inscribed slabs, Dingle Peninsula

Anascaul on R559, a better road which crosses the peninsula and takes a more direct route to the town.

TRALEE (or Traigh Lí, i.e. Lee Beach) pop: 16,700 Busy capital of County Kerry, subject of ceaseless attack and destruction over the centuries. Consequently, little survives of its long history apart from a few Georgian buildings. **Tourist Office** in Godfrey Place.

Since Tralee is big, and not especially interesting, it could be by-passed without stopping (follow signs Killarney). Leave town on N21 at first (direction Limerick, Killarney), soon veering right onto N22, which goes back to Killarney. Alternatively look for the back road: from Tralee take N70/T66 (direction Castlemaine), taking a minor left turn which goes via Ballyhar to Killarney.

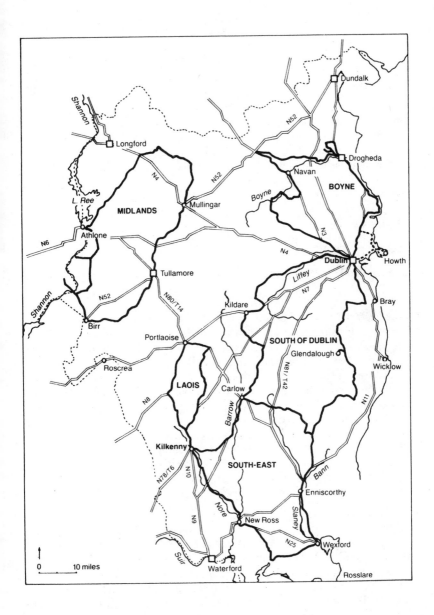

Despite having the richest, greenest, lushest of Ireland's countryside, **Leinster** (pronounced Lenster) is the Republic's most industrial and urbanised province. It is populous and developed compared to much of the rest of the country, and because it was for 1,000 years the chief seat of foreign rulers, it absorbed much outside influence. The Anglo-Norman colonists, who took over the Viking settlement of Dubh Linn (dark pool) at the mouth of the river Liffey, were able to rule and 'civilise' only a small area around the town—equivalent perhaps to present-day County Dublin—which came to be known as The Pale. Later, as the Normans were assimilated and their power weakened, the English moved in and assumed control, extending their rule by 1600 over most of Leinster province. For both groups, everything 'beyond the Pale' remained largely outside the reach of their authority. Nevertheless, the nearness to Dublin proved a moderating influence on the ancient and agrarian Irish culture. Yet there are, even now, countless interesting and enjoyable rural journeys to be made all over Leinster, even within a half-hour of Dublin. Much of the province is flat and well watered, alternating prosperous farmland with bogs and woods, while the hills of Wicklow provide a striking contrast with the rest.

South of Dublin

2–3 days/160 miles (260km)/from Dublin

Although right on Dublin's doorstep, the Wicklow Mountains provide an uncrowded, tranquil escape from the city's noise and traffic. Apart from the quiet villages, heathy summits and green valleys, especially worth pausing to see are the neat gardens of Powerscourt and the beautifully located monastic ruins of Glendalough. Turning back towards Dublin, the route takes in calm and undramatic County Kildare, one of eastern Ireland's most interesting and unappreciated counties—John Betjeman's 'Lush Kildare of scented meadows'. Note that all along this route, the normal confusion of Ireland's roadsigns is exacerbated by the use of new 'EEC-funded' signposts—which lack the courage to give road numbers, and state distances only in kilometres, which are not used by the Irish. However, it must be admitted that they are clearer and easier to read, with English names given in roman type and Gaelic in italics.

DUBLIN (formerly Dubh Linn, 'dark pool', although official Irish-language name is now Baile Átha Cliath) pop: 600,000 within city boundary; 1,000,000 including suburbs. Capital of Ireland, on river Liffey where it reaches Dublin Bay. Central area of attractive Georgian terraces. Birthplace and home of dozens of noted writers, including Oscar Wilde, George Bernard Shaw, James Joyce, Brendan Behan, Jonathan Swift, W.B. Yeats, Sean O'Casey, Samuel Beckett. A few things to do and see:

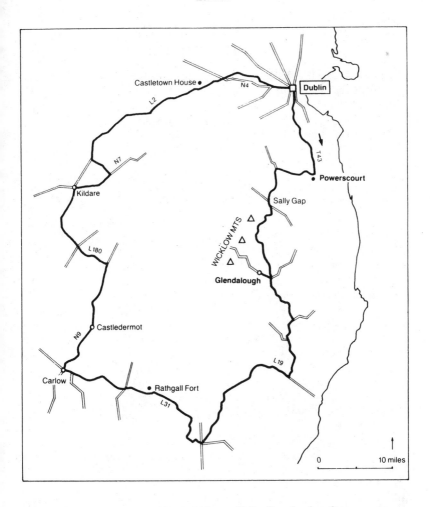

stroll down main thoroughfare O'Connell St (lovely shopfronts; see post office, where Irish Republican flag first flown during Easter Rising); have tea at Bewleys; browse in Fred Hanna's bookshop (nr Trinity College); see a play at the Abbey Theatre; relax in one of many old-fashioned pubs of character; inspect Book of Kells in Trinity College Library (open at different page every day); see Celtic art in National Museum and Irish painting in National Gallery (one of Europe's largest art collections); go on a tour of Dublin Castle (inside, more a palace than a castle); travel on the DART train along foreshore; watch the video at the Guinness factory and enjoy a free pint afterwards; see the mummified bodies in the crypt of St Michan's church; see also: Christchurch (CI; founded by Danes, 11C) and St Patrick's Cathedral (CI; 12C). **Tourist Office**: 14 Upper O'Connell St. Hotels: **Shelbourne** (grand, expensive—01–766471), **Buswells** (relaxed, comfortable—01–764013). **Puerto Bella** restaurant, 1 Portobello Road (01–720851), small, imaginative, not overpriced, is a personal favourite. **Patrick Guilbaud's** restaurant, 46 St James' Pl. (01–764192), has achieved international acclaim.

From central Dublin to the Wicklow countryside takes only about 20–30 minutes by car. Turn off the South Ring Rd onto Ranelagh Rd, which continues along Sandford Rd. Turn right onto Milltown Rd (signposted Enniskerry). Turn left over river at a big junction onto Dundrum Rd. Follow signs to Enniskerry and Dundrum. At **STEPASIDE**, with its tall TV aerials, Dublin's extensive suburbs are at last left behind.

The road suddenly becomes a pleasant minor country route, T43/R117, with mountain views. It passes by the 'Three Rock Mountains', steep little rocky peaks. There are patches of dense woodland. A winding descent reaches **ENNISKERRY** (Ath Na Scairbhe), a pleasing village in a picturesque valley setting: approaching it, pass the pale Catholic church on a bend; then, at the crossroads, turn left (signposted Bray, Bré) down into the central triangle of the village. It's just a touch smart or chic, with clothes boutiques faintly incongruous in such a rural location. **Powerscourt Arms Hotel** is well placed beside the little river. A road on the right climbs up past the Protestant church with its high copper spire green with verdigris, and (in road to right) an attractive little old forge. At the top of the hill is the entrance of **Powerscourt estate and gardens** (open mid-Mar. to mid-Oct.). This superb estate contains a stylish Japanese Garden, formal terraced gardens, and a spectacular 400ft waterfall (also accessible separately 4 miles away by road).

Follow signs 'Glencree 13' up a minor road among hills with trees and green fields, sheep and cows, masses of gorse and gorgeous flowers crowded into hedgerows. Eventually reach high rocky moorland. At a junction, take a left signed to 'Sally Gap 5'. This is the summit road, an old military road built by the British to hunt out Irish rebels after the 1798 uprising. This high stretch has open peat-bog and heath on both sides. At the bleak **Sally Gap** crossroads, carry straight over onto an unmarked road.

After some miles descend into a wide glen, with a waterfall at its head and a rushing little river in a rocky bed at its heart. This is the Glenmacnass valley. At a junction turn right onto R755 (signposted Glendalough). Go through the tiny tourist centre **LARAGH**, and (via left fork) on to **GLENDALOUGH** (Gleann Dá Loch), which, although it does have a tiny touristy hamlet at its centre, is not so much a single place as a whole area of small and endearing ruins. These are the remains of a monastic community founded here 6C by St Kevin, of the Leinster royal line. It prospered until the Viking raids began, 11C, at which time it was damaged and went into a decline, but managed to survive. The community was still there in 1398, when it was attacked and again suffered badly, this time at the hands of the English. There may have been monks still here even in 16C, by which time much of the monastery was probably falling into ruins.

Judging from the size of the buildings, this was never a big community by medieval standards, though certainly large for the early-Christian period; its main significance now is the age and condition of its oldest ruins. The setting is remarkably beautiful, along the banks of hidden loughs in a wonderful wooded valley, opening to give mountain views. Unfortunately, on a busy day this lovely place is not really able comfortably to absorb the number of visitors that come here. During my visit there were two coach parties of Irish families and I heard American, French, German, Japanese and English voices as well.

What remains of the Glendalough monastery is in two sections, corresponding roughly with the two lakes, the Upper Lough and Lower Lough. The best approach to seeing Glendalough is to start with the group on the east side of the Lower lake. Go first of all either to the Visitors' Centre or to the **Royal Hotel** (0404–5135; serving snacks and meals). Ignore unsightly amenities for tourists scattered about this area. The Visitors' Centre (entrance fee) offers a video on the site's history, and a guided tour, but it is perfectly possible, indeed more enjoyable, to do it yourself at your own speed.

To see the main items of interest:

1. From the hotel, walk through a fine double archway (formerly two storey), which was from 9C to 12C the main gatehouse of the monastic lands, into a graveyard.

2. Within the graveyard is the not-very-interesting ruin of the small 'cathedral'—the 9C/11C monastery church.
Behind the cathedral are:

3. 'The Priest's House', a tiny, intriguing and lovely ruined 12C building. Notice blocked archway with Romanesque decoration.

4. An unfinished 12C High Cross.

5. A Round Tower, 9–12C, in excellent condition and from this position there are superb views of both lakes.

6. Beyond the Round Tower, outside the graveyard, St Mary's Church, supposedly Kevin's grave, a simple structure (10C?) with granite west doorway and unusual lintel.
Return to the main path within the graveyard, and continue past the cathedral to:

7. '**St Kevin's Kitchen**', not a kitchen and nothing to do with St Kevin, an exquisite little building of two unconnected rooms, with stone roof, and lovely shape and proportions; estimated 11C, the short round chimney-like tower (which accounts for its nickname) being probably of slightly later date; inside is a 12C cross.

8. Beside St Kevin's Kitchen is a fragment of St Kieran's chapel, which must have been a very similar building.
Cross a stream on a wooden bridge, and find on the other side:

9. An unaccounted-for bullaun (hollowed-out stone); despite the legend that St Kevin milked a divine doe, catching her miraculous milk in this hollowed stone, to my own eye this looks suspiciously like an ordinary milling stone.

10. A footpath goes both ways from this point, following the stream; downstream it leads to 12C Romanesque St Saviour's Church, with intriguing carving; either walk upstream along the path, or return to the

'St Kevin's Kitchen'

road and drive, to the Upper Lough group of ruins. Approaching the Upper lake from the road, a track goes into a park-like area, passing across the head of the beautiful lake, with steep hillsides falling into the dark water.

11. To the left of the track is the 'caher', a circular stone enclosure presumably considerably older than the rest of the site, although that is not certain.

12. Passing in front of the 'caher' are boundary crosses of the monastic lands.

13. After the lake, to the right of the track, a footpath crosses the stream and goes up to the ruins of 'Reefert Church', its name coming from *righ fearta*, kings' grave; it was used as a burial place by the ó Toole clan.

14. Around the lake are a number of other items, most of them natural phenomena (St Kevin's Bed, etc.), which have acquired a legendary connection with the monastery.

Return from Glendalough to Laragh, where turn right (signposted Rathdrum). This makes its way through delightful leafy woods along the Avonmore valley or **Vale of Clara** (T61). No need to pause at **RATHDRUM**, situated along the steep side of the river valley, and unattractive with its single long narrow main street. After the town, turn right for Avoca. This goes into a broader, more open glen, with trees and green fields rising up the pretty slopes. [A signpost points left to 'the Mottee Stone' (Norman landmark, from French *moitié*, half, indicating the half way point from Dublin to Wexford) and also Avondale House, the childhood home of early nationalist politician C.S. Parnell, and Avondale Forest Park. The 18C house, though now a forestry school, also preserves a Parnell museum.]

The road passes next to a confluence of two rivers, the Avonmore and Avonbeg, beside which is an establishment calling itself a 'Restaurant Bar Craft Shop and Nightclub' and flying the Stars and Stripes. It's called 'The Meetings'. The confluence was described in Thomas Moore's poem, 'The Meeting of the Waters'. The road (T7) now runs through the Vale of Avoca. Cross the bridge over the river, which has an amazing rust colour (caused by copper and other minerals, including gold). On the other side, unpretentious **AVOCA** (or Ovoca; pron. Av Oker, to rhyme with English 'ochre') presses against a dramatic escarpment. Just at the far end of the bridge there's a good pub. Turn left through the village to reach the Avoca Handweavers, a cluster of whitewashed cottages turning out the finest textile goods, all made traditionally. Avoca not only has what claims to be Ireland's oldest mill, but reckons to have Ireland's highest pub (south of village) as well.

Cross back over the Avoca bridge to rejoin T7 and press on to **WOODENBRIDGE**, a tiny village clustered around each end of a (stone) bridge over the river. There really is gold in this water, that's no blarney, and it was at this precise point that in 1745 a 22-ounce lump of gold was found. That caused something of a goldrush, in the course of which a total of 2,600 ounces is known to have been discovered. Do not cross the bridge, but take the Aughrim road by passing in front of the **Woodenbridge Hotel** (0402–5146), a popular local haunt which is marvellously quiet if there are no receptions or the like.

Although at first the Aughrim road is picturesque, making its way narrowly between the tree-shaded river and steep wooded slopes, the countryside soon undergoes a great change, becoming less hilly and somehow plainer. There's no real reason to cross the bridge into unattractive **AUGHRIM**, although it does have a couple of good pubs. Continue through the flatter green pastureland. At a crossroads which gives Tinahely to the right, Gorey to the left, and Carnew straight on, take the Carnew road.

At **CARNEW** (Carn An Bhua), the road meets R725, and this tour meets the *South East* route. If you want to combine these two into one, continue from Carnew towards Ferns—see p. 112. Otherwise, turn onto R725/L31 (direction Tullow, Carlow). Follow signs carefully to stay on this country road as it meanders towards Carlow.

Shortly before Tullow, **Rathgall Stone Fort** (Gaelic *rath gall*, foreigners' enclosure) has concentric ramparts. **TULLOW** itself, on the river Slaney, is a straightforward small country town, perfectly agreeable. It once had an important Augustinian priory, but nothing at all survives of it except a single cross in the graveyard. Keep on R725/L31 to Carlow, or if preferred, take R418/L31^A to Castledermot.

CARLOW pop: 12,000 County town of Co. Carlow, on river Barrow. The conspicuous tall, grey, slender spire of its cathedral heralds the town from some distance away. All in all it seems to have been an ill-fated place. Formerly at the outer limits of the Norman Pale, it was heavily defended against the Irish, who attacked it frequently throughout the Middle Ages. On 25 May 1789, over 400 rebels against English rule were shot or hanged here, and their bodies thrown unceremoniously into a gravel pit. The ugly courthouse is distinctive with its Ionic columns and portico, and ringed by an axe-head fence. The 13C castle was reduced to ruins by a suitably crazy doctor who wished to use the building as a lunatic asylum and believed that a few sticks of gunpowder would make the building more suitable! What survives is still impressive. Only the neo-Gothic cathedral (1828) seems to give the town any grace though. Worthwhile excursions: Brownes Hill (2½ miles north east)—magnificent dolmen with largest headstone in Europe, over 100 tons; Killeshin Church (2½ miles north west—lovely Romanesque chapel).

On busy, two-lane major highway N9 (direction Dublin), go on through a flattish unspectacular landscape—just a few gentle hills—of rich, intensely green pasture on which cows and sheep graze dreamily. Cross a little stone bridge into **CASTLEDERMOT**. It seems incredible now that this little

Castledermot

place was once an important ecclesiastical and political centre. On the left at the entrance to the village, ruins of 'Castledermot Abbey', an early-14C Franciscan friary, stand on private property. A right turn (signposted Round Tower and High Cross) leads to the completely ordinary parish church; what isn't so usual is that just in front of the church entrance is a beautifully proportioned Romanesque doorway, almost all that survives of a monastery founded here in 8C. The door of the new church attempts to be a copy of the old. Adjoining the church is a Round Tower: it's lost its top and seems to have been 'castellated' rather clumsily. Two weather-worn but still impressive High Crosses stand in the graveyard, one each side the church. Back on the main road, farther on through Castledermot's straggling ribbon development, a small square tower to the left has become known as the Pigeon House, although in fact it is a 11/12C remnant of a Crutched Friars dwelling. Castledermot's old **School House** (0503–44282) has been converted into a small high quality restaurant (where, if you're feeling rather strapped for cash, the choice includes 'Recession' menus!).

At **MOONE** (pron. Maoin), a few miles farther towards Dublin, there's an unusually tall High Cross (rather hidden away: turn left, through stone gateway onto the Athy backroad, and follow this for several minutes), or rather, it stands on an unusually tall base, depicting the apostles and Biblical scenes. Return to the main road and continue another 4 miles to the edge of Crookstown, where take the left turn, signposted to Kildare (L180/R415). Cross a narrow bridge, and at a T-junction with no signpost, turn right. After this point Kildare is well signed along minor country roads. On meeting N78, turn right and immediately left. The countryside becomes increasing flat, rustic, prosperous, with some fine thatched cottages. At a crossroads, carry straight on. At length a Round Tower in the distances signals Kildare.

Arriving at the outskirts of the town, it is interesting—before going into Kildare itself—to turn sharp right as signposted (i.e. head a little out of town again) to the **Irish National Stud and Irish Horse Museum** (open Easter–Oct.). In the same estate, also deserving a visit, are the pleasing Japanese Gardens. Close by, indicated down a little lane, St Brigid's Well is an ancient sacred spring and a shallow well: a really beautiful spot. Christianised by Brigid, apparently at that time the spring used to flow more freely than it does now. The usual statue of the saint stands overlooking the magic water, with exhortations to say the Rosary. In AD490 Brigid established a monastic community around which eventually grew the town of Kildare.

Go back into **KILDARE**, which, for no discernible reason and despite being on a busy main road, has a cheerful feeling about it. The Round Tower, which in this flat landscape can be seen from a distance, stands in the grounds of a small cathedral at the heart of the town. Its doorway with decorative arches is unusual, and a flight of wooden steps gives access, making this one of the few Round Towers which can be entered. The Tower's top is missing and it has rather silly 19C battlements instead; however during my visit a public collection was under way to pay for the restoration of the original conical cap. The cathedral itself, mostly 17C, incorporates a fortified square tower from its predecessor, built in 1229. In the graveyard there's a broken High Cross, probably from an even earlier period.

On the Dublin side of town (on N7) is the main gateway to the Irish National Stud. Travel out of town towards Newbridge, about 5 miles away. The road crosses **The Curragh**. The word means marshy grassland in Irish, but this one was drained long ago. It's a large area (approx. 5,000 acres) of close green turf studded with clumps of gorse, and is used for training race horses. Part of it is devoted to a racetrack of national (and international) importance, also known as The Curragh.

NEWBRIDGE (or Droichead Nua) is the racing capital of Ireland, but also happens to be an unappealing industrial town. Turn left as signposted onto R416/L107 to Milltown, where pick up another minor road (R415/L180; turn right) to **PROSPEROUS**. On reaching busier R403/L2 on the outskirts of this village, turn right (direction Clane); 1 mile along here is **Curryhills House Hotel** (045–68336), with modernised unpretentious rooms, a pleasant bar and above-average restaurant. Curry Hills refers, of course, to nothing more oriental than the nearby low hills overlooking The Curragh. More in need of explanation perhaps is the name Prosperous: it dates from the optimistic enterprises of the Micawberish Lord Robert Brooke who in 1780 founded the village as a cottage-industry handloom cotton weaving venture. The people were brought in to do the work, and here they (or their descendants, at least) still are, but the cotton weaving did not prosper. While already bankrupt, Lord Robert had Curryhills House built as a present for his brother.

Carry on beyond the hotel to Clane, where turn left at a T-junction and right at a fork. Follow a pleasant country road to **CELBRIDGE**, where signs point the way to **Castletown House**, which is virtually in the centre of this busy small town on the river Liffey. The house stands majestically at the end of a long, imposing avenue of limes. A huge and sombre Georgian mansion, built in 1722 for William Connolly, the Speaker of the Irish House of Commons, it has tremendous dignity. It was the first of the magnificent no-expense-spared mansions, the 'big houses', which symbolised the confidence of the Protestant Ascendancy in Ireland after the Battle of the Boyne. Curving wings with columned arcades enclose the neat forecourt. Inside there is superb plasterwork and Italianate design (the architect was Galilei).

Take the road to **LUCAN** (pron. Loo-kn), a ghastly congested spot (by-pass under construction) on the busy main highway (N4) back into Dublin. An alternative to using this main road is to turn left at the traffic lights *at the bottom of the hill* (and not before) in Lucan, cross the Liffey, and then veer right onto the 'lower road' as it is called—the back road to Dublin—which enters the city through Phoenix Park.

The South East

2–3 days/140 miles (220km)/from Kilkenny (or Rosslare)

'The Sunny South East', people call it, and the climate is indeed drier and more pleasantly balmy than in the rest of the country. Landscapes are tamer too, and devoted to rich and contented-looking cattle farms. This corner of Ireland also has one of Ireland's most interesting and well-preserved medieval towns, Kilkenny, which deserves more than just a passing visit. The route starts and finishes there, but can easily be adapted by anyone arriving at the port of Rosslare. Equally, travellers coming from Dublin can combine this tour with the neighbouring route South of

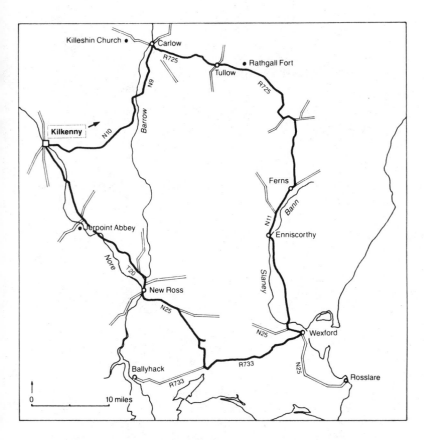

Dublin. The south east, despite or because of its relative prosperity, had a long history of steadfast opposition to foreign rule. The Normans never succeeded in imposing their government thoroughly onto this region, and the English, both before and after Cromwell, met stiff resistance. In 1642, Kilkenny became the capital of the Confederation which declared the Irish nobility independent of English Protestant rule. The 1798 rising, inspired by the general revolutionary mood which affected Europe and North America after the French Revolution, had its impact on many parts of Ireland, but in this area the revolt led to particularly determined and destructive fighting. Then again in this century the Easter Rising of 1916, a turning point in the struggle to persuade the English to leave Ireland, was especially virulent in this part of the country. Yet, as elsewhere, now that the fighting's done and their battle won, one finds the people in these counties as free of rancour, as warm-hearted and welcoming, as they could possibly be.

KILKENNY, though a busy and important provincial capital (pop: 9,500), has an old central area on the right (west) bank of the river Nore of easily walkable dimensions. An immediately likeable town, it consists

Kilkenny Castle

principally of a winding and hilly network built around a picturesque main street which makes erratic progress from south to north, calling itself variously Castle Rd, The Parade, High St, Parliament St and Watergate. At one end stands the great stone bulk of Kilkenny Castle and at the other rises the graceful cathedral of St Canice—both, like most of the old town, built of a fine grey local limestone. Between these two great landmarks there are numerous other interesting old buildings and attractive traditional shopfronts, and little alleys leading off. Parking is a problem, but there are usually spaces if you continue beyond the castle, and it's not far to walk back.

The massive castle dominates the town visually and historically; it stands determined and unyielding beside the river, which provides one of its defences. From outside, the building combines a sturdy medieval four-cornered format with clear evidence—the windows and chimneys, for example, and the gatehouse—of plenty of later work. Go through the main gate (1685) to discover that the castle is in fact smaller than it first appears and has extensive parkland (16 acres) with neat lawns and gardens. The castle's grand interior (with tea room) doesn't look at all medieval, and now displays a collection of paintings and some rich tapestries. Note too the magnificent fireplaces and marvellous timbered ceilings. Kilkenny was one of the earlier Norman castles in Ireland, built in 1191 by William, Earl of Pembroke, on the site of a fort of the ancient Kingdom of Ossory, and rebuilt in grander style about a century later. It soon came amicably into the domaine of one of the first and most powerful Norman families to make their home in Ireland, the FitzWalters, Earls of Ormonde, appointed by Henry II to the prestigious ceremonial post Chief Botilers (or Butlers) of Ireland. The heir of the title decided to adopt the title as a surname. They had arrived from Caen in the 1100s, but settled first at Gowran before making the move to Kilkenny in 1391. Despite the 1366 Statute of Kilkenny which had set out to preserve the Anglo-Norman identity and prevent integration with the Irish, the Butlers were a typical example of the process of Normans merging into Irish society: the 3rd Earl of Ormonde spoke Irish fluently, formed alliances with native ruling clans, and later the Butler family linked itself completely into the Irish nobility through marriage. Astonishingly, the castle remained in the Butler family until as recently as 1967.

Kilkenny Castle was the setting for the occasional parliaments of the Irish nobility, especially during 14C. The important mid-17C Irish Confederate parliament (in its later stage supporting a Catholic English monarchy) also met here. That only lasted a few years before Cromwell, after a long and destructive battle, managed to take control of the town in 1650. The Butlers conceded defeat and were allowed to retain the castle, without a garrison, although every other Norman family was banished to Connacht. Today the castle makes only three sides of a square—the fourth side was knocked down in 1659 to make the place less militarily useful.

Opposite, in the handsome former stables of Kilkenny Castle, the Kilkenny Design Workshops (restaurant) sell superb top-quality cottage-made traditional craft goods: tweeds, knitwear, fabrics, stoneware, pottery, ornaments and jewellery.

From the castle, walk the few yards to the junction with Rose Inn St on right, which leads down to the river and John's Bridge: the **Tourist Office** (056–21755; walking tours; permanent exhibition on 16C Kilkenny) is in Shee's Almshouses, Rose Inn St. Or instead of turning right here, cross straight over into the picturesque High St, with its arcaded grey Tholsel (1761) ornamented by a curious octagonal tower. A few yards behind it, 13C St Mary's Church, now a church hall, has good medieval stonework and notable 17C tombs. Continue along the main street, which changes to Parliament St, in which can be seen the beautiful arcaded facade of a Norman merchant family's 16C dwelling, Rothe House, with its cobbled courtyards, a well, and inside, amazing roof-timbers. It now contains a local museum. Almost opposite, the courthouse is an 18C rebuilding of medieval Grace's Castle. At the end of the street, cross Dean St and climb steps to St Canice's Cathedral, which gave the town its name—*Cill Choinnigh*, Canice's Church. Built on the site of its 6C predecessor, the present impressive building (CI) dates from 13C and retains much good medieval stone work. Beside it stands a slender Round Tower.

A turning along Dean St leads to the 'Black Abbey', the 13C Dominican friary which was attacked and damaged after the Dissolution and then again by Cromwell. The Dominicans, with amazing fortitude, continued as an Order at Kilkenny throughout all this even without their premises, and in 19C they restored and returned to the Black Abbey. In the other direction, 'St Francis Abbey', the 13C Franciscan friary, was likewise damaged and restored, but did not recover from the ravages of Cromwell's soldiers.

Across the river on the left bank see 13C St John's Church and fragments of the original ramparts of the town. Close to John Bridge is Kilkenny College, a Georgian replacement of the earlier college building on the site. Many distinguished politicians, academics and writers were educated there. Jonathan Swift (1667–1745), for example, was a pupil from the age of six onwards, and formed a lifelong friendship with another scholar, William Congreve (1670–1729), both of them becoming writers acclaimed in both Ireland and England. Another pupil was the Irish writer George Farquhar (1678–1707).

There are several appealing bars and eating places in town, such as: **Tynan's** Bridgehouse Bar, **Edward Langtons**, and more modern **Flannery's** (056–22235) family-run hotel and restaurant—these three are all close to John's Bridge; another is ancient **Kyteler's Inn**, focus of a witchcraft trial in 1324 when proprietress Alice Kyteler, who had become wealthy from her money-lending and inheritances and who had coincidentally and tragically lost four husbands, was gound guilty of witchcraft and sentenced to be burned at the stake. She escaped to England on the night before the execution, and with the injustice and cruelty typical of the age, her maidservant was burned in her place. A good restaurant with rooms is the Georgian **Lacken House** (056–61085), on the Dublin road, while the 200-year-old **Club House Hotel** (056–21994), by the junction of High St and Rose Inn St, is central, reasonable and has some charm.

Take the main Dublin road (N10). Stay on this rather unappealing highway all the way into **CARLOW** (see p. 106)—here this route rejoins the *South of Dublin* route, for anyone who has combined them).

Leave Carlow on N80/T16 (direction Wexford), turning left after barely a mile onto L31/R725 (direction Tullow). For **TULLOW** see p. 105. Stay on the same road (direction Carnew), perhaps pausing at **Rathgall Stone Fort**, see p. 105. At **CARNEW**, turn right onto L19^A/R748 along the minor road (direction Ferns). This is a satisfying little country road through pleasant farm country of green fields hedged with gorse. 3 miles from Ferns fork right as signposted.

Meet N11 at **FERNS**, a small and ordinary village now but once capital of Leinster. Facing you on the other side of the main road are the ruins of an impressive Norman moated castle, currently being carefully and intelligently restored, with none of that usual attempt to deceive the visitor's eye as to what is original and what is reconstructed. According to a perfectly unabashed sign, 'Work will be complete and the castle open to the public in 1987'! Probably dating from about 1200, the castle was the work of early Norman settlers, and stands on the site of the fortress of the Leinster kings. It suffered frequent Danish raids and attacks by the ousted Leinster chiefs.

A striking monument, a modern High Cross, stands outside the castle. An inscription states that it is in memory of Father John Murphy, who was born in the parish of Ferns, and who 'led the brave men of North Wexford, and died with them, for the sacred cause of civil and religious liberty, in the insurrection of 1798'.

Descend through the village, passing the new Catholic church (on right), down to ruins of 'the Abbey', an Austin Priory founded 1160. Obviously a substantial monastic building at one time, today it stands in a green field behind small 19C CI Cathedral of St Eden, which incorporates remains of a 12–13C church on the site. The churchyard of the old Priory, part of it overgrown and evocative, part of it neat and tidy with new graves, was the churchyard of the earlier church and now serves the same role for the new cathedral. A number of High Crosses of the original Priory still stand there.

At the bottom of the hill, where the road leaves the present-day village of Ferns, an old holy well and spring has had an arc built over it (1847) using sculpted stones from Clone Church and Ferns Cathedral. According to a sign, the well was blessed, or Christianised, by 'St Molinz, died 697, in honour of St Aedan (Maedoz), died 632'. The first cathedral to be built at Ferns (7C) was named for this latter saint from Clonmore, who was also known as St Mogue or St Maedoc Edan. A sign in the village points the way along the major road to Enniscorthy.

Though not a large town (pop: 5,000), **ENNISCORTHY** has several ugly old manufacturing premises and modern agricultural factories along its waterfront and is not of prepossessing aspect. Its lovely setting though, rising steeply beside a big bend in the wide river Slaney, redeems the town. An old stone bridge crosses the Slaney, which is navigable at this point. The town centre is up the hill, away from the river. There are some interesting old buildings in the narrow streets which climb away from the river. One attractive little place, in Slaney St, is **The Antique Tavern**, a tiny one-room bar which serves excellent, inexpensive food. Slaney St reaches Market Sq., the central esplanade, in which a monument recalls the 1798 uprising, which became a terrible battle here: the English besieged the town with a force of 13,000 soldiers, killing 500 local men.

Off the square, the mock-Classical 19C building called The Athenaeum, now a community centre, was the HQ of the local Irish Volunteers, the Republican group during the 1916 Easter Rising. That too became especially fierce here. Turn towards the impressively tall spire of RC St Aidan's Cathedral (built in the midst of the Famine, 1843–8) which dominates the town from high on the hill. A few minutes away, turning back down towards the river, the town's castle, flying its green nationalist flag, is an imposing four-storey keep with slender towers. It was built at the end of 16C, on the site of a similar mid-13C Norman fortress. In 1649, Cromwell personally led the attack to capture the castle and the town. Considering what it suffered, the building appears to be in remarkably good condition, but that is partly because it was extensively restored in 1903. It now houses a local history museum and **tourist office**.

Return to the Slaney, and cross the river on the old bridge. Leave town on the main Wexford road (N11). Gorse and tree-covered hills rise from the wide river valley. At **Ferrycarrig Bridge**, just before Wexford, the road crosses the Slaney where it meets Rosslare Bay. This strategic—and beautiful—location, where formerly, as the name makes clear, a ferry made the river crossing, was guarded on both sides by the Normans. This was the area where they made some of their first landings and settlements. Beside the bridge, on the left, is the square 14C fortification which guarded the east bank. But across the water, on a ridge of higher ground, stands a Round Tower—does that mean there was a monastery here? No: the Round Tower was built in modern times to commemorate Wexford men killed in the Crimean War. It was constructed from the stone of the ruined Norman castle which had protected this side of the river. Dating from 1169, which makes it very early on the timescale of the Norman presence in Ireland, the castle had been part of a settlement called Castrum de Carrick, which disappeared during 14C; the spot is still known by the rather Norman-sounding name of Shan-a-Court.

Cross the bridge and take the little turning immediately on the right to see the Round Tower. And far more interesting, also down this turning just a few paces farther on, is the new Irish National Heritage Park. In 35 acres, this open-air museum contains reconstructions of a number of historical Irish features. Most notable at the moment is a full-size *crannóg* just as they would have been when inhabited—it's easy to see that this must have been quite an effective means of defence.

Continue into Wexford.

WEXFORD (or Loch Garman) pop: 12,000 County town, important harbour and manufacturing centre. A large town of unattractive low-level buildings, and a long narrow winding High Street, with some traditional painted shopfronts. In Barrack St (continuation of the High Street) is the spot where the Norse built their first stockade here in AD 850: they called it Waesfjord, 'muddy harbour'. Taken over by the first Anglo-Norman arrivals in 1169. In later years the town became a stronghold of opposition to the English takeover: Cromwell was very harsh with the place when he conquered it in 1649. That didn't prevent some further bloody clashes during uprisings in the 1790s, especially the 1798 Rebellion (to which there is a monument in the little market square called The Bullring).

At the southern end of the High Street are ruins of St Selskar's Priory, an Augustinian monastery; it was founded in 13C, but the present remnant is of a high, square 15C tower adjoining a 19C church (key from Mr Murray, 9 Abbey St Lower, close by). Behind the Priory are remains of some towers and walls of the town's 13C fortifications, including a large square fortified gate-tower properly called The West Gate, but sometimes locally called The Castle. Earlier fortifications, 11C, can be seen by the church off Mallin St, and there are other fragments around town. The main through-road follows the waterfront, where fishing trawlers are moored at the quays. A nice feature is the semi-circular Crescent of the Pool (now called Crescent Quay—with **Tourist Office**), the original Norse harbour. A statue in the crescent commemorates the American Navy's first commodore, John Barry (1745–1803), born in County

Wexford. Wexford Harbour itself is known for its many swans, and on the other side of the water is the muddy waterfowl reserve known enticingly as The Slobs.

[From Wexford it is 12 miles on N25 to **ROSSLARE HARBOUR**, the ferry port with services to Fishguard and Le Havre. Off this road, see Rathmacknee Castle, a 15C tower house and bawn.]

To leave Wexford, follow signs, to Arthurstown, L159. This goes through flatter, rougher country than before. At **WELLINGTON BRIDGE** (can be spelled as one word; also known as Clonmines) at first turn right (signposted Duncannon) then right again (seems more like straight on) over a level crossing.

[Anyone wishing to continue from this point to Waterford instead of returning towards Kilkenny should stay on the Duncannon/Arthurstown road, which passes Bannow Bay. Across the narrow Bay can be seen the eerie and ghostly ruins of **Clonmines of the Seven Churches**, a 14C abbey of this community which was submerged by the Bay's drifting sands and had to be abandoned in 16C. The road is straight and rather boring: go on to Arthurstown, where a sharp descent reaches beautiful Waterford Harbour. Take the road to Ballyhack, a busy little harbour village over-looked by a tower house. From here a small car ferry goes to and fro across the water all day long, connecting with Passage East, 8 miles from Waterford.]

Continuing the route from Wellington Bridge, R736/L160 goes through soothing soft green grass-covered country. A turning off to the right leads into **FOULKSMILLS**. This plain, rustic village has a watermill, one of the last still in use, and (a couple of miles beyond—ask directions in village) a marvellous rambling 17C farmhouse offering B&B and evening meals, **Horetown House** (051–63633). It's still a working farm of 200 acres, offering an amiable welcome, rooms with basic facilities and antique furniture, abundant and well-prepared meals, and all at modest prices.

L160 eventually meets N25, where turn left (direction Cork, New Ross). J.F. Kennedy Park, signposted off the road to left, is a memorial park and arboretum in memory of President Kennedy, whose family came from this area—they apparently fought against the English in the 1798 uprising, or so people hereabouts assert on their behalf. The claim is probably true, for the whole district was staunchly nationalist for centuries up to the 1922 independence.

NEW ROSS, on the river Barrow, has too much traffic for comfort. It's a busy, hectic industrial river port. Turn right up Quay St (signposted Town Centre). Along this narrow main shopping street, the Tholsel is made of unfaced stone blocks, the first of them being laid in 1749 on the anniversary of the Battle of the Boyne (though it was almost completely rebuilt in 1906). On the wall a plaque erected by the IRA recalls Michael O'Hanrahan, a native of New Ross and a leader of the 1916 Easter Rising, after which he was executed in Dublin. Opposite the Tholsel a monument honours the memory of all New Ross citizens who died in the 1798 rising, which included, on 4 June in that year, horrifying scenes of door-to-door slaughter in the town.

Climbing further up Quay St, discover some good little coffee shops and bars, and remnants of the town's once-sturdy fortifications. At the summit of the hill, a church stands among ruins of a Franciscan priory. To its right is a 14C tower of the town ramparts, while to the left are the broken remains of 15C Maiden Gate, the old entrance into the town. A sign leads higher to Old Ross, with a Norman motte and bailey.

Return to the riverside, and at first head north on N79 (direction Enniscorthy), but on reaching the left turn (T20/R700) which crosses the river, go over the bridge and through Mount Garret, with its little castle. Stay on the same road (direction Thomastown, Kilkenny), through some-times high heathy country with good views. Descend into the Nore valley, crossing the river on the ten-arched 18C bridge of pretty **INISTIOGE** (pron. Inisteeg; or Tiogh's Island, Teoc's Island, etc.). The village has remains of its 13C priory and Norman fortifications.

Carry on up the Nore to little **THOMASTOWN**, named for one of the Welshmen who comprised so much of the Norman 12C invasion force. Thomas FitzAnthony Walsh made quite an important little place of his town; it was walled and fortified with a castle. Cromwell destroyed most, not all, of those sturdy defences. Ruined fortifications still stand at both ends of the bridge across the river. Parts of a 13C church managed to survive, and have been adapted into a newer CI church. Inside the RC church is the old high altar from nearby **Jerpoint Abbey**. Just a few yards along the Waterford road, the ruins of this splendid Cistercian monastery definitely reward a visit. The monastery seems to have been founded by a king of Ossory (i.e. the Kilkenny region) some time about 1158, originally as a Benedictine house. Then, in 1180, for some reason it was admitted as a Cistercian community, and soon began to distinguish itself as a great centre of civilisation and learning. The Statutes of Kilkenny, forbidding fraternisation between Irish and Normans, threatened to make life diffi-cult for the community, but the abbots resolutely ignored the new law, paying heavy fines for their intransigence, but never agreeing to segregate the two 'races'. The 15C additions to the buildings indicate that it was very prosperous at that time. 'Dissolved' in 1540, the monastery building and land passed into the hands of those Norman potentates of Kilkenny, the Butler family, Earls of Ormonde. The ruins of what survived have been carefully and effectively restored. What remains to be seen are the chapterhouse and other rooms along the side of fragments of cloisters.

From Thomastown, after passing or pausing at the delightful Water Garden at Ladywell (exotic and aquatic plants, tea room) on the edge of the village, continue on T20 back into Kilkenny.

Jerpoint Abbey

Laois

1 day/65 miles (105km)/ from Kilkenny

This quick look around County Laois (pron. Leesh, and sometimes spelt Leix) starts and finishes outside the county in Kilkenny, which makes a better touring base than anywhere else along this route. Though bordered by higher land, Laois is largely flat, low country with areas of bog and other areas of rich pasture: 'Spreading Leix the hill-protected', as John Betjeman described it.

Leave **KILKENNY** (see p. 109) on N77 (direction Portlaoise), travelling through gorgeously abundant greenery as the road heads away from the

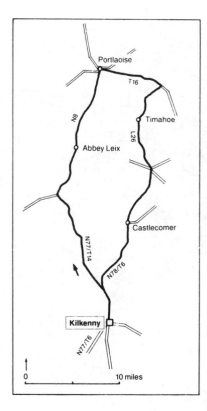

town. **Dunmore Cave** beside the road (signposted), digs far into the limestone terrain, and has a legendary significance as a place of dark and evil, and it was therefore perhaps almost appropriate as the setting of a massacre of Celts by Vikings in 928. It has several caverns linked by passages, and some impressive rock formations, and there is a visitor centre at the cave entrance.

At **DURROW**, laid out around a big village green, turn onto major N8 towards Portlaoise. Before reaching Abbeyleix village, the gardens of 18C **Abbey Leix House** (signposted; open to the public) contain the 13C grave of Malachi ó More, a chief of the Leix kingdom. The 12C Cistercian monastery (founded by his relative Conor ó More) from which nearby **ABBEYLEIX** (pronounced Abbey Leesh) takes its name has long ago disappeared, leaving this very likeable small town (pop: 1,400) of tree-lined streets.

Stay on the main road into **PORT LAOISE** (pron. Port Leesha; can be spelt as one word, also known as Port Leix), County town of Laois, formerly known as Queen's County after Queen Mary, the town (pop: 4,100) was originally a fortress set up by Philip and Mary as a garrison for conquering the powerful local ó More clan, which it did not manage to do with much success. Fragments of the original ramparts survive. At first they gave it the name Fort Protector, then Fort Leix, then Maryborough, then Port Leix. All these changes did not alter the basic fact that the place has little to recommend it. Leave on N80/T16 (direction Carlow).

Four miles outside town, left of the road, there was for centuries a great fortress strategically placed on the **Rock of Dunamase**. It was held by the 12C Leinster king Dermot MacMurrough, then his son-in-law Strongbow the Anglo-Norman, and passed to the Leix clan ó More. It proved a difficult prize to keep for either side in the 17C wars with the English, and was reduced at that time to its present sad ruins. Carry on to the accurately named **STRADBALLY**—'Street Town'—which consists of little more than a long high street. There's a good museum of steam engines.

Turn right, away from the main road, towards **TIMAHOE**, which has an excellent example of a Round Tower, probably 10C. Despite its age it looks strong, sturdy, remarkably well preserved, and it has rather more

The Round Tower at Timahoe

ornamentation than is usual with these strictly functional structures. Take the Swan road (L26/R426) and at Swan stay on this minor road to reach **CASTLECOMER** (or Caisleán an Chomair). The little town's name refers to an old Anglo-Norman fortress, the motte of which can still be seen. But the present town (pop: 1,600) results from a 17C development by a Planted family. It was heavily attacked soon after completion, and then again during the rising of 1798. At that stage it was a mining centre but now has a good deal of charm.

Continue along N78, which turns to merge with N77 (near Dunmore Cave) and return into Kilkenny.

The Midlands
(Longford, Westmeath, Offaly)

2 days/145 miles (230km)/from Birr

Although it has many interesting associations with 19C English and Anglo-Irish writers, Ireland's central flatland is, to be frank, not the most enchanting region of the country. In many parts, though far away from major cities, thanks to industrialisation, towns and villages overgrown with new housing, and relentless main roads, it feels barely rural. Yet, as this quick tour shows, the tranquil heart of the country can still be found here, and there are enjoyable journeys to be discovered among its lakes and lanes, peat bogs and rich fields of pasture.

BIRR (or Biorra), one of the more likeable Midlands towns, was built by an Englishman who was given the land after the Cromwellian confiscations, and it was for a while named Parsonstown after him. He also constructed an impressivly well-defended castle on the ruins of the former Irish fortification. Still very imposing, the castle proved its worth when attacked, as it was several times over the centuries. Its extensive and attractive 18C gardens are open to the public, and another curiosity in the

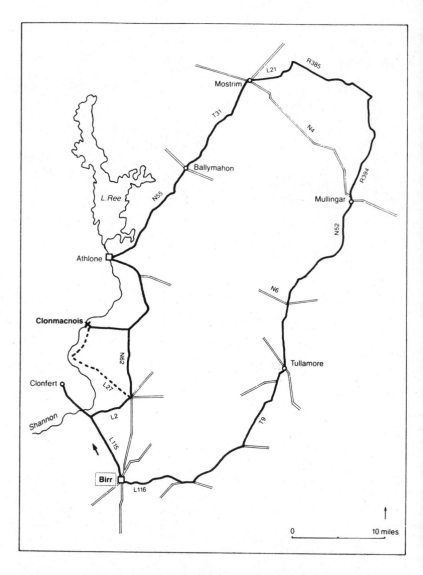

grounds is the remnant of a mid-19C astronomical telescope, once the largest in the world (permanent astronomical exhibition). Accommodation at the **County Arms** (0509–20191).

Take L115/R439 (direction Banagher). This was an area visited by Charlotte Brontë, whose father was Irish, and who married her father's curate, Rev. Arthur Nicholls; they spent their honeymoon at a mansion (now disappeared) near Taylor's Cross. **BANAGHER**, just beyond, well placed on the bank of the great Shannon river, was the small town where Anthony Trollope first lived on arrival in Ireland during his period as a Post Office surveyor. It is perhaps better known for its traditional fairs and its distillery. Trollope's stay in various parts of Ireland yielded some good novels (and characters in some of the others), but the writing he did at Banagher did not receive acclaim. It was while he was here that the town's bridge was being built across the Shannon.

It's worth making an excursion over the river to **CLONFERT** in the province of Connacht. Its ancient and beautiful Romanesque cathedral (follow signs), with excellent stonework (note doorway), once formed part of a major monastic site founded here in AD558, which however was outstripped in importance by Clonmacnois—see below.

From Banagher, take L2/R356, to Cloghan. Follow the minor road through Belmont for about 8 miles to a junction, where turn left for **CLONMACNOIS** (or Clonmacnoise—pron. as it looks), one of Ireland's most outstanding ruined monastic sites. A tremendous amount remains to give an idea of how impressive a place this was. Founded AD545, on what was then a principal highway across the Shannon, Clonmacnois grew to become the country's foremost ecclesiastical centre in the pre-Norman

Clonfert Cathedral doorway

period, an era during which Ireland was—through its monasteries and missionaries—the most important source of civilisation, culture and learning in western Europe. Many Irish kings were buried here, but the last of them was Rory ó Conor, as long ago as 1198. The community, with its fine buildings and rich possessions, and so accessibly placed right on the bank of the navigable Shannon, proved irresistible to the raiding Norsemen, then the conquering Normans. The English took what was left; in 1552 it was plundered by English soldiers stationed at Athlone, who removed all they could, even the glass from the windows.

Nevertheless, the site amply rewards a visit. From the entrance, the main items of interest are:

1. A large number of inscribed sepulchral grave slabs (6–11C), near entrance.

2. 'O'Rourke's Tower', a Round Tower, large but without its top; its exact age is not clear, but it was struck by lighning in 1134.

3. Teampull Conor (Conor's Church), founded about the year 1000 by Cathal ó Conor, much altered and then rebuilt as an 18C Protestant church (the round-headed doorway and windows are original).

4. Teampull Finghin (Fineen's or Finian's Church), adjoining the outer rampart, was founded by Fineen MacCarthy Mór; it has another Round Tower, although this one (built 1124) is clearly not intended as a refuge since its door is on ground level.

5. two richly carved, though now weatherworn, 10C High Crosses—North Cross and Great (or Scripture) Cross.

6. the Cathedral (or Great Church or Teampull Dermot), built 904, rebuilt 14C; inside are the graves of Rory ó Conor and his father Turlough, King of Connacht.

Around the Cathedral are a number of more or less ruined structures (in clockwise order):

7. the foundations of Teampull Kelly (12C).

8. Teampull Kieran (or Eaglais Bheag), a small cell or oratory (probably 9C).

9. Teampull Righ or Ri, all that remains is a plain rectangular structure (12C).

10. Teampull Doolin (or Doulin or Dowling), named—unexpectedly—for Edmund Dowling, who repaired it and made it into a Protestant church in 1689 (though it was originally 10–11C).

11. at the same time, Dowling built another small structure onto the end of Teampull Doolin, and called it, confusingly, Teampull Hurpan (or Hurpain), which had been the original name of Teampull Doolin; this new building collapsed soon afterwards.

12. South Cross, a third High Cross (9C).

Behind this group a causeway goes outside the enclosure to the Church of the Nunnery (1167)—note its fine Romanesque doorway and chancel; farther out, John de Grey's castle, largely destroyed by the Cromwellians, was built in 1212 on the site of the Clonmacnois abbots' residence.

There's an annual pilgrimage to Clonmacnois on St Kieran's Day, 9 Sept., and on the following Sunday.

The Cross of the Scriptures, Clonmacnois

Return along the minor road to the junction; continue to Ballynahown, there turning left (N62/T32) to **ATHLONE**, a large manufacturing town and river port (pop: 10,000) on the Shannon banks. Many people may remember it from years ago mainly as a strange name on the radio dial! That no longer applies though, as the main Irish transmitting centre is now at Tullamore, 25 miles away. Almost nothing survives of Athlone's long past which goes back to the construction of a castle here in 1210 by the Anglo-Normans. Its crucial location at the centre of Ireland, on the all-important Shannon, and between Connacht and Leinster, made it the focus of much fighting from that day onwards, until the creation of the Irish republic. Something of the castle survives on the west bank (and houses a museum), while fragments of a Franciscan monastery founded by Cathal á Conor in 1241 can be seen on the east side of the river. Cruisers can be hired at Athlone for trips along the Shannon and its lakes. **Tourist Office**: 17 Church St.

Travel along N55/T34 (direction Ballymahon). This is Oliver Goldsmith country. Although it is not known with absolute certainty where he was born, or even when—although it was probably 1730, there are places which have been more clearly identified. On this road, **LISSOY** marks the spot of 'The Deserted Village', as described in his poem; and **THE THREE PIGEONS** takes its name from the pub in his *She Stoops to Conquer*. **BALLYMAHON**, on the river Inny, was the village where he lived before leaving Ireland (1752) and going off to become far more famous in London. Just a couple of miles east from Ballymahon, at Pallas, is the likeliest Goldsmith birthplace.

From Ballymahon, stay on N55 to **MOSTRIM** (or Meathas Truim or Edgeworthstown), a village on the busy N4 (Longford–Dublin road). The Edgeworths who give it the alternative name were the local 'ruling family' who dominated the area from 16C onwards. They distinguished themselves in many fields, particularly as ecclesiastics; a macabre distinction is that an Edgeworth was Louis XVI's priest and stood with him during the last moments before his execution. A more renowned member of the family was the novelist Maria Edgeworth, who was in fact born and spent her childhood in England but came to live at Edgeworthstown in 1782, by which time she was 15 years old. It was here that *Castle Rackrent* and all her other books were written, and where she was visited by Sir Walter

Scott, who openly acknowledged the inspiration he derived from her novels, and by Wordsworth, about whom she apparently developed reservations after his stay. The house still survives, but has become a convent.

Leave the village at first on N55/T31 (direction Cavan), but turn right at once onto L21/R395 (direction Castlepollard). Just before Castlepollard, the sombre and fortified **Tullynally House** stands in its wooded estate. It's been very knocked about, redesigned, and added to, since it was built in 17C as the family home of the Pakenham family. In 18C it was restructured in Classical style, and then in 19C turned into a Gothic castle. **CASTLEPOLLARD** is an attractive little village. T10/R394 (direction Mullingar) heads through quite pleasing country between two big lakes, through Crookedwood, back to the N4.

MULLINGAR, a big and busy local capital (pop: 8,000), was long an important British garrison. It still has a few relics of its former imperial dignity, although the striking modern Cathedral is not one of them. The Town Hall and Courthouse, however, are both 18C. It's a cheerful, bright and breezy market town, which attracts some visitors (unlike most of the Midlands towns) on account of its surrounding lakes and rivers. Accommodation at **Grenville Arms** (044–48563).

Turn right onto T9/N52/R421, the Tullamore road. Pass Lough Ennel; at Kilbeggan (on N6) turn left and right to keep on T9 (direction Tullamore). Just a couple of miles along from here, **Durrow Abbey**, lying off the road, marks the location of a monastery founded by Columcille (St Columba). A richly illuminated copy of the Gospels, the Book of Durrow, now in Dublin's Trinity College Library, was made here in 7C. The site preserves a strange 10C cross and ancient St. Columba's Well. **TULLAMORE**, on the Grand Canal and the Tullamore river, is the county town of Offaly, arguably the most attractive of the Midland counties. The town itself is largeish and industrial (pop: 8,000). It remains, as it has always been, an important agricultural centre, and has two marketplaces. There are a few buildings of interest, notably the 18C Market House and 19C courthouse and CI church.

Leave town on N52/T41 (direction Birr), but where this main road veers right, carry straight on (T9/R421), taking a back road to Birr. This skirts the picturesque Slieve Bloom Mountains, uplands which mark the southern limit of the Midlands plains, and perhaps the most scenic countryside on the whole route. After Kinnity, make sure to keep towards Birr: at the junction where T9 heads round (left) towards Roscrea, take R440/L116 (right) back into Birr.

The Boyne

1–2 days/130 miles (205km)/from Dublin

Leinster has seen enacted some of the most crucial events in Irish history, few more so than that fateful battle on the banks of the river Boyne (1690), which finally assured England's dominion over Ireland. The many

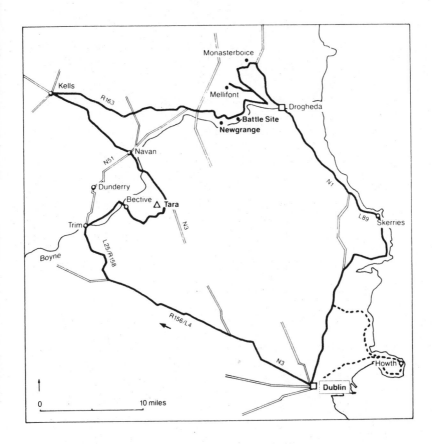

ruined castles in this region are a reminder of Cromwell's invasion just a few years before (1647), during which every Catholic opponent of English Protestant rule was defeated and dispossessed. This productive valley had a vital place in the development of the Irish people for thousands of years before that though. The Hill of Tara, rising south of the river, was for tens of centuries the official 'parliament' of the Kings of Ireland. It was no coincidence either that in 1843 O'Connell chose Tara for a huge public meeting during the campaign for repeal of the Union with Britain. Some of the greatest of Ireland's influential monastic communities were founded along this valley too. Much longer before, Europe's Neolithic civilisation had left its most impressive traces around Newgrange, overlooking the Boyne river.

This route stays largely within the boundaries of ancient Meath, which during the era of the Celtic kings was one of the *five* provinces which there were then. During the Anglo-Norman invasion it was 'granted' to the knight Hugh de Lacy, and later the Meath kingdom became absorbed into Leinster as Counties Meath and Westmeath. Most of this part of Ireland, lying north of Dublin, is quite flat, abundantly rich and fertile, well-watered with delightful streams. It makes for easy and relaxed touring.

For **DUBLIN** see p. 100. Leave the city centre by heading to the main Navan road (N3) on the north side of Phoenix Park, or alternatively go through the park to Castleknock (with ruins of Norman castle), where join N3.

Just after Clonee, turn off left (L4/R156) through Dunboyne. Stay on this road to **SUMMERHILL**, a likeable village (with another ruined castle). Anyone who is puzzled to hear, on occasional news items about Chile, the name of a distinguished Latin American family called O'Higgins, may feel the situation clarified a little (or possibly rendered even more puzzling) on learning that the liberator of Chile, a national hero in that country, was in fact an Irishman, Bernardo O'Higgins. He was the son of Ambrosio O'Higgins, viceroy of Peru and Chile, whose family home was at Summerhill. Take L25/R158 on right (direction Trim), which goes through **LARACOR**, where Jonathan Swift was the rector from 1699. Here he was joined in 1701 by 'Stella', a housekeeper's daughter, his closest companion from then onwards until her death in 1728. It is not known if they ever married, or indeed what the nature of their relationship was. Neither Stella nor Swift would recognise Laracor if they came back here now.

Two miles farther on, the river Boyne flows through a pleasing little country town, **TRIM**. It was once enclosed by protective walls, of which only Sheep Gate and ruins of Water Gate survive. The town's principal landmark is the 'Yellow Steeple', ruined tower of a 13C Augustinian abbey. When, in 1173, Hugh de Lacy came with Henry II's blessing to conquer the kingdom of Meath, he built a large strong castle at Trim from which to defend his claims. Though now ruined, it remains an impressive structure with its fine barbican, its keep and a moat which can be filled with water from the Boyne. Under Anglo-Norman rule, Trim and its castle became so important that noble parliaments were held here, and at one stage Richard II imprisoned the future Henry IV in the fortress. Trim has several other interesting buildings. 15C Talbot's Castle served as a school for a while, and one of its pupils was a little chap called Arthur Wellesley—who later became the great Duke of Wellington. He lived in Dublingate St. Also 15C, the Cathedral has a *sheila-na-gig*. Adjacent are the traces of a 13C Franciscan friary.

Deviating slightly from the route, about 4 miles away at Dunderry is Mrs. Healy's **Dunderry Lodge** (046–31671), one of Ireland's handful of really outstanding restaurants. It is housed in handsome converted farm buildings, and serves magnificent French/Irish cuisine at most reasonable prices. Well worth a visit.

From Trim take R161/T26 (direction Navan) along the Boyne valley. **Bective Abbey**, now consisting mainly of impressive 15C remains beside the river, was originally founded by the king of Meath in 1147 for the austere Cistercians. Hugh de Lacy, assassinated 1186, was buried here. At the suppression of the monasteries, it was saved from destruction by being confiscated and turned into a private house by one of the English administrators charged with enforcing the Dissolution of the religious houses.

Cross the Boyne on the adjacent bridge, go through Bective village and on to Kilmessan, where turn left for the **Hill of Tara**. Not particularly striking if seen simply as a hill, Tara has a central place in Irish history and mythology. Today it's just a mound of green in a sea of green fields. On the hill itself traces of a number of earthworks can be made out. Earth ramparts encircled its base, and indeed the whole hill was in effect a ring-fort. The summit, separately ringed, is known as the Rath na Riogh (Royal Enclosure). One of the two mounds within this area is now known to cover a passage grave dated about 1800BC.

Many people contemplating Tara like to envisage a time, a past golden age of Irish freedom and independence, when this country was ruled by brave and noble warrior kings whom they call the Kings of Tara. The reality isn't *quite* like that! But it's not altogether wrong either.

From at least the Bronze Age onwards, to judge from its earthworks, this hill had some religious and perhaps political importance. The evidence is that at an early stage Tara became the seat of the King of Meath, and, every three years, was the place where all the other Irish kings, priests, and lawyers assembled in a great *feis* (assembly). Gathering in camps and wooden buildings including a Great Hall, they examined the state of their nation; discussed, and if possible settled, disputes between them; and engaged in propitious religious rites. Under the combative system of rulership which prevailed in Celtic Ireland, there was no royal line in the modern sense: even provincial kings were constantly being required to justify—militarily—their pre-eminence. The kings (local chieftains, really) were always at each others throats too, making claims to each other's territory. When it came to Ireland as a whole, no clan leader could automatically command allegiance from any other, so there was no overall king. However, in practice, provincial ruling clans did tend to be able to hang on to their regional power, and on the national level there did tend to be one ruler who would emerge for a while as a High King—although there was no entitlement to pass on the position, and even while it was held the High King would have to 'watch his back' in case of any competitor who would like to take the title away from him.

Christianisation (6C) apparently weakened the force of Tara, whose power was connected to a spiritual significance which the site had and which was constantly reinforced with religious ritual. Nevertheless the *feis* continued to be held until about the year 1022, after which the growing political significance of the Church shifted the power base in Ireland. Although even that was almost 1,000 years ago, the name of Tara still casts a spell in Ireland. During the uprising of 1798, the Irish assembled here and the hill became the scene of a battle with the English. In 1843, during the campaign against the Act of Union with Britain, O'Connell announced a public meeting to be held here, on the 'middle of nowhere' Hill of Tara: the crowd numbered over 100,000. However, thanks to its 'mystical' reputation, Tara has also suffered all sorts of damage and desecrations in the last 100 years, for example the putting up of a statue of St Patrick at the top of the hill, or, worse, the excavations carried out by a 19C Christian sect who called themselves Israelites and came here to search for the lost Arc of the Covenant.

The main street at Kells

Leave the hill behind and join N3; turn left to **NAVAN**, a large, busy, workaday town (pop: 11,000—though only 4,000 within official boundaries). The location, at the confluence of the Boyne and the Blackwater rivers, does not fulfil its promise, and the place is surprisingly dull and unprepossessing. At one time it was enclosed by ramparts and had an important abbey, but both have vanished.

Stay on main N3, and follow the Blackwater valley to **KELLS** (or Ceannanus Mór), an agreeable town on a hillside. It occupies the site of a former great monastery, founded 6C, which flourished until a succession of damaging Viking raids in 10–11C. Nevertheless it continued to survive right up to the 16C Dissolution of the Monasteries imposed from England. Yet almost nothing remains of it now. A substantial but broken High Cross (called the Market Cross) stands at the town centre crossroads. It is heavily carved with Biblical scenes, which unfortunately are so weatherworn as to be indistinguishable. In the grounds of St Columba's Church (CI)—which has a curious detached belfry—there are two other High Crosses and fragments of others. One of these Crosses has a feature quite unusual in Ireland: an inscription in Latin (they are normally in Irish). Also in the church grounds there is a Round Tower (10C or 11C) lacking its top, as well as remnants of a stone sundial, and some interesting 18C gravestones.

Beyond the church an unusual small building, its walls turning towards each other to become a high steep roof made all of stone, stands next to a large, ugly modern structure. This odd and delightful little thing dates in its entirety from 11–12C. It is locally known as St Columba's House, and is popularly believed to have been a domestic dwelling in which Colmcille, alias St Columba (who founded Kells monastery), resided and 'wrote the Book of Kells'. In fact these ideas are somewhat off the mark. The Book of Kells, a magnificent illuminated copy of the Gospels (original in Trinity College Library, Dublin; facsimile in Kells at St Columba's Church) was not made until 8C, some two centuries after Colmcille's time. The little stone 'house', too, dates from 300 years after his death, and besides is believed by historians to have been a church rather than a dwelling. Inside, it does seem more like a small church. I wouldn't envy anyone who lived in such a place! It consists of a tiny stone room (perhaps previously two rooms one above the other), in which a tall ladder climbs up to a tiny attic.

On Kells 'pattern' day, 9 June, a procession goes to St Colmcille's Well, out of town.

Continue from Kells: go down the main street to the edge of town; take the left fork (signposted Slane, Drogheda). This little country road makes a lovely drive. The pre-Christian religion seems to have clung on strongly in this district. For example, between villages **ORISTON** (on the road) and Donaghpatrick (just off to right), the Hill of Tailte was the site of the Aonach Tailteann Games, a sort of Gaelic Olympics with (like the Greek Olympics) a religious significance. The Games were maintained as a local custom until 12C. Another unexpected cultural throwback was the Teltown Marriage Custom practised at nearby Teltown village: couples were 'married' for one year (or longer if all went well during that period) at the end of which they could, if they liked, return to the Hill and be ritually 'unmarried'—that was still being done in the last century. I wonder how the residents of Teltown voted in Ireland's 1987 divorce referendum!

At a junction (with L5/R162; Navan signposted to right), cross straight over (direction Slane). This minor road eventually joins N51. Approaching Slane, you first reach Slane Castle, now with a restaurant and nightclub. Drive through the castle gateway (on N51) to see the rather imposing edifice, built 1785, now rather commercialised, set in pretty, gentle countryside beside the Boyne. The restaurant is open at weekends, with tours of the castle on Sundays. **SLANE** is a quiet little crossroads village (note the four Georgian houses at the central junction). A road leads up to the summit of the Hill of Slane, from which there's a marvellous panorama. The fine ruined 'Abbey' at the summit was founded for Franciscans in 1512 on the site of an early-Christian religious and educational establishment. It was not abandoned until 1723, and the cemetery is still used. A spiral staircase goes up to the top of its church tower, for a superb view.

This is supposed to be one of the many spots where St Patrick came in person to proclaim Christianity with a great hilltop fire. Apparently he won at least one convert, now called St Erc, whose 'hermitage' is a 16C Gothic building in the Slane Castle estate, near the Protestant church. The walk to it is attractive. Erc, it is said, as part of his gloomy religious devotions, used to stand all day long in the Boyne river.

Leave the village on N51 (following signs to Newgrange). Soon after Slane, on left, a sign pointing to 'Ledwidge's House' refers to the birthplace of a Great War poet, Francis Ledwidge. Farther on, left turns are indicated to Knowth and Newgrange.

All these possible turnings bring you eventually to **Newgrange**, the site of a remarkable passage grave, one of the most impressive Neolithic (i.e. New Stone Age, 3000–4000BC) monuments in Europe. Newgrange, and its neighbours Knowth and Dowth, all about 1 mile apart, comprise a single burial area known as Brugh na Boinne. Entrances to the Knowth and Dowth tumuli are usually closed. Newgrange is the largest of the three. Its toll booth has information leaflets about the site. Come at opening time or in winter to avoid the coachloads of tourists.

From outside, all that can be seen is a grass-covered mound, partly supported by a wall of stone slabs, rising in a large grassy enclosure. A ring

Neolithic carving at the Newgrange burial chamber

of individual stones encircles the mound. An entrance in the wall leads past the Threshold Stone, intriguingly carved with spirals, directly into a narrow passage lined with stones, many of them also engraved with spiral shapes. This leads to a chamber with three recesses. The whole length of the passage, with the chamber, amounts to less than one third of the mound's diameter. In recesses are 'basin stones' which contained the remains of the persons who had died; during the excavations little trinkets and personal treasures made of bone or stone were found in the basin stones as well—perhaps placed by family and friends of the dead. At dawn on the winter solstice, from that day to this, the first rays of the morning sun fall on a small decorated opening above the passage ceiling, allowing the light to pass through and illuminate the chamber for a few seconds.

From Newgrange follow signs 'Drogheda'. Reach a T-junction where turn right. The fine Georgian mansion Townley Hall, immediately on the left, is now an agricultural college and a youth hostel. Soon after, at a crossroads with signs 'Mellifont' and 'Drogheda', a more obscure small sign points to 'Battle of the Boyne 1690 (Viewing Point)', and on right, another small sign to 'Battle of the Boyne 1690 (Jacobite Camp)'. The smallness of the signs no doubt reflects the unwillingness of the Irish to recall what happened here.

First of all, stop in the small car park at this junction and walk (across a small enclosed picnic area) to some steep steps which climb up to the viewing point. Here the whole battle area can be seen, and a viewing table offers a complete explanation of the course of the **Battle of the Boyne** which took place on 1 July 1690 (or 16 July as it would be in the modern calendar). Though a small affair in military terms, it was to affect the course of history in Ireland, England and Europe from that date onward.

It happened like this. James II, the rightful heir and a Catholic, had come to the throne in England, despite strenuous efforts to keep the monarchy Protestant. He pursued an unpopular policy of replacing Protestants with Catholics in all key posts, and was also a firm believer in the outdated notion of the Divine Right of Kings. James had a daughter, Mary, who was married to the sickly and unlikeable William of Orange, the Protestant Dutch ruler. (His other daughter, Anne, also opposed the Roman Catholic religion.) Meanwhile Louis XIV of France (a Catholic fanatically opposed to Protestantism and pursuing a policy of brutal physical persecution in France) was in a belligerent mood, on the verge of war with several nations. The Dutch felt justifiably threatened by him, and William of Orange was worried that the English might support the French.

Parliamentarians and ousted Protestant men of importance in England formed close links with William, who would in any case, they believed, rightfully be the next man on the English throne. Then, rather surprising everybody, James II had a son. The birth of the new baby acted like a catalyst. William of Orange was invited by his many and powerful Protestant allies to invade England and take the throne by force. He came over the Channel with his soldiers in 1688. Poor King James saw town after town cheerfully 'surrendering' to the Dutchman and his English wife (and her sister, for Anne had also joined the invading force).

With his tail between his legs, James escaped to France, and asked for support from Louis XIV, who willingly agreed to help—especially since the English, under their new king now called William III, had just declared war on him. Unfortunately he could only spare a small force at that moment, as he was overstretched fighting everybody on several fronts. So James, with his little army of Frenchmen, decided to return to England via Ireland, because it was a Catholic country where he thought he could gather more support. But James' attempt to rally support in Ireland for his Catholic monarchy was not as successful as it might have been because (never a man to recognise where his best interests lay) he wasn't prepared to promise to restore all their confiscated lands to the Irish nobility, and in any case the Irish by this time were already moving towards the idea of absolute independence from England, and an Irish parliament. His 'divine' view of himself meant that James could not agree to any of these Irish aspirations. Quite a few Irishmen did join him though, and altogether his strength amounted to about 25,000 men.

It was just here at the Boyne river that James and his makeshift army encountered William with 36,000 soldiers. The viewing table shows the positions of the two sides. The battle was all over within the day. William was wounded, and his gallant General Schomberg was killed. James' side retreated and was pursued; they suffered several more defeats, notably at Limerick, and not long after, James gave it all up as a bad job, went back to France, and stayed there for the rest of his life.

Today, at the place where William's soldiers crossed the Boyne to attack James' forces, sturdy Irishmen—masters now (through the ballot box) of their own nation—stand contentedly fishing in the tranquil waters. If James had won, would their lives be better?

If James had won, Ireland and England would both have been Catholic countries, united under a Catholic monarch. With his belief in the Divine Right, he would have tried to check and overthrow the moves towards parliamentary democracy. Louis XIV's plans for French Catholic domination of Europe would have progressed. The period of religious wars in Europe would have been vastly prolonged. France and England would have been nominal allies instead of, as happened, enemies. Except of course . . . that James' day, and the day of everyone like him, was over. Even if he had won the war at the Boyne, perhaps it would only have led to another Civil War in England and another execution of the monarch. Indeed, it is impossible — despite the awful consequences for Ireland of James' defeat (or rather, William's victory) — to say that anything would have been better if he had won.

Nevertheless, The Battle of the Boyne was the key event as far as the politics and power struggles of Ireland in modern times are concerned, simply because it confirmed absolutely the Protestant supremacy over Ireland. It also meant that in the English mind, Ireland and its Catholicism were their enemy and a constant threat. The immediate consequence of the English victory was the confiscation of more land from the Irish and the imposition of the Penal Laws, designed to punish and control the Catholic population of Ireland.

Continue from the Battle site on T26/51 into **DROGHEDA** (pron. Droyeda; or Droichead Átha) pop: 24,000. A large busy industrial town with too much traffic. Important port on navigable stretch of Boyne. Imposing St Lawrence's Gate, near far side of town, is part of once extensive fortifications. Other remnants are near Mill Mount (an Anglo–Norman motte). On 10 Sept. 1649 Cromwell and his men managed to enter the town after a seige and, in one of the most notorious incidents of Cromwell's unsavoury Irish campaign, massacred over 2,000 of the residents. It later became a major English garrison. A few interesting 18C and 19C buildings can be seen: the old Tholsel, the courthouse, St Peter's Church (CI — note that there is an RC church with the same name).

From Drogheda, a circular trip can be made to see the ruins of two important medieval monasteries. Travel back along T26/N51 (direction Navan) as far as a right turn, T26/R168 (direction Collon). A few yards along here take a left onto the road to **Mellifont Abbey**, the first Cistercian community in Ireland, founded 1142. It quickly acquired considerable influence. In 1172, Henry II came here and met ó Neill, powerful chief of the clan which ruled Ulster, and obtained his promises of subservience and loyalty. Though largely reduced to the bare stumps and skeleton of its buildings, even these show that this was a place of awesome size and dignity. Its original name was Mainistir Mór. 'The Great Monastery'. Surviving in better condition than the rest are the chapter house (or 'St Bernard's Chapel'; note roof interior, good stonework); the huge gatehouse; and an enchanting 'lavabo' or washroom, formerly octagonal but with only five sides still standing. ·

Return to the Collon road and turn left (towards Collon). Turn right after a couple of miles for **Monasterboice**. This was an older and perhaps much larger monastery than its neighbour—founded as long ago as the 5C by a St Buithe. Here too most of the buildings have fallen into ruins, but what remains is impressive: a 9C Round Tower, which may be entered, and is still exceptionally tall (100ft) even though its cap is missing; two crumbling churches, the older one dating probably from 9C; a granite sundial; and some ancient grave slabs. But the most striking relics of the monastery are three superb High Crosses, two of them magnificent examples, tall and richly carved.

Return on adjacent N1 into Drogheda; cross the river and continue on this major road through uninteresting **BALBRIGGAN**. From here follow signs to 'Skerries' along minor L89/R127, which soon becomes a scenic seashore road. Little **SKERRIES**, on a promontory ahead, looks attractive and inviting. Arriving at the village, follow signs to the harbour, where there are several places of refreshment as well as a greensward for walking by the rocky shore. There are misty views of the Mourne Mountains in Ulster. Stay on the same road, to picturesque **RUSH**, a smaller, less spoiled, more genuine little harbour. The coast road turns west to **LUSK**, where an imposing fortified 15–16C church tower, incorporating a very early Round Tower (maybe pre-8C), dominates the village.

Take the Dublin road (L90/R127). This rejoins major N1. By-pass (or enter, if preferred) Swords.

SWORDS pop: 12,000 Now too large and crowded for comfort, the town grew up around an important monastery, founded 550. It was renowned for its wealth, and suffered accordingly from frequent raids. All that remains are: the Round Tower, one of the oldest (in grounds of CI church); fortified tower of abbey church, 14C; ruins of the Archbishops' Castle (or Swords Castle), dating from about 1200.

From Swords, N1 heads straight back into Dublin, passing the airport on the way. A more attractive alternative way back into the city is along the coast road through **MALAHIDE** (resort with castle) and **HOWTH** (pron. Hote or Hoath; pleasant harbour resort and suburb, with castle). Follow the road round Dublin Bay into the city centre.

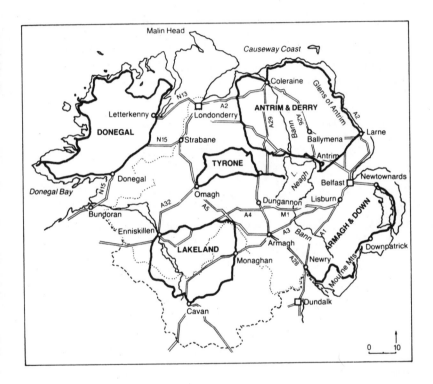

Ulster has been 'different' from the rest of Ireland for centuries—since long before the 1921 creation of Northern Ireland. It had its own legends and its own customs, and during the various waves of colonisation it remained the most entirely Gaelic, the most deeply entrenched in old traditions, of Ireland's four provinces. That, no doubt, was why it was the object of the most strenuous efforts to eradicate the power of that old Gaelic culture. From Queen Elizabeth I's time onwards, the whole of Ulster was intensively 'planted' with Protestant colonists. In the rest of Ireland, the Plantation was confined to seizing the property of Irish Catholic landowners and giving it to English landlords. In Ulster, by contrast, following the confiscation of the lands of the Irish nobility (who fled the country in the notorious Flight of the Earls, 1607) whole towns and villages were built or rebuilt for Scottish and English settlers of all classes—these 'Plantation towns' usually remain distinctive with a broad Mall and a main square often known as The Diamond. Other typical relics of this period include *bawns* (fortified farmhouses), and the simple barn-style churches of the Presbyterians, who brought many customs with them from Scotland.

The policy of 'planting' Protestants, sensible as it may have seemed to the English colonists at the time, lies at the root of Ulster's present troubles, although in more recent times it is undoubtedly the Protestant refusal to abandon their privileged position in Northern Ireland society, and the bitter Catholic reaction to that, which has perpetuated the problem.

In the early years of this century, during the turbulent run-up to the creation of Northern Ireland, the British Government was eager to exploit the presence of the violently pro-British Protestants in Ulster as a way of preventing the formation of a united independent Irish state. In 1920, the majority Nationalist feeling was that in order to secure peace and an independent Irish nation it would be acceptable to see Ireland divided into a 'Free State' and British province (there was however a considerable minority view on both sides which would be satisfied with nothing less than the whole island).

To establish where the frontier between the two would be drawn, in 1921 there were negotiations between Irish leaders and the British Government. Among the options were to keep the whole of Ulster under British rule, or to keep just the four counties of Londonderry, Antrim, Armagh and Down, the only ones which had shown a clear Protestant majority in recent General Elections. It was eventually decided to settle upon a Northern Ireland of six counties, as being the largest possible area in which Protestants would still have an unassailable majority over Catholics. Military considerations may have played a part in the British thinking too: the four counties could have been easily surrounded by any future anti-British army on Irish soil, whereas with six counties the British would have a defensible salient into Irish territory. The two anti-Unionist counties brought into Northern Ireland were Tyrone and staunchly-Nationalist Fermanagh. The other three Ulster counties—Donegal, Cavan, and Monaghan—were allowed to be part of the new Irish Free State, which later changed its name to the Republic of Ireland.

One of our Ulster routes is in the Republic, three are in Northern Ireland, and one crosses from one to the other. It is interesting to note the many visible differences between British Ulster and Irish Ulster: in Northern Ireland there are many more two-storey houses (as against traditional Irish one-storey dwellings), better roads, more understandable roadsigns, little Gaelic writing anywhere, far more churches and chapels, larger and more modern-looking towns and villages, and—though the North like the Republic is very rural—a good deal more industry. In the small towns, although there is little evidence of the tension between the Catholics and Protestants, visitors cannot fail to notice such oddities as the kerbstones and telegraph poles painted red, white and blue by Protestant 'Loyalists', Union flags and Ulster flags flying from lamposts, police stations and government offices swathed in protective fencing, and fully armed British soldiers incongruously on patrol in busy shopping streets.

Yet in everyday things resemblances between Northern Ireland and the Republic outweigh the differences, with similarities in everything from mannerisms and mores to food and drink. Northern people on the whole are as friendly, likeable, sincere and ingenuous as in the South, and the countryside of drumlins, lakes, bogs, magnificent glens, and hilly fields of green pasture recognises no border. Indeed some of the North's landscapes and scenery are among the best that Ireland has to offer.

Antrim and Derry

2–3 days/165 miles (260km)/from Belfast Airport or Larne

This journey takes in, along Ulster's northern coast, some of the most sublime scenery in Ireland. County Antrim is mostly high, rolling hills of heath and moorland; nine beautiful valleys, called the Glens of Antrim, cut through these uplands while the hills themselves descend majestically—sometimes in high, sheer cliffs—into a turquoise sea. Inland, the route crosses the wild open moors of the Sperrins in mountainous County Londonderry (or Derry), before returning via the shores of Lough Neagh into Antrim. Londonderry, county and town, were both officially called Derry until James I, as part of the 'Plantation' policy, presented most of the county to a group of City of London companies. It is now known by either name although the town is correctly known, by decision of its council, as Derry City.

Although this route starts at Belfast's Aldergrove Airport (or Larne, for people arriving by ferry from Scotland), it does not approach within ten miles of that troubled city. Indeed our road remains mainly in quiet country areas, along the way passing through tranquil Catholic and Protestant small towns.

From the airport take A5 (changes to A57, and then joins A8) to **LARNE**. Many remnants of Stone Age habitation have been found in the area of this now-uninteresting port town, and at the harbour (terminal of ferries to Scotland) are 16C ruins together with a modern copy of a round tower. There is no need to go into the town to reach the coast road: instead, on the outskirts of Larne, follow signs to Pound St; continue along Victoria Rd; turn left (signposted Glenarm) onto A2.

A2 is the coast road, clinging to the edges of the high hills as they turn down into the sea. Constructed in the early 1830s, it is an extraordinary engineering achievement, particularly in this first stretch. Views are spectacular. At **GLENARM**, there are quarries and stoneworks, but even

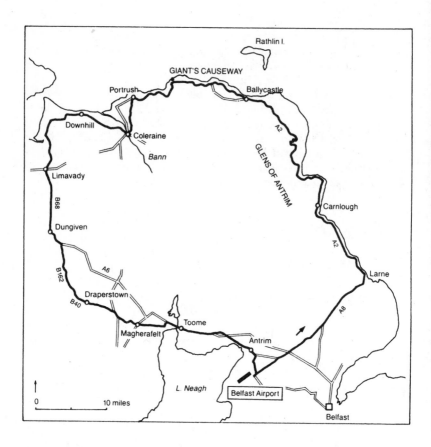

these cannot mar the beauty of its situation. Turn right (direction Carnlough), crossing a fortified bridge. The countryside is lush and intensely farmed, but rugged too, with green fields creeping up the lower slopes of moorlands hills which descend sometimes steeply, sometimes shallowly, towards the waves.

At **CARNLOUGH** there is a tiny harbour between stone walls, an agreeable 17C inn of considerable character, called **The Londonderry Arms** (0574–885255; good food, lodgings and local music), and a **tourist office** (at post office). The waterside road continues around Garon Point. The peaks inland from here have clear views of the Scottish coast. **WATERFOOT (or Glenariff)** crosses attractive Glenariff river where it runs into Red Bay. Upriver are waterfalls and a Forest Park; Glenariff has the most pleasing scenery of all the Glens of Antrim.

Turn right in Waterfoot/Glenariff to stay on A2 (direction Cushendall). In little **CUSHENDALL**, the curious fortified square tower of red stone on the central crossroads used to be a gaol and is now a private house. Turn left at the tower (direction Cushendun). Off the road (2 miles on left) soon after the village is a cairn commonly known as Ossian's

Grave (after Ossian or Oisin, an important figure in Ulster's Gaelic legends). Although there is a narrow coast road from **CUSHENDUN**, I prefer here to stay on A2, which heads inland for a few miles. This gives a chance to see the bog and heath on the rounded summits of the Antrim hills, as well as having fine views in all directions.

The road skirts peculiar **Loughareema**, a 'lake' which is filled to the brim in rainy weather, then just empties away as the water disappears into the limestone beneath. After the planted woods of Ballypatrick Forest (with marked 'scenic drive'), A2 gently descends into **BALLYCASTLE**. Before entering the town, the road passes interesting ruins of **Bonamargy Friary** (on left; various spellings). Built 1500 for Franciscans, damaged in 1584 by one of the local ruling MacDonnell family, it was at once repaired by a more devout member of the clan, Sorley Boye MacDonnell. He and his descendants (who became the Earls of Antrim) lie here in the MacDonnell family vault. After the Friary, the road reaches a T-junction, where turn right for the town. This small but bustling resort is strikingly placed, rising up a hill which ends abruptly in an escarpment overlooking the sea, with fine views of cliffs around Ballycastle Bay and of Rathlin Island out to sea.

Rathlin emerges sheer and rocky from turbulent water hardly a dozen miles from the Mull of Kintyre on the Scottish coast. The short crossing from the mainland to Rathlin is notoriously difficult and dangerous; boat access is possible in fine weather only. Nevertheless the island has not been altogether by-passed by history. It was attacked by Danes and Vikings, St Columba almost drowned right beside it, and it was here that Robert Bruce, fugitive king of Scotland, sheltered in a cave and found inspiration and hope from watching a spider which, undaunted by having her web damaged, simply set about making a new one. Although this took place in 1306, visitors are still shown a plausible 'Bruce's Cave'. The island attracts vast numbers of seabirds, which can best be seen (and heard!) from Bull Point, at the western tip.

Ballycastle's rocky shore plays a part in several of Ulster's Gaelic legends. *Carrig Uisneach*, at the foot of the cliffs, is claimed as the place where Deirdre and Naoise landed when Conchubar tricked them into returning to Ireland (he later killed Naoise and Deirdre killed herself). And the tempestuous Waters of Moyle, where the Children of Lîr were condemned to spend centuries in the shape of swans, was the channel which separates this part of Ireland from the Scottish coast. On a more cheerful note, Ballycastle is the setting for two enjoyable and interesting traditional fairs: the *Fleadh Amhran agus Rince* in June, three full days of music, dance, and boozy merriment, and the Ould Lammas Fair in August, a festive two-day cattle fair which was established by special charter in 1606.

Leave Ballycastle on A2. Soon a brown sign indicates a right turn towards The Giant's Causeway; follow these signs. They lead along coastal B15, passing **Carrickarade Island** (or Carrick-a-rede, etc.), a rocky fragment just offshore, connected to the mainland by a rope bridge swinging in the breeze (60ft long, 80ft drop). Though terrifying, this is crossed diligently throughout the summer months by tourists of all ages, and turns out to be fairly safe. At **BALLINTOY**, the next village, turn right at the sign for Ballintoy Harbour. The narrow road passes an unusual little white Church of Ireland church before winding steeply down to a tiny harbour among spectacularly treacherous rocks. There are caves, a waterfall splashing down, and all in all this looks a most improbable place for a harbour. The chaotic offshore rocks are part of the basalt outburst which formed The Giant's Causeway.

Return from the harbour to the through road (B15) and continue toward the Causeway, following the brown signs (which lead back onto A2 and then onto B146). To the right of the road, perched on a ledge of rock above the sea, **Dunseverick Castle** is a tiny ruin of a medieval fortress on what has probably been a royal site since the Iron Age. A National Trust plaque gives details of a ripping yarn about the history of the castle. A footpath (the North Antrim Coastal Path) leads from here along the cliffside with dramatic views, to The Giant's Causeway and beyond. This is the best way to see the whole of this marvellous Causeway Coast, which is under National Trust supervision. When the Spanish galleon *Girona* struck rocks on this shore at Port-na-Spaniagh in 1588 it went down with a tremendous loss, not only of life, but of treasure. In 1968 a team of divers exploring the coast came up with immense quantities of gold and silver coins, gold chains, rubies, rings, and superb ornaments made of jewel-studded gold, now displayed in the Ulster Museum, Belfast.

Follow signs to **The Giant's Causeway**, one of few places in Ireland to have become at all developed as a real tourist attraction, yet even here—thanks to intelligent National Trust management—commercialisation is minimal and provision of amenities unobtrusive.

The Causeway consists of huge masses of extraordinary pillars of basalt rock, mostly hexagonal, clustered together honeycomb-style, which march down from the shore cliffs into the sea. There are distinct sections, which have been called the Little, Middle, and Grand Causeways, and there are several individual features in the rock formation which have been given names, such as the Wishing Chair, the Key Stone, and the Organ. The Causeway figures in Irish legend as the stepping stones thrown down by the giant Finn MacCoul as he made his way to Scotland—hence the name. As if to provide further evidence for this theory, similar columns emerge from the sea at Fingal's Cave on the Scots island of Staffa, Fingal being the Scottish name for Finn.

This site has been attracting foreign visitors at least since the early 18C. William Thackeray, very impressed, described it as 'a remnant of chaos' left over from the creation of the world. In fact it is the result of molten rock shooting out a volcanic fissure about 60 million years ago; the regular shapes are due to high pressure and rapid cooling.

At the top of the access road which descends to the Causeway itself is a Visitor Centre with both free displays and a pay-to-enter audio-visual exhibition about the Causeway Coast and its formation. There's also a pleasant tea room.

From the clifftop above the Causeway it is possible to get a good overall view. For a closer look, walk down the access road to the Grand Causeway (about 20 minutes one way). Private vehicles are not allowed on the access road; although inconvenient this undoubtedly helps preserve the character of the site. A minibus provides access for those who do not wish to walk. Circular footpaths—either 2 or 5 miles—give a chance to see much more.

From the Causeway, follow signs to **BUSHMILLS**, on the A2. To judge from its UVF grafitti and red, white and blue kerbstones, this unattractive small town must be staunchly Unionist. But it is famous— and for good reason—for a product popular throughout Ireland, and throughout the world: Bushmills' Irish Whiskey made by The Old Bushmills Distillery Company. The Distillery was legally licensed in 1608 and claims to be the oldest in the world. It is open to visitors on weekdays, and makes an interesting tour as it is one of the few distilleries where one can see the entire process from mashing the malt to bottling the finished product.

Stay on A2 (direction Portrush), which passes the impressive ruins of **Dunluce Castle** poised dramatically on a crag of the beautiful seashore cliffs. The ancient Irish probably had fortifications on the site, but the

The Giant's Causeway

141

present castle was originally built about 1300 by the Earl of Ulster, Richard de Burgh. The local MacDonnell family under Sorley Boye MacDonnell captured it in 16C, and the castle was enlarged by his son James. The English, unable to dislodge them, decided instead to name Randall MacDonnell, another son of the redoubtable Sorley Boye, as Earl of Antrim and Viscount Dunluce. Later Earls of Antrim abandoned the castle for more modern quarters in 17C.

The road heads to **PORTRUSH**; A2 merely skirts the edge of town. Turn into town if you want to see more of this resort, which on the whole is not remarkable, although its small older central area built around a little harbour is fairly attractive. Ramore Head, a promontory into the sea, is effectively part of Portrush, having a small greensward backed by tall boarding houses. From the harbour and the Head there are lovely views along the coast and out to the string of offshore rocky islets called The Skerries. Popular eating place: **Ramore Restaurant and Wine Bar** at the harbour. Portrush's most distinctive landmark is the red-brick town hall, built in an imitation of many styles.

Turn inland on A28 to Coleraine, in County Londonderry.

COLERAINE (pronounced as Coal Rain) pop: 16,000 Large industrial (and university) river port on the Bann, rather disfigured by smoking factory chimneys. River crossed by two busy bridges, one a handsome structure of 1844. Earliest relics of man in Ireland found here (flint tools of 6650BC). Town originally 5C, acquired in 1618 by City of London companies. The high oval earth mound of Mountsandel (1 mile south of town on east bank) is the site of the fortress of Finan, an ancient King of Ulster, and later also of John de Courcy, 12C viceroy of Henry II. Few other remnants of the town's past survive. Upriver, just south of town, **Salmon Leap Restaurant**, in a modernised 17C building, is a popular, congenial eating and drinking establishment with live music and good food at modest prices.

The Bann river on which Coleraine stands flows from the Mourne Mountains in the far south of the province, through Lough Neagh, right up to this northern coast, and it traditionally divides Northern Ireland into two distinct regions. East of the river, Counties Down and Antrim, is the area with an undisputed Protestant majority. West of the Bann is the region in which Protestant and Catholic are more equally divided, and which hard-line Protestants tend to view as irremediably rustic and 'Irish'.

Cross the river Bann and leave town on A2 (signposted Castlerock). The road runs between fields of rich pasture dotted with plump, contented-looking sheep. At a crossroads on A2 1 mile south of Castlerock, Hezlett House is a long single-storey thatched rectory of 1691, having a cruck roof, i.e. constructed of pairs of curved timbers balanced against each other. Straightaway after, a hilltop mausoleum comes into view. This is the signal that on the right, set back a little from the road, is the National Trust property **Downhill Estate**. This consists of the rambling ruins of Downhill Castle, built in the late 1770s as home of the wealthy 4th Earl of Bristol (also Bishop of Derry), well known for his flamboyance, eccentricity, and love of foreign travel—many hotels on the Continent were named Hotel Bristol in his honour! Although it had already been damaged by fire in 1851, only as recently as 1949 was his castle partly demolished, when the Downhill lands were broken up to allow coastal development, for example at the resort of Castlerock.

The conspicuous mausoleum is of the 3rd Earl, whose statue used to stand on top of it. Blown down in high winds, it now reposes against Bishop's Gate, one of the entrances to the grounds. Arriving on A2, the first part of the Downhill estate to be reached is Bishop's Gate; this leads into a delightful park with a footpath. It is a pleasant ½-hour walk along here, to the cliffs overlooking the sea, and to the construction called Lady Erne's Seat, and beyond to the graceful rotunda known as Mussenden Temple (1783). Around its dome a Latin motto asserts how very agreeable it is to be standing safely on dry land watching ships struggling desperately in a stormy sea! Despite this startling view of life, the no doubt well-meaning Anglican bishop allowed the basement of Mussenden Temple to be used for Mass by local Catholics. Throughout the estate, Classical influence is strongly in evidence, possibly the result of the Earl of Bristol's journeying. Across the road from Downhill Estate is Downhill Forest, with footpaths.

A2 descends to little **DOWNHILL**, which has a good view of Mussenden Temple, standing on its cliff edge above. The road, at first running at the foot of dark cliffs (with two waterfalls, near Downhill), reaches unattractive flatter ground and continues into **LIMAVADY** (pop: 8,000). Turn right into town following signs 'Dungiven B68'. Limavady is charmless; its Crown Buildings gives an idea of modern fortress architecture. W.M. Thackeray was rather taken with a barmaid here, 'Sweet Peg of Limavady' (1842), and in 1851, Jane Ross of 51 Main St, jotted down a tune—later to become known as 'Danny Boy', perhaps the best known of all Irish folk tunes—as it was being played by an itinerant fiddler.

B68 leads through enjoyable undulating farm country with sheep on distant hills and the higher slopes of the Sperrins ahead. At **DUNGIVEN**, an uninteresting large village in a lovely setting, the road meets A6, where turn left (direction Belfast). In the village there are ruins of a fortified mansion (1618) of the Skinners' Company, one of the guilds to which County Derry, as it then was, was given. On the outskirts of Dungiven a muddy, rutted track on the right gives access to the ruins of an 11C Augustinian priory, restored late 14C, with an ornate little tomb (1385). Adjacent are ruins of a 17C *bawn*, fortified Plantation farmhouse.

At a fork some 1½ miles from Dungiven, take the right turn signposted 'Draperstown 10'. After some distance turn right again (also marked 'Draperstown 10'). This is the B182. Note that this would be a difficult road to attempt at night, and in any case there would be no point in coming this way after dark since scenery is the essence of it (if it is getting dark, continue along A6, through Glenshane Pass instead). Our narrow mountain road climbs over the Sperrins, a broad open landscape of deserted hills covered with heathy moorland and peat bogs. It descends again into pleasant farmland. After unappealing Moneyneany village, turn left into 'Derrynoyd Road'; this is in fact the B40 to Draperstown, unsignposted. The village of **DRAPERSTOWN**, constructed by the Drapers' Company, has the immensely wide main street typical of Plantation towns.

Carry on straight across the main road, taking B40 to the village of Desertmartin (on A29), and from there take a left to stay on B40, continuing into **MAGHERAFELT** (pop: 5,000). Here is another Plantation town, this time owned and rebuilt by the Salters' Company. It has a large main square and wide main roads, and interesting 9C courthouse. Stay on B40, as far as The Creagh on A6, where turn right; at Toome Bridge, the road crosses back over the Bann at the point where it leaves Lough Neagh. Continue through **RANDALSTOWN** (pop: 3,600), industrial centre, formerly known as Mainwater, with 18C former Markethouse, a number of 19C churches, and unusual oval Presbyterian church of 1790.

It is hardly 6 miles on A6 into Antrim, passing on the way Shane's Castle on the shore of Lough Neagh. Shane's Castle and its grounds have become something of a tourist centre. Ruins survive of a mansion: orig-

Mussenden Temple

inally the 16C fortress of Shane O'Neill, it was rebuilt (by John Nash) in 1812, destroyed by fire in 1816, rebuilt again (by Lanyon) in 1865, and again destroyed by fire in the rebellion of 1922. The conservatory survives and houses a collection of camelias. In the grounds there is an incongruous assortment of 'attractions' including a head of deer, an area set aside as a bird sanctuary, a small permanent funfair, a café, and a narrow-gauge steam railway which runs from Shane's Castle to Antrim.

ANTRIM pop: 23,000 Industrial but not unpleasant town on the Six Mile Water close to Lough Neagh (daily cruises). The Church of Ireland building dates from 1596 and retains some Renaissance windows. At the end of the main street are a quaint courthouse (1726) and the Tudor gateway of a former Plantation castle (castle itself burned down 1922, its gardens are now a public park). A perfect 9–10C Round Tower, 92ft high (badly signposted; locally 'the steeple') stands in unprepossessing surroundings just off the out-of-town ring road, and is reached by a turning off Oriel Rd.

Follow signs to return to the airport, 5 miles south of Antrim. Or to return to Larne, take A6 to Templepatrick, where pick up main Larne road (A5/A57/A8).

Tyrone

1 day/90 miles (145km)/from Omagh

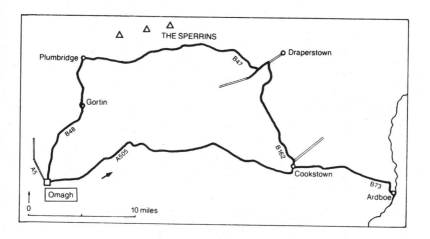

County Tyrone is largely taken up with bogs and hilly moorland. The rustic English spoken by its 'planted' (i.e. Protestant) population has proved of great interest to scholars, as it preserves many Elizabethan idioms unchanged. However Tyrone, like neighbouring Fermanagh, does not have a distinct preponderance of Protestants in the population, the denominations being more evenly matched, and the 'Irishness' of the county and its people more pronounced than in most of Northern Ireland. For example, the farmhouses and country cottages follow the long, single-storey style more familiar south of the border. The whole county is scattered with impressive remnants of prehistoric habitation.

OMAGH pop: 14,600 Industrial and market town in attractive location on rivers Drumagh and Camowen where they meet to form the Strule. 19C 'Victorian Gothic' Catholic cathedral, with two unequal spires, dominates skyline. Adjacent to it is a Classical courthouse (1820), now heavily guarded. **Tourist Office** in High St.

About 5 miles north of town on A5 (not part of our route) are Mellon House (former farmhouse, birthplace of Thomas Mellon, who emigrated to America, became a judge and founded a huge business empire) and the Ulster American Folk Park (permanent exhibition illustrating the remarkably strong 19C links between Ulster and USA).

Take the main Cookstown road (A505) out of Omagh. On both sides rise hills of heath and bog. To the right, after Creggan, a signpost points the way uphill to a court tomb (chambered megalithic grave). A far more striking site lies to the left of the road a little farther along: **Beaghmore** (signposted)—a remarkable group of seven stone circles, twelve cairns, and a number of other stone monuments which together once formed an important ceremonial area. Long preserved under a blanket of peat bog,

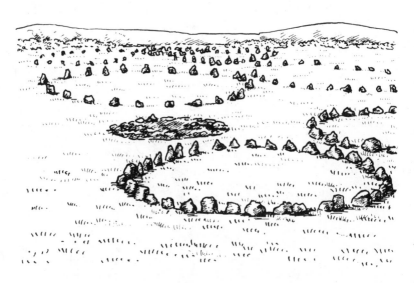

The stone circles at Beaghmore

these survivals of Bronze Age culture were uncovered in the 1940s, and are among the best of many such archaeological finds in the bogs. It is believed that more await discovery at Beaghmore.

Continue along A505. **Wellbrook Beetling Mill** (National Trust; signposted), just off the road, is an impressive water-powered 18C beetling plant in full working order. This part of County Tyrone was noted for linen manufacture, and part of the preparation of the finished cloth was beetling, a deafening process of hammering the linen to give it a smooth texture. Just beyond Wellbrook, Drum Manor Forest Park is a recreation area of wooded grounds (with butterfly reserve) around remains of a mansion.

A couple of miles farther, the road reaches **COOKSTOWN** (pop: 7,600), local commercial centre for a dairy-farming district. The town consists, curiously, of almost nothing but a single straight main street over 1¼ miles long and 130ft wide. Its principal landmark is the conspicuous 19C Catholic church, about half-way along.

A worthwhile excursion from Cookstown is to the shore of Lough Neagh, 10 miles east. Take B73, which runs all the way to Newport Trench, on the shore of the lake. Covering 153 square miles, **Lough Neagh** is by far the largest lake in the British Isles, and looks more like a sea than a lake. It contains great quantities of fish, especially eels. Its waters are also noted for a certain 'petrifying' quality: objects placed in the water quickly become hardened with mineral deposits. The shores of the lake are mostly low and marshy, and provide a perfect breeding ground for all sorts of annoying insects, including some which are found nowhere else. A few yards south of Newport Trench along an access road (signposted) **Ardboe High Cross** stands on the lake edge. This 10C Celtic cross, part of the remains of a 6C monastic community, is exceptionally tall—over 18ft—and (though the upper section is damaged) is richly carved with Biblical scenes, with Old Testament on one side and New Testament on the other.

Return to Cookstown and take minor B182 (direction Lissan), a picturesque little road which runs below Slieve Gallion, an attractive hill area with some good walks. Where the road meets B47 (with Draperstown signposted to the right), turn left towards Plumbridge (for Draperstown see p. 144). B47 veers sharply right (signposted 'Scenic route via Glenelly Valley'), but an amusing deviation is to continue straight ahead in search of the signposted **SIX TOWNS**. It turns out that there is nothing, not even a hamlet, at the place called Six Towns. There is however a single house, with a tiny extension on which is written 'Six Towns post office', and a phone box. It is possible to regain our route by turning right shortly after this house, but it might prove simpler to return to B47.

This runs through the open moorland of the Sperrin hills, passing close to Sawel Mountain (680ft), highest peak in the almost deserted landscape. For several miles this delightful road follows the picturesque valley of the small Glenelly river. It passes Goles Forest (marked footpaths), and the Sperrin Heritage Centre (refreshments and information). At rustic **CRANAGH** hamlet, there is petrol and a post office.

B47 at length descends into the village of **PLUMBRIDGE**, where turn left onto B48 (direction Gortin). Do not be tempted by the signs leading straight through Plumbridge to 'President Wilson's House'—they give the impression that this home of President Woodrow Wilson's grandfather is just around the corner; in fact it is 10 miles away. **GORTIN** (pronounced Gorshun) has the wide main street and neat appearance of a Plantation village. Go straight over its crossroads (staying on B48; direction Omagh), after which the road follows a beautiful steep-sided and wooded valley, part of the Gortin Glen Forest Park. The entrance signposted Forest Park, on left, goes into an extensive recreation area with marked footpaths and drives. A 'History Park' is also under construction here.

Stay on B48 for the return into Omagh.

Donegal

3 days/210 miles (330km)/ from Donegal

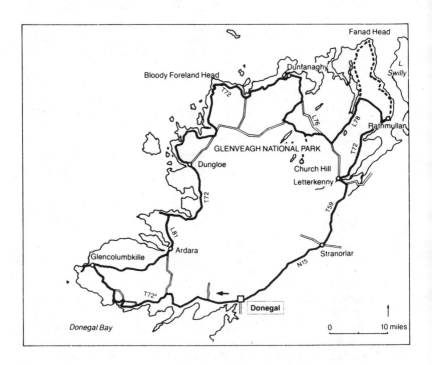

The whole of County Donegal is cut into peninsulas by a coastline deeply indented with rocky fjord-like bays. Inland, unspoiled green glens and cool clean rivers score through magificent uncultivated hill ranges. Much of it inaccessible, almost uninhabited, this is one of the loveliest regions in the country.

County Donegal has an unusual position. The most northerly county in Ireland, it is very much part of Ulster not only geographically but in culture, tradition, and history. Yet it is not part of Northern Ireland. At the time of the partition the majority of its population were anti-Unionist and were relieved to find themselves part of the Republic. Indeed, today Donegal is one of the most 'Irish' parts of Ireland, profoundly rural, with large Gaelic-speaking areas. This distant corner feels equally remote from Belfast and from Dublin, and close only to the wind and waves of the Atlantic Ocean.

DONEGAL (pop: 1,800) is a small, bright, unpretentious provincial town, attractively located on a bend in the river Eske where it reaches Donegal Bay. It has a picturesque little harbour on the Eske estuary. As with many Ulster towns its main 'square' is called The Diamond—but in this case the Diamond is a triangle. On all three sides are shops selling excellent thick sweaters, traditional homespun cloth and Donegal tweed, all of the highest quality and a good deal cheaper than they would be anywhere else.

Donegal's Irish name is *Dún na nGall*, Fort of the Foreigners. The foreigners in question were the Vikings who raided this coast mercilessly and eventually established a stronghold here. During the 1,000 years (6C–16C) that north-west Ireland was disputed between the ó Neills and the ó Donnells (themselves originally an ó Neill branch called Cenel Conaill), the town became the capital of the powerful ó Donnell clan, whose territories (called Tyrconnel) eventually covered a large part of Ulster.

In the centre of the Diamond is a monument to The Four Masters, as they are always known: four historian friars who researched and wrote (1632–6) a complete history of the Irish from legendary times right up to their own day. Known as *The Annals of the Four Masters*, this gives considerable insight into the Celtic world before the English takeover. The Masters were Franciscan friars, whose monastery, locally called Donegal Abbey, stands now as a group of handsome ruins by the Eske estuary. It was founded by the ó Donnells in 1474, destroyed (accidentally) in Anglo-Irish fighting 1601.

With the 17C English conquest and confiscations, Donegal became the property of Sir Basil Brooke, who built the Diamond and rebuilt the town centre around it. He took up residence in the small 15–16C ó Donnell castle, which can be seen adjacent to the Diamond. The last ó Donnel had partly destroyed the building before leaving for Europe in the Flight of The Earls (1607), so Sir Basil had it entirely restructured as a fortified Jacobean house. A very appealing and interesting little 'domestic fortress', it is currently being restored.

There are two good middle-range hotels on the Diamond, the **Hyland Central** (073–21027) and the **Abbey** (073–21014). Out of town on an offshore island reached by causeway, there's a superb, luxurious little hotel-restaurant, **St Ernan's House** (073–21065).

From the town centre take T72/N56 to **MOUNTCHARLES**, a village high on a hill with good views of Donegal Bay. Stay on this road as it gently follows the coastline. **DUNKINEELY** is a plain and simple village with a small ruined castle visible. Continuing west, the scenery is attractive and wild, with gorse-covered hills interspersed with woods, many little rivers and streams, and frequent glimpses of the sea. At **BRUCKLESS**, what looks like a Round Tower in the churchyard is actually a 19C belfry. At a junction, continue along coast road T72^A (direction Killybegs) while T72/N56 heads away to the right (to Ardara/Ard An Ratha). The road descends into **KILLYBEGS**, which has a delightful waterside location; it is a large village seriously devoted to fishing, with trawlers in the harbour and a dockside fish-processing plant. It is known too for good quality carpet weaving. After Killybegs this quiet road climbs again, with sheep on one side and marvellous views of Donegal Bay on the other.

At a roadsign where the right turn would be to Kilcar 6km, take instead the left fork towards Muckross Head. Follow this superb back road which rises above the shore. It returns towards the larger road at Kilcar (Cill Charthaigh), where again choose the back road on the left (direction An Charraig/Carrick). This edges between wild sea cliffs and bleak inland summits. The hillsides are dotted with white sheep and tiny hamlets of white cottages. Throughout western Donegal, on these small traditional dwellings the thatch roof is netted and pegged down with ropes (*sugans*) to stop it being blown off.

The road has now entered a Gaeltacht region, and will remain in it for much of the rest of this route. The first officially Irish-speaking village we reach is **AN CHARRAIG (Carrick)**. If you feel like some exercise, this makes a good starting point for a walk to the top of Slieve League, from which multi-coloured cliffs descend in a sheer drop of nearly 2,000ft. Rejoin T72^A at An Charraig, turning left and crossing a bleaker countryside of peat bogs to **GLEANN CHOLM CILLE (Glencholmcill, Glencolumbkille)**, or, to translate, Columba's Glen, which sounds altogether prettier. This small, sparse village rests beside a beautiful stretch of coast, where waves of the open Atlantic beat against a rocky shore. A narrow climbing road heads round Glen Bay towards Malin More, with some good sea views along the way. St Columba and some of his disciples are thought to have spent time near Glencolumbkille. Every year on 9 June the local people make a procession called *An Turas*, The Journey. It takes them about 2 miles through the surrounding country to pause at 15 ancient cairns and crosses and relics which are called the Stations of the Cross. The House of St Columba, north of the village above the sheer cliffs of Glen Head, is a small hillside oratory. Inside, St Colmcille's Bed and Chair are stone constructions; nearby is St Colmcille's Well. Altogether, more than 40 prehistoric relics have been identified around the village. The Folk Village is an unusual and interesting museum, with real cottages furnished and equipped to represent daily life at different stages during 300 years of Irish history.

A road, with a few sheep on it and fewer cars, crosses a bare headland of rock and peat to reach **ARD AN RATHA (Ardara)** (pronounced Ard-a-ráh), an old-fashioned village with some tourists. It produces top quality cottage-industry tweed and woollens. Some residents will show visitors how they make the cloth on hand looms. The **Nesbit Arms** is a good spot for a meal or snack. Take L81/R261 (direction Naran/Narin). After Ardara the countryside is green and rocky, with rough little fields and gorse and the sea within view. **NARAN (Narin)** is a lovely spot, and its beach forms a broad sandy causeway (covered at high tide) out to an island on which are two ruined churches in an enclosure, but the 'fishing village' itself is now litttle more than a collection of holiday cottages and chalets. Its neighbour **PORTNOO**, just as attractively situated, and with a minia-ture harbour, has more character. Take the road signposted to Maas, through which continue onto T72/N56 towards An Clochan Liath/ Dungloe. Cross the tidal estuary of the Owenwee river which empties into Gweebarra Bay. **AN CLOCHAN LIATH (Dungloe, Dunglow)** (all the same place) is a pleasing little coastal town; it has no beach but there are useful places here to find refreshments.

Carefully follow signs to Ailt an Chorráin (or Burtonport); the road is numbered R259 or T72 but no longer N56 (do not yet follow sign to Croithli/Crolly, unless you want to cut off this part of the coast drive). This atmospheric coastal road makes its way round **The Rosses**, a large, flattish, wild and windy rock-strewn gorse-covered heathland of pools and water channels. Pass Ailt an Chorráin (or Burtonport) which lies to the left of the road. Follow signs to Croiscli (or Croithli or Crolly or Croichshlí—all one place, pronounced approximately as Crolly), where pick up—briefly—L130/N56. Turn left on R357/T72 (direction initially An Bunbeagh or Bunbeg) across the **Gweedore Peninsula** out to **Bloody Foreland Head**. This gets its splendid name not from some great battle, as one might almost expect in this part of the world, but from the redness of the rock at this headland in the evening light. The Gweedore is very similar to The Rosses, though seemingly more densely inhabited.

Continue through An Fál Carrach (Falcarragh), after which the coun-tryside becomes lusher, to **DUN FIONNACHAID (Dunfanaghy)**. This village on a huge sandy river estuary, part of Sheep Haven, has three hotels. One of them, the middle-range **Carrig Rua** (074–36133), is well placed on the very edge of the tidal estuary; it has a convivial bar, comfortable rooms, and is a popular spot for hearty unpretentious good food. There's 18-hole golf next to the hotel. *Carrig rua* means 'red rock', Just across the road is another good family-run hotel, well-equipped, welcoming and popular, **Arnolds Hotel** (074–36208). West of the village, the strange 'McSwyne's Gun' (i.e. MacSweeney, see Doe Castle below) is a natural hole into which flood tides descend with a sudden explosive roar—hence the name. Stay on T72/N56 to Creeslough, via **Ards Forest Park** (on left). A mile or so left of the road is the lofty surviving keep and defensive perimeter wall of **Doe Castle**, 15C stronghold of the gallowglass MacSweeneys. It was much fought over in the following centuries, eventually coming into the hands of the English. One noted inhabitant was an 18C general, George Vaughan Harte: returning here from cam-paigns in India, he brought with him a loyal Indian servant who continued to wear Indian dress and reputedly used to sleep outside the general's door

Glenveagh Castle

every night to protect him from the hostile Irish. The castle was still inhabited until the end of the last century. At Creeslough turn right onto a minor road where you see a sign to Glenveagh National Park. Follow signs through bog land to the Park entrance.

Glenveagh National Park is almost 24,000 acres of protected wilderness within the deep valley of the river Beath (or Veagh) where it forms a long narrow lake. Mountains thickly cloaked with brush and heath and woodland of oak and birch rise steeply away from the valley.

Surprisingly, in the midst of the park is a 'Castle', in fact an extraordinarily extravagant 19C mansion unsuccessfully imitating a medieval fortress. It is, at the same time, a luxurious residence, overlooking the grandeur of the glen and the cool, steel-blue water of Lough Beagh. Behind the house are pleasing, unusual gardens including a fascinating old-fashioned vegetable garden. (Free minibus service from Park entrance to castle.)

Beyond the Castle, bridle tracks and footpaths give access to the remoter glen and woodland where red deer and falcon may be sighted. The scenery is magnificent, unspoiled, and uncrowded (visitors in any case tend to remain close to the Castle).

The biggest danger to the park, wardens told me, is the rhododendron. A constant battle is fought to contain the spread of this foreign invader which kills every other plant, is poisonous to animals, and has already taken over hundreds of acres of Park territory. A task force of volunteers is employed to keep it under control.

The whole Glenveagh estate was originally brought together by John George Adair, gentleman farmer and land speculator, who bought Glenveagh in the Encumbered Estates Court (where the property of bankrupt landlords was sold towards paying off their debts) in 1857. Although he had as a younger man been a keen advocate of tenants' rights, Adair seemed to have abandoned all those principles by this time. He was a harsh landlord who employed harsher agents to deal with the many tenants who were trying to make a bare living from the Glenveagh lands. These occupants of the estate were, in the usual Irish practice of that period, tenants-at-will (i.e. they had no right to remain on the land, no rent control, and all improvements which they made to their property became the property of the landlord). After a dispute between tenants and Adair about sheep stealing (it was later discovered that Adair's own agent was responsible), Adair evicted every man, woman, and child living on the Glenveagh estates and had their dwellings destroyed. He then had Glenveagh Castle built, but on its completion went to live in America with his American wife. He bought a majority share in a Texas ranch and died in Texas in 1885. Strangely enough, after his death, Mrs Adair came to live at Glenveagh Castle, created the gardens, and gave lavish house parties. It subsequently was bought and sold on the open market before coming into the possession of the American millionaire Henry P. McIlhenny who presented the whole Glenveagh estate to the nation.

National Park open Easter and end May to end Sept. Car park. Restaurant. Morning coffee/Afternoon tea at Castle. 3hr guided walks (Tues and Thurs) if required. A Visitor Centre at the entrance has a permanent exhibition on the local peasant history and economy, and explaining how climate past and present has created the Glenveagh landscape.

Just outside the Park area and administered as part of it (but approached separately via Church Hill on R251/L82; 6 miles from Park entrance) is the **Glebe Gallery**, a startlingly good collection of paintings mostly by the French Impressionists and some by Jack B. Yeats. These are displayed in a fine Regency-style house. The house and collection were presented to the nation by owner Derek Hill, whose own paintings are also on view. Glebe Gallery stands on the shore of Lough Gartan, an area strongly associated with St Columba. He was born in a house close to the Gallery; a stone in the National Park marks the spot. Columba or Colmcille was born in 521 of noble parents but decided upon a religious life. Despite this vocation he was a hot-tempered and violent man who at one stage in his eventful life went to war to defend his right to copy another monk's work secretly, and was exiled from Ireland as a result. He took up residence on the Scottish island of Iona, where he founded a monastery and seems to have become genuinely penitent.

From the Park gates, turn right along R251/L82 (direction Cill Mhic Neanainn/Kilmacrenan); at a junction join R255/L77 to continue towards Kilmacrenan. This is bleak, open bog land. Where this back road meets large L76/N56, turn right (direction Letterkenny). **CILL MHIC NEANAINN (Kilmacrenan)** is a modest crossroads village; turn left here, and immediately left again, following signs to Milford and Kerrykeel.

The road from Kilmacrenan to Milford is a delightful, leafy country lane, startlingly green and fertile after the bog. It looks onto Lough Fern on the right. **BAILE NA NGALLÓGLACH (Milford, Millford)** is a sprawling place, more town than village. Take the road signposted Kerrykeel, along another attractive lane with views of Mulroy Bay on the left. This picturesque inlet, open to the sea only along narrow, twisting channels, looks more like a lake with islands. We have now come onto the **Fanad Peninsula** region.

KERRYKEEL (or Carrowkeel or An Cheathrú Chaol), though something of a holiday centre, is a very small village. Here a left turn goes up to **Fanad Head**, a rewarding drive to a panoramic headland; from Fanad Head turn south again along the shore of Lough Swilly (another long sea inlet) towards Rathmullan. Alternatively, carry straight on at Kerrykeel,

Rathmullan village

cutting straight across the peninsula to Rathmullan. We have now left the areas in which the Irish language is likely to be heard.

RATHMULLAN (or Rathmullen) village is an exquisite little place on green fields of pasture beside the water of Lough Swilly. Its 'Priory', founded 1516 by Owen MacSweeney for the Carmelites, is now just a small, uncared-for ivy-covered ruin, though beautifully situated. In 1587 English forces, under orders to take hostages, moored off Rathmullan posing as wine-merchants. They took captive 15-year-old Red Hugh ó Donnell, heir to leadership of the ó Donnell clan. He was imprisoned in Dublin Castle but managed to escape. The experience encouraged him later to abandon the ancient rivalry between the two leading Ulster families, the ó Donnells and the ó Neills, united the clans in a fierce struggle against the English invaders. Their fight was, of course, unsuccessful; Red Hugh fled to Spain, and in 1607, ó Neill set sail for France from Rathmullan with about 100 members of the ó Donnell and ó Neill nobility, abandoning their lands to the English Plantation of Ulster. This hopeless exodus, an irrevocable turning point for Irish culture in Ireland, became known as The Flight of the Earls. (There's now a Flight of the Earls Interpretation Centre in the village).

Just north of the village, standing in splendid grounds beside the beach of Lough Swilly, graceful comfortable rambling 18C **Rathmullan House** (074–58188) is an excellent country house hotel. It's a member of the Relais et Châteaux federation and has been a winner of the National Garden Award. Proprietors Bob and Robin Wheeler are friendly and likeable. Excellent food served in pleasant dining room.

Take the waterside road south along the lough to **RAMELTON** (or Rathmelton). Cross the old stone bridge into the small, handsome Plantation town. Francis Makemie (1658–1708), founder of the American

Presbyterian church, was born in Ramelton and preached here before emigrating. Built on a hillside rising from a river which runs into the lough, it has a little harbour with some fine old warehouses. A number of Georgian houses also survive, and there is a ruined 17C church with an unusual east window. Continue south towards Letterkenny on R245/T72, which travels inland away from the lough.

Industrial, unappealing **LETTERKENNY** (Leitir Ceanainn) (pop: 6,450) sprawls along a single long main street which rises steadily up a hillside (Gaelic *leitir*, hillside). It has an imposing late-19C cathedral, and beneath their bland renderings many of the town's houses are solid old stone dwellings. **Tourist Office** on Derry Road. [Letterkenny would make a good base for a look round the superb landscapes of the **Inishowen Peninsula**, perhaps up as far as Malin Head, most northerly point in Ireland, which is mentioned almost daily on the BBC shipping forecast and 'weather reports from coastal stations'.]

Take N13 (direction Lifford) out of Letterkenny, crossing the river Swilly, and turning right onto N56/T59 (direction Donegal). After about another 8 miles, at a T-junction in Kilross, follow the Donegal road round to the right. Continue into **STRANORLAR**, which has merged with neighbouring **BALLYBOFEY** to form a single unassuming workaday town (pop: 3,000). They stand one each side of the river Finn. Join N15 (direction Donegal) here. Beyond Ballybofey, this main road enters higher and more barren, but still attrractive country, before passing through the Barnesmore Gap, a high, bleak, long valley, and descending into Donegal.

Lakeland

2 days/110 miles (180km)/from Enniskillen

Ireland's lake district is inexpressibly beautiful; broad cool landscapes of hill and water. Its scenery seems to possess a secret, virginal freshness. Opaque grey-blue expanses of lake are enclosed by unadorned, unfarmed slopes, while overhead big airy skies filled with cloud in movement express the same mood. Amazingly few people visit the region so it has not been at all debased by the crowds and commerce of tourism. So far only keen fishermen have discovered it, and they come to help themselves from an apparently inexhaustible supply in the perfect clean unpolluted waters of thousands of square miles of lakes and rivers.

This route wanders over the border between Northern Ireland and the Republic. This does not entail any difficulty or formalities, although of course some sort of identification must be carried.

ENNISKILLEN (or Inniskillen, etc.—various spellings; pop: 10,500), county town of Fermanagh, has the most extraordinary location, very pleasing because of all the water: it stands right on the edge of Lower Lough Erne, with the old town centre on an island in the river Erne which

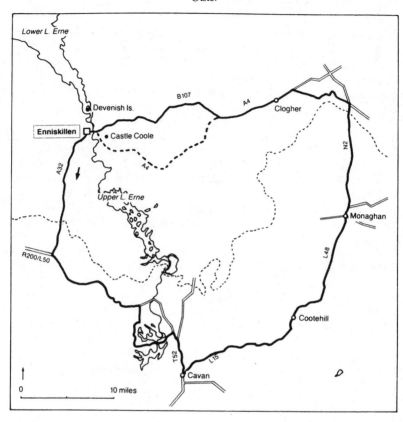

connects the Lower Lough to the Upper. A single main street extends from the East Bridge to the West Bridge, changing its name as it proceeds (E. Bridge St, Town Hall St, etc.). The towers of a sturdy little Town Hall of 1900, and the Cathedral and church spires, are principal landmarks. The centre is all a Control Zone so to explore the town it is best to park in one of the many well-signposted car parks.

Now staunchly Protestant, though in a largely Catholic region, Enniskillen was originally a fortress of the Maguire clan. After the Flight of the Earls (1607) it was confiscated and given to a Sir William Cole, whose family have since borne the title Earl of Enniskillen. Two noted British regiments, the Inniskilling Dragoons and the Royal Inniskilling Fusiliers, take their name from this loyal town.

The War Memorial (by the E. Bridge), scene of a notorious IRA explosion on Remembrance Sunday, 1987, appears little damaged by the incident. It is perhaps worth pointing out that, despite this exception, provincial Enniskillen is not troubled by violent factionalism, and has a peaceful, friendly, quietly busy air. There are several attractive public houses along the main street as it goes from E. Bridge into the heart of the old centre, which lies in a slight hollow and is indeed called the Hollow.

One of the nicest of the bars in this part is called by the name of proprietor, William Blake—no relation to the poet. Mercifully, no attempt has been made to modernise 'Blake's of the Hollow' as it is known, which dates from 1887. The street rises to the Protestant Cathedral of St Macartan (1840, but with tower of 1637). Inside, set into the west wall, is a flagstone called the Pokrich Stone which used to lie in the graveyard; it is a tombstone of 1628, with the inscription half one way up and half the other!

Over the road is the Catholic church. After this point the main street leaves the commercial centre of town and descends to the West Bridge. A turning to Castle Bridge leads to handsome remains of a waterside castle, now consisting only of two round towers of a fine water-gate (16C) and parts of the keep (15C), and containing a military museum. Beyond the West Bridge is Portora Royal School, a public school where both Oscar Wilde and Samuel Beckett were pupils. A **Tourist Office**, called the Fermanagh Lakeland Visitor Centre (signposted), is on the town centre's big by-pass road.

Just outside Enniskillen to the south (on A4, direction Belfast) is **Castle Coole** (National Trust), the late-18C mansion built for the Earl of Belmore by James Wyatt. It stands grandly at the end of a long drive in impressive grounds. Structural problems have led to the house having to be almost rebuilt, which caused controversy at the time of its reopening in 1988; some say the works have only improved the effect of the sumptuous interior while others are less impressed. Among the 'anti's' are the present (8th) Earl and Countess of Belmore themselves, who moved out of the house in disgust after its alteration. The problems, according to the National Trust, are due to some confusion over what the building ought to look like: the 1st Earl of Belmont had the house built and decorated in an elegant neo-Classical style, while the 2nd Earl moved towards a heavy and rich Regency appearance. The original elaborate plasterwork and furnishings from both periods have been restored to the house. Go and see for yourself whether the restoration has been a success.

An exceptional place to stay in the Enniskillen area is **Jamestown**

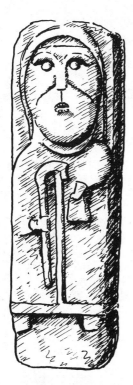

White Island figure

House (036581–209), about 7 miles north from town just past Ballinamallard on B46. This elegant country house is a private home with 140 tranquil acres of woods and pasture and 1½ miles of river. A few paying guests are accommodated in comfortable rooms. Food is of a high standard, using fresh local ingredients, served generously, and drinks are charged only at off-licence prices.

Lower Lough Erne, a lovely spread of dark water and little islands extending away north and north east of Enniskillen, can be explored by rented cruiser (available from Enniskillen) or can be circled by road. The best views are from the west side (A46). With so many islands, and lakeside woods and fields, there are constant variations of scene. An important site in the lake, definitely worth the trip, is **Devenish Island** (or simply Devenish, since the word means Ox Island), reached by a small ferry from a jetty on the east side of the lake about 3 miles from town on A32 (Omagh road). The ferry runs in summer only, although off-season a boat can be provided 'with 2 days notice'. On the island are clustered together the evocative waterside ruins of a 6C monastery, an unusual Celtic High Cross, and a perfectly intact Round Tower over 80ft high. Up in the north of the lake, joined to the 'mainland' by causeways, **Boa Island** has a weird double-faced pre-Christian stone idol, and at **White Island**, close inshore on the lake's eastern side, several odd and slightly eerie stone figures stand in a row against the interior wall of a 12C church.

Leave Enniskillen on A4 (direction Sligo), forking left after 3 miles onto A32 (direction Swanlinbar). The hilly farmland along this road gives way to a countryside which is hillier, rougher, more wooded, less farmed. Away to the left is the convoluted shoreline of island-filled Upper Lough Erne. Dervla Murphy cycled through all this country and wrote 'I have fallen in love with Fermanagh—especially the rough border stretches, all mountains and moors and wide silent lakes.' Right of the road after 4 miles, **Florence Court** (National Trust; signposted together with Marble Arch Caves) is the extensive estate, gardens and fine 18C house originally belonging to Lord Mountflorence. **Marble Arch Caves**, another 2 miles farther away from the main road, are a system of passageways and caves formed by an underground stream (guided visits in summer).

A32 continues south to the border, where on the day we came this way an Irish soldier was chatting and laughing with an English soldier, and the two of them just waved us on without a glance. Straight away the inferior roads and signposting of the Republic become apparent, but also the more rustic and simpler atmosphere. Follow signs to Cavan; note that at **SWANLINBAR**, just across the border, the roadsign gives the road number as T53 or L50 but the maps give this road as T53 or R202, with L50 passing east-west through Derrynacreeve, about 3 miles away (but not signposted). Pass through Derrynacreeve, and **BALLYCONNELL**, a small town with a pretty 17C church. After tiny **DRUMASLADDY** turn right on a road signposted Drumlane Abbey 2½ miles and Killeshandra

12km (T52 or R201). Along here the country becomes greener again and less hilly.

At **MILLTOWN,** another tiny village, there is a junction where the road bends, and a track leads half a mile to 12C ruins of **Drumlane Church** (signposted), which are in fact remnants of an Augustinian Friary and part of a Round Tower. Follow direction Killeshandra along a winding road; at a fork, take a very minor road on left signposted Butler's Bridge. At first this little back lane has grass growing in the middle, but improves slightly, though it remains severely pot-holed as it makes its way across the extraordinarily chaotic inlets and indentations of the meandering river Erne. Cross Urney Bridge, a high-sided narrow stone bridge. At the middle-of-nowhere junction immediately afterwards, bear right (while the left goes to Baker's Bridge). Arriving at a main road (N3), turn right (signposted Butler's Bridge and Cavan). At Butler's Bridge, stay on N3 (bears right; direction Cavan).

CAVAN (pop: 3,250), county town of Cavan, is dominated by the tall spire of its odd-looking new church. Originally an ó Reilly stronghold with a castle, little of note has survived the fierce 17C battles for control of the town. It is not really necessary to go into the centre of Cavan at all since our route continues on R188/L15, which leaves town on the north side (direction Cootehill). The road emerges from Cavan's housing estates into an attractive landscape of drumlins with fields, pasture and copses.

COOTEHILL is a small agricultural Plantation town, its wide main street half-blocked by double-parked tractors. It is an agreeable, bustling little place, with one or two interesting (if not terribly old) buildings, for example the (CI) All Saints' Church which stands proudly at one end of the main street, and the Allied Irish Bank building next door. The town takes its name from the Coote family who owned all this land. Note that Monaghan is not signposted in Cootehill other than as 'Monaghan Customs Post L45' on a sign at the junction with L15 by Connolly Bros bar (in the wall of which, incidentally, is set a tiny post box, with the initials VR for Queen Victoria but now of course painted green—a pretty symbol of Irish independence).

Take this road, which simply becomes the main road to Monaghan. It circles the walls of Bellamont Forest, also part of the estate of the Coote family. The road rises towards, and passes, an immensely tall and incongruous column erected 1807 on the death of local MP Richard Dawson.

ROCKCORRY (or Buidheachair) is a pleasant village with an interesting and unusual little church. One notices that in this part of the country many of the older houses are made of dark unfaced stone.

The tall church spire in **MONAGHAN** is visible for some time before one arrives at this likeable county town (pop: 6,300). A former stronghold of the local ruling MacMahon clan, little survives from before the 17C takeover of the town by the English. Beside the central crossroads is the handsome neo-Classical courthouse (1829) of pale dressed stone. An interesting contrast is the old Market House (houses **tourist office** mid-

May to mid-Sept.), a neat little Classical-style grey stone building (1791). Behind it are other solid grey stone 18C buildings, one of which, the impressive former Council Office, now contains the Monaghan County Museum. Among items displayed in the museum is the skilfully decorated bronze Cross of Clogher dating from 1400 (our route carries on to Clogher from here). Seven miles south east of Monaghan on N2 is the village of Clontibret which in August 1986 was invaded by a violent mob of Northern Ireland Loyalists. However, our direction is northwards (leave town on N12, direction Armagh; turn left onto N2 outside town, direction Aughnacloy).

Travel through green drumlins, crossing the border at **AUGHNA-CLOY**. Here we have wandered into County Tyrone temporarily. This was clearly once rather a fine-looking village, with many interesting 18C shops and houses, but now seems neglected, almost abandoned. However, twice a month (1st and 3rd Weds) there's a big street market along its wide main street, which rises across a ridge with good views of distant Slieve Beagh (1225ft). Leave the village on A5, but soon turn left onto A28, and continue to the crossroads village **AUGHER**. An early Plantation castle **Spur Royal**, built here in 1615 on the site of a previous fortress, has been restored as a comfortable modern private house which takes paying guests (06625–48589). This area has seen many discoveries and successful excavations of cairns etc.; an example is the chambered cairn or passage-grave at Knockmany (signposted, 3 miles north, past Spur Royal), where, however, stones with early-Bronze Age carving have been badly defaced by somewhat more modern carving in the form of people's initials. At Augher, signs point south of the main road to MacCartan's Church and Carleton's Cottage. These both may be of interest to readers and admirers of the Irish peasant writer William Carleton (1794–1869); the simple white thatched cottage where he grew up as one of a family of 16 is now preserved and makes an interesting visit; small St MacCartan's church is where his long-suffering parents are buried. If you turn off the main road to see these places, it is possible to continue on back lanes to Clogher. Otherwise stay on A4.

The simple village of **CLOGHER** climbs a steep hill at the summit of which, confusingly, is St MacCartan's Cathedral. The MacCartan so celebrated hereabouts was a disciple of Patrick, and was made a bishop, with Clogher as his seat, as long ago as 5C. The Cathedral, rebuilt 9C and 18C, much restored 19C and 20C, shows little sign of its long history apart from two damaged 9C High Crosses in the churchyard. A signpost points the way to the chambered cairn at Knockmany (see above). From Augher and Clogher stay on A4 as it travels through pleasant green drumlin country, with lofty Slieve Beagh on the left.

At Five Mile Town turn right at a confusing junction onto B107 (direction Tempo), and follow signs first to Tempo and then to Enniskillen. Or one could instead continue on A4, perhaps taking in Castle Coole (see p. 157) before arriving at Enniskillen. For much of the way from Five Mile Town to Enniskillen the country is a dense mass of drumlins.

Armagh and Down
1–3 days/100 miles (160km)/from Newtownards to Newry

Counties Down and Armagh, lying broadly south of Belfast, consist mainly of a well-tamed countryside of farms, market gardens and orchards, and lightly industrial small towns with an English look about them and a largely Protestant population. Much of the area is frankly not very interesting for touring, and indeed this route barely touches upon County Armagh at all for that reason. But the Ards Peninsula and, even more so, the Mourne Mountains do make an excellent rural tour. The Mournes in particular deserve something more than just a quick look. They would make a satisfying area for a long, leisurely stay.

Both the Ards Peninsula and the Mourne Mountains are within easy reach of Belfast (or Belfast Airport). For anyone wanting to make this a circular tour from Belfast, the starting point Newtownards is only 10 miles from the city, while from Newry it is under 40 miles on the main highway A1 back into Belfast.

NEWTOWNARDS (pronounced Newton'ards) pop: 20,500 Unappealing industrial town, which grew up around a Dominican priory founded 1244 by Walter de Burgh. Ruins of priory church in Court Sq., off Castle St. See also: octagonal 'Old Cross' market tower (junction of Castle St and High St); fine 18C Town Hall overlooking large marketplace (Conway Sq.; Saturday market). Conspicuous out-of-town landmark is the 135ft tower on Scrabo Hill.

Newtownards stands at the head of **Strangford Lough**, a large sea inlet with many islands, which cuts off the narrow **Ards Peninsula** from the rest of the mainland. Leave town on A20 (direction Portaferry), which immediately brings you onto the Peninsula. As the road curves round, staying as close as it can to the edge of the Lough, many curious little islands can be seen which are in fact the tops of submerged drumlins.

After about 4 miles a sign on the right says Mount Stewart, and points across the road into a gateway. Now National Trust property, the house and gardens of **Mount Stewart** used to be the aristocratic family home of the Marquises of Londonderry, including one of the most detested men in Irish history, Lord Castlereagh (1769–1822). Detested, because although he was an exemplary landlord and generous philanthropist, as well as a distinguished diplomat and politician, his most lasting contributions to his native country was the work he put into the Act of Union (1800) which destroyed all traces of Irish autonomy and had disastrous consequences from which people ate still suffering today. The house itself is 18C with later additions, wonderfully grand, and contains many interseting possessions of Castlereagh and other Marquises of Londonderry.

The landscaped gardens are superb; enriched with gorgeous collections of plants and planned views and extravaganzas of topiary, with many odd pieces of stone work representing such improbable creatures as dodos and dinosaurs and duck-billed platypi. Also in the grounds is **The Temple of the Winds** (separate entrance a little farther down the road), an elegant octagonal building of 1780, copied from a more ancient version in Athens. Gardens, house, and temple are open most afternoons from Easter to end Oct.

GREYABBEY, reached soon after, is a simple village on the edge of which (signposted) are the roofless remains of the church of a Cistercian monastery of 1190. It was founded by Affreca, a princess of the Isle of Man, who married John de Courcy, the conqueror of Ulster. The aisleless church contains much handsome stonework (note west doorway), and effigies of a 13C lady and a 14C knight. The ruins, standing beside a more recent parish church, are known locally as 'The Abbey'.

Stone carving at Mount Stewart

162

Follow the road round to **PORTAFERRY**. This is a nice little harbour village standing on the channel where Strangford Lough narrows to join with the sea. The village has a good Aquarium with exhibits of the Lough's underwater wildlife, which includes seal and some huge, long-lived fish. On the quayside—known as The Strand—there is an appealing place to eat, drink, or stay overnight: **The Portaferry Hotel** (02477–28230). From the waterfront a tiny car ferry crosses over to Strangford on the far side of the channel. At both ends of this ancient and strategic ferry crossing there are substantial remnants of old tower house fortifications. Tower houses—tall, grim, defensive fort-like dwellings built on private land or in strategic locations—were a feature of life in this part of Ireland from the Anglo-Norman period right into 17C. From Portaferry there's a good view of one of them: Audley's Castle on a hillock just north of Strangford.

The ferry journey makes a brief but pleasant interlude. It chugs briskly across the swiftly moving water, reaching the other side in just 10 minutes or less; tickets are sold on board without ceremony. Strangford Lough is tidal, and twice a day hundreds of millions of tons of water pour through this bottleneck channel. The original Viking name, *Strang fjord*, refers to the strength or force of the current. Yet the water is not rough. The boat operates every day of the year except Christmas Day, starting at about 7.30 or 8am (9.30 on Sundays) and running every half-hour until about 10.30 or 11pm.

STRANGFORD is a quiet, agreeable fishing village. It has a ruined tower house (16C) overlooking the harbour, and an appealing little main square with the Protestant extremists' Orange Hall on one side and the Roman Catholic church on the other! Take A25 (direction Downpatrick), and after just 2 miles a sign points out a right turn to **Castle Ward** (National Trust), a most peculiar mansion dating from the 1760s. It was built for the first Lord Bangor and his wife. *She* insisted on the neo-Gothic style, *he* on the neo-Classical. The archtect earned his fee by cleverly making the south suit the master and the north suit the mistress. Although for that reason alone the outside rewards a visit, the interior too deserves a look: another insight into the extravagance of Lady Bangor's taste can be gained from a glimpse at the ceiling in her boudoir. And note the Victorian laundry in an outhouse. There is much else to see in the extensive grounds: a cairn, a Palladian temple, a 17C castle, and, on the bank of Strangford Lough, the ruins of **Audley's Castle**, a tower house dating from

Saul church

1500. Castle Ward House is closed except in summer, but the grounds are open all year round.

This district, from Strangford to the other side of Downpatrick, and the whole of this **Lecale Peninsula** which lies south of Strangford Lough, is often known as St Patrick's Country, for it was here that Patrick came some time in mid 5C (generally presumed to be about AD432) on his return to Ireland from France (or Gaul, as it then was) and where he subsequently did most of his preaching. It seems probable that it was in this area too that he lived as a slave in earlier years, before escaping to France.

It is only 5 miles from Castle Ward to Downpatrick on A25, passing through orderly well-kept rolling farmland, but an alternative is the minor road (on left, signposted Saul), which goes into Downpatrick by way of the village of **SAUL**, where Patrick lived in a monastic community which he himself had founded. Traces of a 12C monastery, Round Tower and a 20C Anglican church ('Celtic Revival' style) now stand on the original site. Patrick almost certainly died in the monastery here, but is believed to have been buried on the summit of a hill at nearby Downpatrick.

Despite being the administrative capital of County Down, **DOWNPATRICK** is only a small town (pop: 8,500), and has quite a pleasant character. It has several fine old Georgian houses, some unusual with their rough unfaced stone facades. The busy shopping streets end with views of lovely green gorsey hills. This was always an important place, going back for thousands of years. Originally called Dun (Gaelic, 'fort'), it became associated with Patrick after he had converted the local Celtic chief, Dichu, who gave him the land at Saul on which to build a monastery. The town's centre is the junction of Irish and Market Streets; follow Irish St round into English St, which climbs up to the Cathedral.

Since before 6C, Down has been an important religious centre, with a monastic community on the site of the present cathedral. For some 400 years (8–12C) the settlement was harrassed by constant Danish raids. After John de Courcy's takeover of the region, the Irish monks were ejected and replaced by English, but their buildings were destroyed in 1245—by, one is surprised to learn, an earthquake. Successively rebuilt and re-destroyed (in 1316 and 1538), the present cathedral building was erected in 1790, retaining many parts of earlier structures. In front of the cathedral stands a weatherbeaten 10C High Cross, while in the graveyard there is a tomb-like slab engraved 'Patric' which gives the misleading impression that it marks the site of St Patrick's grave. This is completely spurious—no one knows where Patrick was buried, although somewhere on this hill is considered as a distinct possibility.

For a more serious and factual look at Patrick's life and times, pop into the very interesting and useful Down Museum almost next to the cathedral. As well as prehistoric finds and several items of 'Celtic gold' found in the area, it houses The St Patrick Heritage Centre. The museum's premises, with two gatehouses and two separate buildings surrounded by open courtyard within high walls, reflect their original function as the old County Jail (1790). Clean and neat and restored as it is now, the building has quite a pleasing appearance despite its former use. Among prisoners held here was the 'Society of United Irishmen' activist Thomas Russell, who was hanged not from a gallows but from the prison's main gateway, in 1803. He is buried in the churchyard of the parish church farther down the street, an inscribed stone marking his grave. The church incorporates a 16C tower believed to have been part of John de Courcy's castle on the site. One of the most interesting churches in this religious town is the unusually-shaped Non-Subscribing Presbyterian building in Stream St; built in 1710, its interior has preserved many original features of that date.

Near Downpatrick

Struell Wells (1½ miles; take Ardglass road B1; turn left after hospital; signposted): an intriguing group of ancient healing wells with ruins of 17C bathhouses (the men's still has its roof). Patrick is supposed to have blessed the wells—certainly he would have known about them, as they are very close to Saul where he lived. Even the claim that he blessed them in some way shows that these waters (from an underground stream) had religious significance; a sort of spa, but with connotations of mystery and magic. Even today, Mass is said here on Midsummer night, which would appear to owe little to Christianity.

Inch Abbey (just on northern edge of town off Belfast road A7): ruins of a 12C Cistercian monastery on the site of an earlier monastic building, in an attractive setting overlooking the river Quoile. The name comes from *inis*, an island, and the abbey stands between drumlins which are protected by marsh on one side and the Quoile on the other. The access lane is in effect a causeway.

Take A25 (direction Newcastle, Newry), quite a busy main road but running through attractive green farm country, neat and pretty. At Clough pick up A2 (direction Newcastle—easy to go wrong here). On the approach to **DUNDRUM** there are lovely views over Dundrum Bay, and a ruin can just be seen hidden among trees on a hilltop beside the village. This is **Dundrum Castle**, poised on rock and enclosed by a dry moat carved out of rock. The name of the village—Gaelic 'ridge fort'—suggests that there may have been something like a castle standing here for some considerable time. Although nowadays Dundrum is nothing but a village in what we see as a beautiful location, in past centuries it was evidently perceived as a strategic military site, one of many coastal strongholds necessary for effective control of Ulster. The present ruins are of a castle built by John de Courcy (12C). It was in two parts, the Upper Ward, being the fortress proper, and the Lower Ward, which was a walled and fortified area of outhouses, servants' dwellings, and gardens. It was besieged with varying degrees of success by rivals for local power, including Lord Grey in 1538 who described it as 'One of the strongest holds in

Ireland, and most commodious for defence of the whole country of Lecayle both by sea and land.' Eventually Cromwell (1652) captured and dismantled it, although a fine circular keep survives, along with other curiosities like two latrines which emptied through chutes in the outer wall.

After leaving Dundrum, take right turn B180 towards the Mourne Mountains, rising ahead. Pass through **MAGHERA**, a rustic hamlet (but with a riding centre) to **BRYANSFORD**, where there is one of the entrances into the extensive grounds of Tollymore Forest Park. The Park, formerly the estate of the Earls of Roden, is now a leisure area of pine woods enlivened by several elaborate oddities and follies of Gothic stone work. Three roads go into Bryansford village from three different directions, and all are numbered B180—the sort of signposting more familiar south of the border! Take the one which goes to Newcastle.

NEWCASTLE (pop: 6,250), on the Shimna river, is the holiday resort of the **Mourne Mountains**. A bright, clean, sedate town, it has an attractive seafront and a number of curious examples of modern and early 20C architecture. Beside the town rises the Mourne's highest peak, **Slieve Donard** (2805ft), an easy climb (take footpath from Donard Park south of town). From the top, it has been asserted, the view extends into all four countries of the United Kingdom—but it happened to be exceptionally clear on the day I tried it and I wasn't convinced, although certainly the Scottish coast and the Isle of Man were clearly visible. The view was marvellous.

A2 continues as a glorious coast road, with the rounded heathy summits of the Mournes close by on the right. At **MULLARTOWN** a road on the right is signposted Silent Valley. Take this road inland, into the quiet hills. (If you miss this turn, alternatives follow within minutes.) The narrow unfrequented road runs between distinctive dry-stone walls of rounded boulders. The country seems all but deserted, with yellow grass-covered hills sometimes glistening with a silver lace of trickling water. The Mourne Mountains used to be a self-contained ungovernable area styled by its hardy inhabitants as The Kingdom of Mourne. An important part of their income is supposed to have come from smuggling, the goods being landed at the coves and beaches where, as a popular song puts it, 'the Mountains of Mourne sweep down to the sea'. Most of the Mournes are inaccessible to vehicles, which is as it should be. Though not a large area, it retains the feeling of a separate identity, a separate world. The Silent Valley and its lake (reservoir) are best explored on foot, an excursion which requires proper walking gear and preparation. To continue our route, follow signs to Spelga Dam. At a junction, turn right onto B27, and at a fork stay on B27 (still direction Spelga Dam). All this is through the most beautiful hill country, with high wide views across uplifting scenery, ever changing from pasture to heath to grass-covered slopes. Eventually the road passes the Spelga Lake, from which flows the Bann river which virtually cuts Northern Ireland into two (see p. 142).

Aim now for Rostrevor on the coast: B27 continues towards Hilltown, first reaching a turning on the left (a picturesque minor road which goes direct to Rostrevor) and then, a junction with B180, where follow the road round to the left for **HILLTOWN**, a quiet, unimportant village well-placed at the edge of the mountains. Take either the direct minor road, or at Hilltown turn onto B25, for **ROSTREVOR**, a pleasant village on the coast which marks the end of the most rural part of this route. Attractive wooded Rostrevor Forest rises from the village up the slopes of Slievemartin, on which lies Cloghmore (Gaelic, 'great stone'), an immense 40-ton boulder. It was either dumped here during glacial action or thrown across Carlingford Lough by the giant Finn MacCoul, or both—take your pick.

Turn left at Rostrevor onto A2 (direction Newry), the main coast road which follows the bank of Carlingford Lough, a large sea inlet. In a couple of miles it reaches the head of the Lough at **WARRENPOINT**, an industrial small town with docks along the waterside and good views of wooden hills dropping to the lake edge. Becoming a busy dual carriageway, A2 none the less enjoys beautiful scenery as it runs beside the Newry Canal. On the way it passes **Narrow Water Castle**, a small square castellated tower house in a square walled enclosure.

NEWRY pop: 19,000 Unattractive industrial town on the Armagh-Down county boundary, victim of a certain amount of recent political violence. Much fought over in the past as well, for its strategic location at 'The Gap of the North' between Louth and Ulster. Too much damaged over the centuries to retain a great deal of historical interest. But see: St Patrick's Church (1578), first Protestant church in Ireland, the building which inspired Jonathan Swift's sour comment about Newry, 'High church, low steeple, dirty town, proud people'; other 18C buildings survive, eg. the White Linen Hall, and houses in Upper Water St and Trevor Hill; the Town Hall (1893) which stands on a bridge, exactly half in Armagh and half in Down. A number of influential Irish Nationalists were born in or around Newry, including the lawyer Lord Charles Russell (Lord Chief Justice for England 1894–1900), political writer John Mitchell, and Samuel Nielson, a founder of the Society of United Irishmen.

Short Tour West of Newry

Leave town on the main road A1 (direction Dundalk); at Cloghoge turn off right onto B113 (direction Killevy). Signposted on right is Ballymacdermot Cairn. Head into **KILLEVY**. Just outside the village is the access point for **Slieve Gullion** (1894ft), with steep path and drive climbing through a Forest Park to the top of this wedge of upland which dominates the whole surrounding area. At the summit is a neolithic passage-grave called the House of Calliagh Birra (Gaelic *calliagh*, witch). The mountain traditionally has strong mystical/legendary associations, and features in the ancient Irish saga of Taín Bó Cualnge (The Cattle Raid of Cooley, about an attempt by the King of Connacht's men to seize a sacred bull belonging to the King of Ulster).

Also reached from Killevy village are the Killevy Churches on the

Gullion's north-east slope. These are two small intriguing rectangular stone churches standing with their backs to each other. The one on the west side dates from as long ago as 9C or 10C (note: lintel over doorway), while the other is 13C.

Carry on past the churches to Derrylough, turning right onto A25 (direction Newry). This passes **Derrymore House** (on left; National Trust), the eminently picturesque 18C thatched cottage (somewhat grander than that word usually implies) in which the Act of Union of 1800 was drafted by the owner of the house, Isaac Corry, MP for Newry. A left turn immediately after goes into (usually an army checkpoint here) **BESSBROOK**, which is an excellent example of the 'model villages' built for their workers by some philanthropic early industrialists. In this case the builder was Quaker linen manufacturer J.G. Richardson, who established the village in 1845. With a population today of nearly 3,000, Bessbrook preserves its original appearance with little alteration: tiny terraced stone cottages arranged neatly around tidy rectangular greens. 'The Model Chemist' faces 'The Model Newsagent'. Richardson supplied the village with every convenience imaginable in that period, all except a public house—which it still does not have.

Take A25 back into Newry (3 miles).

[If heading towards Belfast from Newry on A1, the towns of **BANBRIDGE**, **DROMORE**, and **HILLSBOROUGH** (where the Anglo-Irish Agreement was signed in 1985) are all well worth a visit.]

LANDMARKS IN IRISH HISTORY

Ireland's is a long story, at times bewilderingly complicated, but a basic grasp of what has happened in this country, how it got like this, greatly increases one's appreciation of the place, the sights, and the people.

700–600BC—Celtic invasion Celts, militarily powerful and artistically advanced, arrive and impose their culture, art, religion and language on the existing population (who had themselves arrived from Britain thousands of years before).

Celtic society Under the Celts, Ireland is entirely rural, divided into about 100 'kingdoms' (*tuatha*) with local tribal leaders who compete for dominance; also highly influential are druids (magician priests), brehons (professional lawyers) and filidh (story-tellers); Ireland eventually separates into provinces each with a dominant clan leader; the first to claim the kingship of all Ireland (the *ard rí*, or High King) is Niall of the Nine Hostages, AD5C.

AD5C—St Patrick About 432 St Patrick, a Briton who had escaped to France from a period of slavery in Ireland, returns to embark on an evangelical campaign in Ireland to increase the number of Christians; his success has become legendary, although his travels were in reality not very extensive and were concentrated in the area where he had been a slave, around Downpatrick in Ulster.

7–9C—the great monastic period Many monasteries founded; they become the only thing comparable to towns in Ireland, and attract all art, culture, wealth and learning; often ruled by father-to-son abbots; the first towns grow around them; Irish missionaries influential throughout Europe, where they establish important monasteries.

795—Viking raids begin Vikings (or Danes or Norsemen) plunder monasteries causing damage and killing monks; they begin to colonise the coast, acting as traders between the Irish and other nations.

940–1014—Brian Ború Following in family footsteps Brian Ború becomes a local chieftain in Co. Clare; sets out to wage war against Viking colonisation; by 984 he controls all Southern Ireland; 1002 becomes High King; 1014 is killed at Clontarf in a battle which terminates Viking/Norse expansion in Ireland.

1169—(Anglo-)Norman invasion begins Leinster chief Dermot MacMurrough seeks military aid against other Irish chieftains from Normans, who are settling England having conquered it in 1066; in exchange for MacMurrough's allegiance, Henry II allows him a force of Normans (1169); Raymond le Gros comes with a second larger Norman force to aid him further (1170); Richard FitzGilbert de

Clare, Earl of Pembroke ('Strongbow') also agrees to help in exchange for the right to marry MacMurrough's daughter and succeed him as king of Leinster; Strongbow conquers large areas including Dublin (1170) and to prevent him from taking over Ireland on his own account, Henry II stations garrisons in main towns and appoints provincial lords to conquer and rule as his representatives (Ulster remains largely independent).

14–15C—the Geraldines   Norman and Irish nobility become intertwined and Ireland becomes increasingly independent of the English (i.e Anglo-Norman) monarchy; renewal of Irish culture and monasticism, and Irish-speaking Norman earls (the Geraldines) become the dominant class (and are the first to raise the issue of Home Rule).

1534—Tudor invasion begins   Henry VIII despatches forces which regain control of Ireland; he makes local chiefs who promise loyalty into earls; he orders all monasteries to be 'dissolved', i.e. closed down, but this proves difficult to enforce; under Mary Tudor (1553), English settlers 'planted' on confiscated Irish land; under Elizabeth I (1558) attempts made to impose English Protestantism on Ireland meet much hostility (Ulster remains untouched by Tudor invasion).

1594 uprising   English 'planted' population of Munster driven out.

1607—the Flight of the Earls   From 1594 to 1607: the war for Ulster—English versus Ulster clan leaders, notably the long-dominant Hugh ó Neill, Earl of Tyrone, and Red Hugh ó Donnell of Tyrconnell; in 1607 the Ulster Irish nobility, accepting defeat, leave Ulster for Spain and France, permanently abandoning their land; their properties (about one million acres) seized by English Crown.

1609—Plantation of Ulster begins   Former possessions of Ulster earls 'planted' with large numbers of Protestants from England and Scotland.

1642—The Confederation of Kilkenny   1641 Rebellion—organised risings led by ousted Irish nobility against the English Protestant administration in Ulster and Leinster; the rebels capture several towns and soon control most of Ireland, killing many 'planted' Protestants; 1642—The Confederation (an independent ruling parliament of Irish nobility) established at Kilkenny; meanwhile Civil War in England, and the objective of some Confederates becomes support for a Catholic (or tolerant High Church) monarchy in England against a Protestant (or intolerant Puritan) parliament.

1649—Cromwell's invasion   Following the execution of Charles I in England, the Protestant parliament under Cromwell's leadership reigns supreme; Cromwell comes to Ireland to end the Confederation, eradicate royalism and bring the country completely under English Protestant control; he has resounding success, with much gratuitous slaughter, and destroys fortifications of conquered areas.

1652—Cromwellian Confiscations begin   Almost all Irish-owned land confiscated and 'planted' with English 'adventurers' (people who put up money for Cromwell's invasion on the hope of being given land afterwards) and soldiers; Irish nobility banished West of the Shannon where some Irish landowners allowed to own small areas; Catholic priesthood abolished (many hanged).

1690—Battle of the Boyne   See p. 130; 1660—the return of monarchy to England causes a resurgence of rebellion in Ireland; 1689—many Irish support James II (Catholic) in his conflict with William III for English Crown; Seige of Londonderry: James II tries to take the largely Protestant city, which resists to the point of starvation but is saved by William's troops; William's victory at the Boyne ensures absolute English Protestant supremacy.

1695—Penal Laws introduced   Catholics excluded from: government, civil service, army, teaching, legal profession; and not allowed to: teach their own children, send children to school of their choice, own any weapons (which made them vulnerable to highwaymen), buy land, take a lease for more than 31 years, own a horse worth more than £5 (i.e. a horse that one could ride); any existing Catholic landowners had to leave the property to all their children equally (to make Catholic holdings smaller); all Catholic clergy banned except parish priest if took oath of allegiance to English Crown. Catholic church continued to function in secret. Less repressive laws against Presbyterians also passed.

1699–1779—Irish Trade Restrictions   All Irish industry and trade prohibited or restricted if liable to compete with English manufacturers; e.g. trade in major Irish products like wool, beer, glass, live cattle, was prevented. Restrictions gradually lifted because of opposition by influential Protestants.

1795—Orange Order founded   Late 18C—emergence of violent political organisations and secret societies among both Catholics and Protestants wanting more Irish autonomy; in parliament, a significant number of Irish Protestants ('Patriots') notably Henry Grattan ('The Irish Protestant will never be free until the Irish Catholic ceases to be a slave') demand more independence for Ireland; 1789—French Revolution inspires much interest among Irish Catholics; 1791—Wolfe Tone (a Protestant) founds Society of United Irishmen, which becomes a nationalist revolutionary organisation; Penal Laws substantially eased; backlash among Ulster Protestants who oppose liberalisation or Irish independence; 1795—after pitched battle with Catholics, extremist Protestants found Orange Order, a violent organisation committed to keeping Catholics subservient.

1798 Rebellion   Society of United Irishmen gets French support for revolutionary uprising—English send large forces to quell; the Rebellion occurs mainly in Ulster and Connacht (quickly controlled and defeated in both), and south Leinster (huge battles with heavy losses on both sides); Wolfe Tone sentenced to death but commits suicide—he is remembered as the originator of Irish Republicanism.

1800—Act of Union   Ireland to be ruled directly from Westminster as part of a United Kingdom of Great Britain and Ireland, and Ireland no longer to be regarded as a separate country; this leads to increased agitation.

1775–1847—Daniel O'Connell ('The Liberator')   A Catholic lawyer (educated abroad), popular larger-than-life orator; leads mass campaign for Catholic rights (the Catholic Association, 1823), and becomes the first Catholic in the British House of Commons; leads huge non-violent campaign against Union (National Repeal Association, 1840).

1842—Young Irelanders   A group of militant Irish nationalists both Protestant and Catholic campaign through their influential newspaper *The Nation* for overthrow of English rule through a combination of constitutional politics and violence.

1845–6—The Great Famine   See p. 9; potato famine kills a million through starvation; another million emigrate; English government refuses aid, but encourages poorly paid public works projects so that destitute workers can earn their bread; landlords evict the starving for non-payment of rent.

1858—Fenians founded   Famine creates a bitter mood; the Fenians, Irish Republican Brotherhood, call for violent revolution; supported by Famine survivors in America and England; first rising 1867 fails; in England, police killed by Fenians escaping from captivity.

1846–91—C.S. Parnell   Protestant Ulsterman, elected to Parliament 1875; staunch Irish nationalist with Fenian backing; campaigns against extortionate rents paid by small tenant farmers (1879, becomes president of Land League); 1880 becomes leader of Irish group of MPs committed to Irish self-government (Home Rule), which is adopted as Liberal Party policy but defeated in Parliament.

1884–1904—Irish Revival   Great resurgence of interest among Irish people in all things Irish; 1884—Gaelic Athletic Association founded to promote traditional Irish sports; 1880s/90s, Irish (mostly Protestant) writers deal actively with Irish themes, some writing in Irish language; 1904—Abbey Theatre founded in Dublin as a platform for new Irish writing.

1916—Easter Rising   1880s/90s and 1910s—severe rioting by anti-Home Rule Protestants in Ulster; 1905—Sinn Féin founded, committed to complete separation of Ireland from Britain; Fenians organise for insurrection; Easter Monday 1916 'Irish Republic' proclaimed from the steps of the GPO in Dublin, with the support of about 1,500 armed men; leaders quickly arrested and 90 sentenced to death, but only 15 executed; one of the leaders not executed was Éamon de Valéra.

1919–21—War of Independence   1918—Sinn Féin win majority of Irish seats in British Parliament; 1919—Sinn Féin set up separate Irish Parliament in Dublin, Éamon de Valéra escapes from prison and is elected 'President of the Irish Republic' by the Dublin Parliament; British send troops to take control; Irish Republican Brotherhood becomes Irish Republican Army (IRA), fights British army and police; police reinforced by 'Black & Tans'—British soldiers who combine police and army uniforms and become notorious for atrocities against Irish towns and villages.

1921—Anglo-Irish Treaty   War ends with Treaty agreement that Ireland will be divided into two; an independent 'Irish Free State' and a British 'Northern Ireland'; the division is effected in 1922.

1922—Civil War   IRA and Irish Parliament split over signing of the Treaty; some ('the Irregulars') want to continue fighting until whole of Ireland has been won; they begin a guerrilla war against the new Irish Free State Government (made up of Treaty supporters); Irish Government gradually eradicates Irregulars, using severe methods reminiscent of the British; Éamon de Valéra abandons the Irregulars, instead forming Fianna Fail party to argue their case in Irish Parliament.

1949—Republic of Ireland proclaimed   Irish Republic officially breaks all ties with British Government and Commonwealth.

1985—Anglo-Irish Agreement   Treaty with British Government gives Irish Government a consultative role in Northern Ireland affairs.

The Mythical Past—and Present

The Gaelic version of Irish history, formerly oral, was preserved in books written during the Middles Ages; there were two principal versions, or sets of legends: the Ulster cycle (probably composed AD1–3C), and the Southern cycle (3–5C) which broadly overlap. The ancient Gaelic pantheon, like the Greek, consisted of partly mythical, partly historical beings, whose exciting exploits often involved non-divine, human but heroic characters. The Southern tradition was developed into more of a story-telling art, and the legends were related in an eloquent ballad form.

In the beginning were successive waves of invaders, all destroyed by great natural calamities. Then came the Firbolgs, who were the first human invaders, and the Fomors, sea-giants under the leadership of Balor, whose eye could destroy whatever it saw.

The Tuatha dé Danann arrived, the people of the goddess Dana: they were a divine race, led by the sun-god Lugh; they fought the Fomors in a great battle at Moythura (near Cong, County Mayo). Lugh put out the evil eye of Balor. Another of the Tuatha was Lîr (or Lêr), a sea-god. He had a daughter, Fionnuala, and three sons, Aedh, Fiachra and Conn. All of them were changed into swans by their jealous stepmother Aoife, and condemned by her to spend 900 years in lakes and the waters off the Ulster coast. But St Patrick arrived, broke the spell, and converted them to Christianity just in time before they died. Aoife was punished by her stepfather Bove Dearg the Druid, who struck her with his wand and turned her into a demon of the air—the thing she most dreaded. It's all told in 'The Three Sorrowful Stories of Erin'.

Another son of Lîr was Manannán, a popular god, patron of sailors and traders, whose home was the Isle of Man. Some believe him to have been a three-legged giant—he is the subject of many legends. Manannán's daughter was the goddess Niamh, who fell in love with Oisin, son of Finn MacCoul (see below).

Meanwhile, the Milesians (1300BC) had invaded Ireland: they were the country's original Gaels, led by the sons of Miledh, a mythical Spanish king. They first beat the Firbolgs, and drove them into the Western Isles. Then they took on the Tuatha dé Danann and conquered them. But the victory was not absolute—and it was agreed that the Gaels would rule the Earth, and the Tuatha would rule 'the underground world'. They survive to this day, as the fairy folk, the little people: pookas (goblins who startle night travellers and make them slip or fall, but only in fun), leprechauns (dapper little penny-pinching, pipe-smoking, problem-solvers), red men (terrifying mischief-makers dressed in red), cluricauns (baffling, tipsy, noctural fellows with silver buckles), butter fairies (who steal cream from milk), and a host of other beings good and bad who live side by side with, but apart from, the human inhabitants of Ireland.

At the same time, or maybe a lot later, there was a great king of Ulster called Conchubar (pron. Conachoor). King Conchubar had a nephew called Cuchulain (pron. Choolin), of miraculous birth (AD1C), who achieved many marvellous things in the defence of Ulster, mainly warding off the attacks of the wild Medb (pron. Maeve), Queen of Connacht. One of the most enduring of Irish legends is the epic tale—Tain bo Cuailgne—of her (unsuccessful) fight to capture the symbolic Brown Bull of Cuailgne (pron. Cooley). Eventually Cuchulain, by this time still aged only 27, was killed by Lugaid, son of another Ulster chieftain, and the daughter of Calatin, a terrible magician.

King Conchubar's story-teller and harpist, Fedlimid, had a daughter called Deirdre. She was incredibly beautiful, but Cathbad the Druid foretold that her beauty would bring disaster and death. Conchubar fell in love with her and to prevent the Druid's prophecy coming true, ordered her kept locked in solitude. Nevertheless she looked through a window and saw Naoise (pron. Neesh), the handsome son of Scottish king Usnach (pron. Usna). And he saw her. Naoise managed to free Deirdre and took her away with him to Scotland. At first Conchubar swore that he would get revenge, but eventually he persuaded them that his anger had passed and he had forgiven them, and urged them to come back and make it up with him. On their return, Conchubar killed Naoise, and Deirdre, grief-stricken, killed herself.

A great warrior bard called Comhal or Cumal had a son (AD3C) who became the best known of all Ireland's legendary characters—Finn MacCoul (various spellings). He was a fierce but noble giant of incredible strength (many of Ireland's natural landmarks turn out to have been made by him). King Cormac appointed him as leader of the semi-mythical Fianna (pron. Feena) or Fenians, a band of warriors set up to defend Ireland from the Vikings. They were all men of exceptional prowess and fighting skill. Finn MacCoul above all; and he stood out, too, for his honesty and wisdom. For all that, the others mutinied against him, and killed him in AD283.

Finn MacCoul fell in love with Grainne, King Cormac's daughter. But she was in love with Diarmait ó Duibhne, Finn's nephew. They fled from Finn's jealousy and anger; for a year and a day they wandered throughout Ireland. To this day dolmens are referred to as the 'beds of Diarmuid and Grainne' and it is popularly believed that there are 366 dolmens (although in fact over 1,500 have been discovered in Ireland).

Finn had a son, Ossian (or Oisin), another great warrior bard. Oisin fell in love with Niamh, daughter of the sea-god Manannán. Oisin was transported by Niamh across the sea to be with her for 300 years. She returned him to Ireland on a magic horse, on condition that his feet must not touch the earth. They did though, and he became a blind old man instantly. Oisin told St Patrick himself all about his great love for Niamh. Patrick, symbol of the Christian era and end of the Gaelic myths, baptised Oisin before he died.

A SHORT BIBLIOGRAPHY

A selection of holiday and background reading for a visit to Ireland would on its own make a first class library. Any booklist for a country so literate itself, and so fascinating to foreign writers, must necessarily be a mere fragment of the total range of possible reading. Here is a personal choice. Writers like Joyce or Behan who wrote on urban themes have not been included. (NB: Some are out of print and available only from libraries.)

Literature—Irish writers

A Pagan Place, *Edna O'Brien* (Penguin; Knopf; Weidenfeld & Nicholson) Life in modern rural Ireland.

At Swim-Two-Birds, *Flann O'Brien* (Penguin) Amazing multi-layered novel within novel with characters ranging from pre-War Dublin students to semi-mythical Irish heroes.

The Plough and the Stars, *Sean O'Casey* (Macmillan) One of several controversial plays of the 1920s dealing with the 1916 Easter Rising and Irish nationalism—the title refers to the flag of the early 20C Irish Citizen Army.

The House of the Titans, 'Æ' (*G.W. Russell*) (1934, Macmillan) The Celtic mythical world described in a long poem.

The Aran Islands, *J.M. Synge* (1907) Life on the western isles.

Playboy of the Western World, *J.M. Synge* (1907) Strange play with improbable story set in poorest peasant society of western Ireland.

Fairy and Folk Tales of the Irish Peasantry, *W.B. Yeats* (1888) Ancient legends retold.

The Wanderings of Oisin, *W.B. Yeats* Poems combining ancient Ireland with his own feelings about life.

The Celtic Twilight, *W.B. Yeats* Collected stories with Irish mythical theme.

The Collected Plays of W.B. Yeats (Macmillan) Excellent plays written 1892–1939 in lyric form with Irish themes or based on Irish myths.

Lady Gregory's several 19C **Translations** (C. Smythe) from Irish of old Gaelic myths.

Castle Rackrent (1800) and **The Absentee** (1812), *Maria Edgeworth* 18C Irish rural life seen through eyes of wealthy landowning lady.

Irish Miles, *Frank O'Connor (real name Michael O'Donovan)* (Hogarth; Macmillan; 1947) Philosophy, politics, history, and bicycling in the Irish countryside—a marvellous travel book.

Traveller's Samples (Macmillan, 1951) and **Domestic Relations** (Hamish Hamilton; Knopf; 1957) and other short stories and plays by *Frank O'Connor*. Pictures of lower middle class life in pre- and post-War County Cork.

An Only Child, *Frank O'Connor* (1964) Recollections of growing up in poverty in County Cork in the early years of this century.

Come Back to Erin, *Sean O'Faolain* (Viking, New York; 1940) Irish life and longings as experienced by the Irish in America.

The Irish, *Sean O'Faolain* (1947) A study of Ireland and its people.

An Irish Journey, *Sean O'Faolain* (Longmans, Green: 1940).

The Man Who Invented Sin, and other stories, *Sean O'Faolain* (1948) Repressive attitudes in the rural West.

Literary History of Ireland, *Douglas Hyde* (1892).

The Macmillan Dictionary of Irish Literature is a valuable reference work, summarising the lives and work of significant Irish writers of all periods.

Literature and travel—foreign writers

The Kellys and the O'Kellys, *Anthony Trollope* (OUP and others) Superbly written 19C novel about love and money, with great insight into the life of both working class and upper class Irish families—acclaimed for its unparalleled frankness and accuracy by Irish writers of the time.

Irish Sketch-book, *W.M. Thackeray* (1842) The lively and observant novelist's journeys in Ireland.

Round Ireland in Low Gear, *Eric Newby* (Collins) Gentle, amusing account of Newby and his wife's disorganised cycling tours of the Republic during the wet winter months.

History and Politics

A Short History of Ireland, *Martin Wallace* (Appletree Press, Belfast) Compact, concise, constantly updated.

The Great Hunger, *Cecil Woodham Smith* (Penguin) An account of the 19C Famine.

Domestic Industry in Ireland, *W.H. Crawford*, and **Landlord and Tenant in 19th Century Ireland**, James Donnelly, short books in the series Insights into Irish History (Gill & Macmillan, Dublin).

The Ulster Question, *T.W. Moody* (The Mercier Press, Cork; 1974) The conflict in Ulster from 1603 to 1973.

Six Generations, *L.M. Cullen* (The Mercier Press, Cork; 1970) Life and work in Ireland from 1790 to 1970.

Divided Ulster, *Liam de Paor* (Penguin) Highly readable, journalistic look at the history of Northern Ireland up to late 1970s.

The Road to Hillsborough, *Anthony Kenny* (Pergamon) History of Northern Ireland up to signing of the 1985 Anglo-Irish Agreement.

An Atlas of Irish History, *Ruth Dudley Edwards* (Methuen, London; Harper & Row, USA) Fascinating complete study showing Ireland from Vikings onwards.

The Green Flag: A History of Irish Nationalism, *Robert Kee* (Quartet Books and others) The story up to 1971.

Ireland: A History, *Robert Kee* (Abacus; Weidenfield & Nicholson) Based on in-depth BBC television series about Irish history from the beginnings right up to 1980—thorough, intelligent, well illustrated.

A Place Apart, *Dervla Murphy* (Penguin) Excellent and educational account of a no-stone-unturned visit to Northern Ireland by this southern Irish travel writer better known for her intrepid travels in remote corners of the world.

Guidebooks

Blue Guide: Ireland, *Ian Robertson* (A&C Black) The definitive guide to everything of historical interest.

The West of Ireland, *Seán Jennet* (Batsford) Readable, knowledgeable, guide to the western counties.

Ireland Guide (published by The Irish Tourist Board, Bord Fáilte) Gazetteer of main towns and principal sights together with masses of other useful and interesting information.

General interest

Granuaile, *Anne Chambers* (Wolfhound Press, Dublin) A factual rather than mythical biography of the 16C Connacht pirate queen Grace ó Malley, alias Granuaile.

Irish Shopfronts (Appletree Press, Belfast), a book of lovely photographs by *John Murphy*.

The Meaning of Irish Place Names, *James O'Connell* (Blackstaff Press, Belfast).

Peig: The Autobiography of Peig Sayers of the Great Blasket Island, *Peig Sayers* (Talbot) Life on a now-uninhabited island off the coast of County Kerry, translated from Irish.

Treasures of Ireland, *A.T. Lucas* (Gill & Macmillan, Dublin) On pagan and early Christian artefacts; beautifully illustrated.

Facts About Ireland (published by the Dept. of Foreign Affairs, Dublin) Masses of clear straightforward information about Ireland including for example, climate, flora and fauna, the legal system, politics, history, art, and so on.

INDEX

Many places in Ireland have several names, or names which may be spelt in a variety of ways. This Index lists only their principal names with the most usual spelling. County names, which are important in Ireland, are given in capital letters.

TRAVEL AND CULTURE BOOKS

"World at Its Best" Travel Series
Britain, France, Germany, Hawaii,
  Holland, Hong Kong, Italy, Spain,
  Switzerland, London, New York, Paris,
  Washington, D.C., San Francisco

**Passport's Travel Guides and
References**
IHT Guides to Business Travel in Asia &
  Europe
Only in New York
Mystery Reader's Walking Guides:
  London, England, New York, Chicago
Chicago's Best-Kept Secrets
London's Best-Kept Secrets
New York's Best-Kept Secrets
The Japan Encyclopedia
Japan Today!
Japan at Night
Japan Made Easy
Discovering Cultural Japan
Living in Mexico
The Hispanic Way
Guide to Ethnic Chicago
Guide to Ethnic London
Guide to Ethnic New York
Guide to Ethnic Montreal
Passport's Trip Planner & Travel Diary
Chinese Etiquette and Ethics in Business
Korean Etiquette and Ethics in Business
Japanese Etiquette and Ethics in Business
How to Do Business with the Japanese
Japanese Cultural Encounters
The Japanese

Passport's Regional Guides of France
Auvergne, Provence, Loire Valley,
  Dordogne & Lot, Languedoc,
  Brittany, South West France,
  Normandy & North West France,
  Paris, Rhône Valley & Savoy, France
  for the Gourmet Traveler

**Passport's Regional Guides of
Indonesia**
New Guinea, Java, Borneo, Bali, East of
  Bali, Sumatra, Spice Islands, Sulawesi,
  Exploring the Islands of Indonesia

Up-Close Guides
Paris, London, Manhattan, Amsterdam,
  Rome

Passport's "Ticket To..." Series
  Italy, Germany, France, Spain

**Passport's Guides: Asia, Africa, Latin
America, Europe, Middle East**
Japan, Korea, Malaysia, Singapore, Bali,
  Burma, Australia, New Zealand, Egypt,
  Kenya, Philippines, Portugal, Moscow,
  St. Petersburg, The Georgian Republic,
  Mexico, Vietnam, Iran, Berlin, Turkey

Passport's China Guides
All China, Beijing, Fujian, Guilin,
  Hangzhou & Zhejiang, Hong Kong,
  Macau, Nanjing & Jiangsu, Shanghai,
  The Silk Road, Taiwan, Tibet, Xi'an,
  The Yangzi River, Yunnan

Passport's India Guides
All India; Bombay & Goa; Dehli, Agra &
  Jaipur; Burma; Pakistan; Kathmandu
  Valley; Bhutan; Museums of India; Hill
  Stations of India

Passport's Thai Guides
Bangkok, Phuket, Chiang Mai, Koh Sumi

On Your Own Series
Brazil, Israel

"Everything Under the Sun" Series
Spain, Barcelona, Toledo, Seville,
  Marbella, Cordoba, Granada, Madrid,
  Salamanca, Palma de Majorca

Passport's Travel Paks
Britain, France, Italy, Germany, Spain

Exploring Rural Europe Series
England & Wales, France, Greece,
  Ireland, Italy, Spain, Austria, Germany,
  Scotland, Ireland by Bicycle

Regional Guides of Italy
Florence & Tuscany, Naples &
  Campania, Umbria, the Marches &
  San Marino

Passport Maps
Europe, Britain, France, Italy, Holland,
  Belgium & Luxembourg, Scandinavia,
  Spain & Portugal, Switzerland, Austria
  &the Alps

Passport's Trip Planners & Guides
California, France, Greece, Italy

PASSPORT BOOKS
a division of *NTC Publishing Group.*
Lincolnwood Illinois U.S.A.